MIT Project Athena

A MODEL FOR
DISTRIBUTED
CAMPUS COMPUTING

MIT Project Athena

A MODEL FOR DISTRIBUTED CAMPUS COMPUTING

GEORGE A. CHAMPINE

Digital Press

Printed in the United States of America.

9 8 7 6 5 4 3 2

Order Number EY-H875E-DP

The views expressed in this book are those of the author, not of the publisher. Digital Equipment Corporation is not responsible for any errors that may appear in this book.

Trademarks and sources are listed on p. 282.

Production: Quadrata, Inc.
Editing: Jerrold Moore
Text design: Melinda Grosser
Index: Marilyn Roland
Jacket design: Dick Hannus
Composition: Compset, Inc.

Library of Congress Cataloging-in-Publication Data

Champine, George A.
    MIT project Athena : a model for distributed campus computing /
George A. Champine.
        p.   cm.
    Includes bibliographical references and index.
    ISBN 1-55558-072-6
    1. Massachusetts Institute of Technology—Data processing.
2. Electronic data processing—Distributed processing.   I. Title.
T171.M44   1990   91-10948
004'.36—dc20   CIP

CONTENTS

—————

FOREWORDS

—

I arrived at MIT in the fall of 1990, midway through the final year of Project Athena. With vision and determination, Professor Gerald Wilson, then Dean of Engineering, together with President Paul Gray and Provost John Deutch, had led this remarkable effort to create a new educational computing environment at MIT. The project challenged the entire MIT community, especially the faculty, students, and Project Athena staff. It succeeded in creating a system that has begun to transform the ways in which our students and faculty approach computing, learning, and information sharing.

I believe that the development of information technology will revolutionize the ways in which many of us work and interact. It is important that MIT prepare its graduates for such an environment and that we explore and implement ways to use information technology to enhance the educational process itself. With over 1000 networked workstations and servers located throughout the campus, Athena seems ubiquitous to this year's first-year students. By the start of classes in the fall, a typical freshman had likely become an Athena user, beginning with electronic mail and messaging and basic text editing. He or she might well have been enrolled in 3.091, Introduction to Solid State Chemistry, which uses the new On-line Teaching Assistant (OLTA) capability. In later years, a typical member of the class of 1994 will probably have created new software on Athena and will likely have taken several of the 200 subjects now using courseware on Athena. Some of the courseware developed in Project Athena is already in use on other campuses around the country.

Project Athena was made possible by the partnership with the Digital Equipment Corporation and the IBM Corporation, and is a model of university–industry collaboration. Working side by side, people from the three organizations created new client–server software technology, including X Window, Kerberos, and many other system and application level programs, all of which were made available to the outside world.

The author of this book, Dr. George Champine, was the DEC Associate Director of Project Athena. His perspective provides valuable insight and a lasting account of the creation of the Athena Computing Environment.

Charles M. Vest
President
The Massachusetts Institute of Technology

From time to time, windows of opportunity open to make major advances in computing technology. One such window was the occasion to participate in Project Athena in 1983. Three unique factors came together at that time to make this an unparalleled opportunity. These factors were

- a major change in computing from centralized time-sharing systems to a distributed network of workstations;
- the desire by MIT to develop a campus-wide world-class computation system for education as well as research;
- the desire by Digital to participate in a very large scale implementation of networked workstations to test its strategy and products.

Nevertheless, the project was clearly very risky because of the many unknowns.

Now, eight years later, Athena has utilized this opportunity to make very significant contributions to distributed computing and has been successful beyond any of our expectations. Through the X Window System, Kerberos Authentication Service, and other similar developments, Athena has changed the world of computing. Athena is one of the first and one of the most successful implementations of the client/server model of distributed computing. This model has now been endorsed by the Open Software Foundation for their Distributed Computing Environment. Athena has emerged as the model of choice for distributed campus computing, and I expect that it will serve as the preferred model of distributed computing for the 1990s.

Project Athena also stands as an excellent example of what can be accomplished when the right kind of partnership is struck between industrial corporations and universities. What Athena accomplished could not have been done in the 1980s by MIT, Digital, or IBM alone. Working together, in the open environment of the university campus, we created the pioneering implementation of the vision of a coherent, powerful, distributed computing system.

On behalf of Digital Equipment Corporation, I would like to thank our two partners in Project Athena, MIT and IBM, for the chance to join with them in undertaking a project too large for any one of us to support alone, but whose benefits far outweigh the costs.

We congratulate the entire Athena team, knowing that the system they designed and built so well will serve as a platform for the major computing advances that will be accomplished in the 1990s.

Samuel H. Fuller
Vice President, Research
Digital Equipment Corporation

Creativity and innovation are the fuels that drive modern high technology companies. Just as the New England textile mills of the last century needed a steady flow of water to power their turbines, today's information-based industries require a steady flow of new ideas to compete in global markets.

Most people agree that innovation cannot be forced. Many believe it cannot be planned for or managed to a fixed schedule. In fact, there is evidence that most organizations are doing very well if they are able to encourage innovation rather than stifle it, and to recognize and reward creativity when it blossoms.

Developing collaborative research projects with universities is one successful strategy to encourage innovation that has been developed and used successfully for years by Digital Equipment Corporation. Project Athena at MIT was Digital's largest and longest running university project. During its eight-year history, Digital engineers spent more than 40 person-years working on site with MIT faculty, students and staff, and researchers from other companies. The trail of innovation leading from the people working together on this project is proof of the basic tenet of those of us who sponsor strong research connections with universities: When industry and academia pool their research talent, both sides prosper.

Project Athena was a success in several dimensions. Thousands of young engineers and scientists learned more about their core curriculum because of innovative learning software developed by faculty and staff. Perhaps even more important, they learned how to use networks of powerful workstations for collaborations in many endeavors. New technology that emerged from the project was turned into commercial products by Digital and other companies. Examples include the X Window System, Kerberos, and Hesiod. In addition, knowledge about how to design, install, manage, and modify an extremely complex network of distributed systems is influencing dozens of other organizations, both commercial and academic, that are on the forefront of computing.

Many of the lessons learned from Project Athena have to do with how bright people from different organizations, with different goals, and with very different cultures can work effectively together despite these differences. George Champine worked for nearly five years at bridging these cultures and contributing in many ways to the success of the project. This book is a great contribution to everyone interested in understanding the vision and the accomplishments of one of the most important university–industrial cooperative projects of the past decade. Equally important are his insights about how this remarkable partnership developed and functioned on a day-to-day basis.

Like most effective technical relationships, Project Athena was based on mutual respect, ongoing communication, a vigorous quest for excellence, and the challenge of growth and discovery. We hope that it can serve as a model for many other successful university–industry cooperative efforts.

John W. McCredie
Director, External Research Program
Digital Equipment Corporation

PREFACE

Tell me and I forget
Show me and I remember
Involve me and I understand

Ancient Chinese proverb

Project Athena at MIT has emerged as one of the most important models of next generation distributed computing in the academic environment. MIT pioneered this new systems approach to computation based on the client–server model to support a network of workstations. This new model is replacing time-sharing (which MIT also pioneered) as the preferred model of computing at the Institute. Athena is unique in that it is one of the first and one of the largest integrated implementations of this new model, perhaps paralleled only by the Andrew project at Carnegie-Mellon University. Athena's uniqueness has led to widespread interest in its design, implementation, and results. This book was written to supply information in a relatively concise form to meet this interest. For those who need more detail, a complete set (2800 pages) of Athena reports through September 1988 was published under the title "Project Athena: The First Five Years" and is available from Digital. This book is abstracted in large measure from those reports but with updated information where available and supplemental information to fill out the picture. This book also provides references to the more detailed papers describing Athena in the Bibliography.

The following characteristics, taken together, make Project Athena unique among the various higher education computing systems:

- magnitude, the largest educational project ever undertaken by MIT with a cost of about $100 million;

Figure 1   Project Athena workstation cluster.

- workstation-based almost exclusively;
- campuswide, with one integrated system that serves the entire campus;
- coherent, in that all applications run on all workstations, providing the same user interface independent of hardware architecture and easy sharing of programs and data; and
- centrally managed and supported.

In the late 1970s the information processing needs of higher education were rapidly moving beyond the capabilities of conventional pedagogical techniques. These techniques—pencil, paper, books, blackboards, and lectures—have all been used for hundreds of years. At the same time, major computer manufacturers were developing high-performance graphics workstations and networks that they expected students could afford within a few years. The MIT faculty believed that a network of workstations with good graphics and communications could overcome the well-known obstacles to learning by providing capabilities for

- easier visualization of abstract concepts;
- powerful simulation tools for classroom demonstration and homework problems;
- productivity aids to allow the student to accomplish more in less time and with better quality; and
- improved education in the area of design, by solving realistic problems using sophisticated computer-aided techniques.

Figure 1 shows part of Athena's largest workstation cluster.

Ultimately, the system was intended to help students obtain new conceptual and intuitive understanding of disciplines. A one-time investment in training and development would become applicable to all uses of the system.

In May 1983, MIT announced the establishment of a five-year program to explore new, innovative uses of computing in the MIT curriculum. This program was Project Athena.

Athena was undertaken to create a computing environment that would make a significant and lasting improvement in the overall quality of education at MIT. Athena's mandate was to explore diverse uses of computing in support of education and to build the base of knowledge needed for a longer term strategic decision about how computers fit into the MIT curriculum.

Athena has a major role in the educational mission of MIT, with the objective of contributing to the quality of the educational process. This role includes instruction, research, and activities outside the laboratory and classroom.

The primary technical objective of Project Athena, as stated early in 1983, was: "By 1988, create a new educational computing environment at MIT built around high performance graphics workstations, high speed networking, and servers of various types" [Lerman 87]. This objective has remained constant over the life of the project. Additional technical objectives were to

- support a heterogeneous hardware configuration;
- provide a user interface independent of hardware;
- provide a software development environment independent of hardware;
- maximize the exportability and importability of software; and
- accomplish these objectives at an ongoing operations cost, including hardware, not to exceed 10 percent of tuition.

These objectives have largely been met.

The support of heterogeneous hardware is necessary because Athena's two major sponsors, Digital Equipment Corporation and IBM, have products with substantially different architectures. The attainment of the cost objective was aided to a considerable extent by having a single user interface and single software development environment independent of hardware. The computational environment includes hardware, data communications, physical facilities, systems software, documentation, user support, applications software, and information resources, such as the libraries and outside databases.

Project Athena has now been in existence for seven years. Today, it is a production system, having fulfilled its objective of providing campuswide access to workstation-based computing at MIT.

Athena is a distributed workstation system in use 24 hours per day with 10,500 active accounts and 1300 workstations. The Athena model of computing is that of a unified distributed system where a single log in provides universal access to a variety of authenticated network services. The distributed services supported by Athena convert the time-sharing model of computing supported by Unix into a distributed system operating environment.

Network services supported include authentication, name service, real time notification service, a network mail service, an electronic conferencing service, a network file service, and an on-line consulting service. The system has extensive failsoft capabilities that permit continuous operation despite equipment failures. The system is designed to support 10,000 workstations by minimizing the use of network bandwidth, mass storage, and labor—all scarce resources. The centralized management approach also helps to minimize support and operations cost.

The workstation types presently supported are the Digital VAXstation and DECstation, the NeXT computer, the IBM RT/PC and RS6000, the Apple Macintosh II, and IBM PS/2 personal computers. Communications is provided by a campuswide local area network. The backbone is a 10 million bit/second fiber optic token ring. Attached to the backbone are 23 IP routers, which support 41 Ethernet subnets using TCP/IP.

The system provides a coherent model of computing in which all applications can run on all supported workstations independent of architecture. Because of the strong level of coherence, the human interface to the system is independent of the type of workstations being used. Differences in equipment are invisible to the user. Only one training course set and one documentation set are needed, no matter what workstation hardware is used. Students need to learn only one system during their stay at MIT, thus improving their productivity. The ultimate objective of coherence is to make the transfer of information limited only by its usefulness, not its availability.

Currently, 16 public clusters of workstations are available for use by students. These public clusters include 10–120 workstations each, and are open 24 hours per day. One of the public clusters is an electronic classroom. In addition to the public clusters, there are 25 department clusters and four projection-equipped facilities. Workstation clusters have been installed in five student residences, with some having workstations in the bedrooms and others having them in common areas. Figure 2 shows the locations of Athena workstation clusters.

At present, 38 Network File System (NFS) file servers, 8 Andrew File System (AFS) file servers, 36 Remote Virtual Disk (RVD) file servers, 135 Postscript printers, three each of name servers and post office servers, and two authentication servers are utilized. In addition to the "generic" Athena monochrome workstations, 15 multimedia workstations support full motion color video and sound. The system has 100 gigabytes of rotating storage in the workstations and an additional 50 gigabytes of rotating storage in network file servers.

The current 10,500 active user accounts (from a total of about 15,000 total accounts) generate about 5000 log ins and about 13,000 mail messages per day. The average student uses the system eight hours per week. In aggregate, the users generated 24,000 questions for the on-line consulting system and printed 5 million pages during 1990. About 96 percent of the undergraduate students and about 70 percent of the graduate students use the system. Athena usage is increasing substantially each semester.

The design of the Athena system was led by Professor Jerome Saltzer of MIT, in association with the Athena staff, which includes among others Ed Balkovich, Tony Della Fera, Steve Dyer, Dan Geer, Jim Gettys, John Kohl, Steve Lerman, Steve Miller, Cliff Neuman, Ken Raeburn, Mark Rosenstein, Jeff Schiller, Bill Sommerfeld, Ralph Swick, and Win Treese.

Initially, about 1500 Institute-owned workstations will be deployed. Later, all students and staff will be allowed to purchase private workstations, and plans call for ultimate system extension to

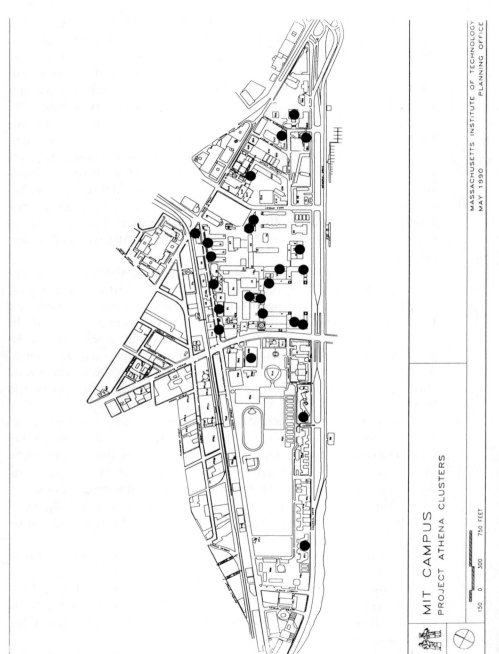

Figure 2 Locations of Athena clusters.

support approximately 10,000 workstations. System software is based on Unix and includes additional MIT-developed software that implements a client–server distributed system.

A significant part of the project is development of instructional software; to date 125 projects have been funded for that purpose. Students use Athena for most courses in some manner. Often Athena is used with personal productivity software, such as word processing, spreadsheets, graphics, and mathematical application packages. In addition, about 200 courses are presently being taught that use MIT-developed instructional software. Some courses require the use of Athena in mid-semester and final exams. Considerable anecdotal evidence shows that Athena has improved the quality of education at MIT, fulfilling its primary objective, even though the instructional software developed to date falls short of what ultimately can be developed.

Another part of the project is development of a multimedia workstation that uses interactive video disk technology to deliver full motion video in an X window simultaneously with conventional computer-generated text and graphics. The multimedia workstation project includes development of an advanced authoring environment, called MUSE, to reduce the cost and skill level needed to develop instructional software.

Athena continued as a free-standing project until June, 1991. At that time it was integrated into the MIT administrative system.

In many ways, Athena mirrors larger campus issues. Some of the more fundamental issues are the proper role of computers in higher education, the role of student housing as integrated into coursework versus a defense against the demands of coursework, and the inherent conflict between the priority given to teaching and the priority given to research (and tenure). To the extent possible, these larger issues are described in this book, with Athena being only one point in the spectrum of tradeoffs that can be made. All campuses are different, and strategies that work well on one campus could end in disaster at another. No claim is made that the approach selected by MIT is appropriate anywhere else. However, the lessons learned may be helpful to others designing similar systems.

Not all sections of this book are likely to be of equal interest to all readers. To help you find the areas of interest to you, we divided the book into four parts: Development, Pedagogy, Technology, and Administration.

The Development part includes Chapters 1 and 2. Chapter 1 describes the process of creating the vision that became Athena, the negotiations necessary to achieve some level of consensus about that vision, and the trigger necessary to start implementation. Chapter 2 then describes the project undertaken to implement the vision, starting with the activities to develop the project's infrastructure.

The Pedagogy part includes Chapters 3 and 4. Chapter 3 describes the instructional software developed for Athena, including the process by which it was funded, and some of the more widely used packages. Chapter 4 describes project–faculty relations. An important aspect of Athena's success, these relations have not always been smooth.

The Technical part includes Chapters 5, 6, and 7. Chapter 5 summarizes the technical aspects of the system, and Chapter 6 presents them in much greater detail. Chapter 6 deals with the system at a technical level and assumes a knowledge of computer systems software and Unix. It also describes the human interface work at Athena and the campus communications system. Chapter 7 describes multimedia workstation development and use.

The Administration part includes Chapters 8–11. As part of the Athena experiment, workstations were put in five student housing facilities; Chapter 8 describes these installations and assesses the results. Chapter 9 describes the financial and organizational aspects of the project. Chapter 10 provides an assessment of the project. Chapter 11 looks at possible futures for the project and the direction chosen by MIT.

Three documents of interest to implementors of campus computing systems similar to Athena are included in the Appendixes: Guidelines for Installation (Appendix II) and Principles of Responsible Use of Project Athena and Athena Rules of Use (both in Appendix IV).

Acknowledgments

Project Athena would not have been possible without the vision of many individuals from MIT, Digital, and IBM and their willingness to take risks. At MIT, the primary driving forces behind getting Athena started were Gerald Wilson, Dean of Engineering, Joel Moses, Head of Electrical Engineering and Computer Science, and Michael Dertouzos, Director of the Laboratory for Computer Science. Moses and Dertouzos gave much of the early direction to technical considerations, including the concept and definition of coherence. Steve Lerman, Professor of Civil Engineering, was Project Director for the first five years and provided the managerial direction necessary to start the project and keep it on track. Jerome Saltzer, Professor of Electrical Engineering and Computer Science, provided technical leadership for the first five years; without him the project might have failed. James Bruce, Vice President of Information Systems, provided continuing support of Athena in the implementation of the campus communication system and in significant contributions in serving on the Athena directors committee. Earll Murman, Professor of Aeronautics and Astronautics, accepted the position of Director of Athena for the last three years and managed the difficult transition from development to delivery of highly reliable and quality computing services.

The responsible people at Digital include Kenneth H. Olsen, Founder, President—and graduate of MIT—who was willing to bet on a vision. They also include Winston R. Hindle, Senior Vice President, who provided continuing support for the pedagogical aspects of the project; Samuel H. Fuller, Vice President of Corporate Research, who argued the case within Digital to fund the project; Dieter Huttenberger, the first Director of External Research, John W. McCredie, Director of External Research, who staffed the Digital part of the project and integrated it into the larger Digital External Research Program; Edward Balkovich, the first Digital Associate Director at Athena who contributed substantially and crucially to its management and design; and Maurice Wilkes (inventor of the first programmable electronic digital computer), who was my immediate predecessor. I joined the project in August 1986 as Digital's Associate Director and participated in its management through its mid-life to the end.

Key people at IBM who made significant personal contributions to Athena include Ralph Gomory, Senior Vice President for Science and Technology; Richard Parmelee, first IBM Associate Director at Athena; and Les Comeau, Manager of Technical Computing Projects.

People who contributed significantly with ideas or in the review of this book include Jim Bruce, Ed Balkovich, Jim Gettys, Dan Geer, Anne LaVin, Jack McCredie, Jerry Saltzer, Naomi Schmidt, and Win Treese. Joel Moses and Mike Dertouzos provided material from their personal files concerning creation of the Athena vision and the early days of the project. Earll Murman provided significant help with the chapter on instructional uses of Athena. Ben Davis provided substantial input for the chapter on the multimedia workstation project. Steve Lerman, Earll Murman, and Jerry Saltzer spent considerable time reviewing various drafts in great detail. All errors, however, are the responsibility of the author.

Special thanks go to Steve Lerman, who developed and contributed many of the ideas described here and recorded with his permission.

These contributions are gratefully acknowledged.

George A. Champine
Cambridge, Massachusetts

Development

O N E

Creating the Vision

——————

The Massachusetts Institute of Technology (MIT), founded in 1865 by William Barton Rogers, from the outset established the objective of combining research and education to the benefit of both in solving real-world problems. The Institute has long had a reputation for outstanding research in many fields, including computers. Since the invention of the computer, MIT has been in the forefront of development and application of computing technology. The Radiation Laboratory there did much of the initial work on vacuum tube circuits for counting and logic that established the technology for electronic digital computers.

MIT started using computers in 1947—with the Whirlwind I computer—only a year after the invention of the electronic digital computer, and went on to develop the notable inventions of core memory and time-sharing. An early research project at MIT that had considerable influence on computing was the Multiplexed Information and Computing Service System (MULTICS), started in 1964. Some of those who worked on MULTICS later worked on Athena, and the Remote Virtual Disk (RVD) software developed at MULTICS was later used by Athena.

The Student Information Processing Board (SIPB) is one of many organizations providing opportunities for MIT students to participate in independent research activities. Originally, SIPB was organized to allocate time on MULTICS to undergraduates who wanted to do private computing. SIPB is now an information services and consulting group for the student community and has played a major role in Athena development.

Presently, MIT has more than 9000 students, about equally divided between undergraduates and graduates, and supported by some 1000 faculty members. A unique feature of MIT is that undergraduates are encouraged to undertake research projects, and most seniors are required to write a thesis as part of the graduation requirements.

MIT has long been well endowed with computing resources for research. To some extent, these research computing resources were also available to graduate students on an ad hoc basis. However, the vast majority of the extensive and highly decentralized computing resources at MIT historically were devoted to research-related activities. This strong research orientation inhibited extensive exploration of computing as an integral part of instruction.

Late in the 1970s, some faculty members began to be concerned about the computational resources available for education, especially for undergraduate education. At that time a student could complete a four-year curriculum in engineering or science without ever using a computer. There was general acceptance of the idea that, in order for MIT to be a first-class educational institution, it had to have a first-class educational computing system. Various committees examined the question and agreed that improvement was necessary.

Identifying the Vision

The earliest document pointing out the need for a campus system like Athena probably was the report by the Ad Hoc Committee on Future Computational Needs and Resources at MIT [Dertouzos 78]. The report was submitted initially in September 1978 and published in final form in April 1979. Chancellor Paul Gray and Provost Walter Rosenblith had established the committee "to consider the **long term** needs of MIT and . . . make recommendations for the evolution and development of information-processing resources at MIT." The committee was chaired by Michael Dertouzos, Director of the MIT Laboratory for Computer Science (LCS). Although formally charged to take a five-year view, the committee decided to take a ten-year view.

It became evident to the committee that information processing technology was changing as rapidly as potential applications. Moreover, computing was (and still is) a capital-intensive activity. Thus

MIT needed to develop a strategy that would efficiently and effectively use its capital investments in this technology. The committee's report was remarkably accurate in forecasting the nature of the oncoming technology, although somewhat optimistic about the time frame.

In 1979, MIT was spending about $10 million per year on computing, divided among

- education (6 percent);
- research (57 percent);
- administration (21 percent); and
- outside users (16 percent, cost recovered).

As the educational use of computing at MIT in 1961 had been 30 percent, its share of resources had dropped substantially over the preceding 17 years. In 1979, the largest single user of educational computing resources on a per-student basis was the Sloan School of Management at $210 per student per year. The largest machine on campus had a performance of 3.5 million instructions per second (MIPS), and the total processing power on campus was about 20 MIPS. (Exactly ten years later, Athena alone had 2000 MIPS of processing power, and an individual workstation can have 27 MIPS of processing power.)

The 1979 report stated that

> The use of instructional computing at MIT is not perceived as leading our peer institutions . . . and is characterized by restricted access and high costs. On balance . . . we are not where we should be: our present path does not lead where we should be headed; and . . . MIT's overall use of information processing can not be characterized as pioneering.

The report went on to forecast—rather accurately—the advent of office automation and campuswide local area networks using glass fiber, graphics, facsimile, digital voice and image transmission, and personal computers. For 1989, it forecasted that

> Students may very well use their several thousand personal machines and other ports to review course material, solve homework problems and submit them, simulate experiments, text edit theses and reports, prepare graphs, perform bibliographical searches, communicate via the campus electronic mail with fellow students or with instructors, or even with students at other institutions, find out what goes on throughout MIT, and check their registration. Faculty may use their personal machine or terminal to do their own research, prepare course material, to disseminate it to students, to review the work of students, colleagues, and administrators in a paperless fashion, to maintain their appointments and phone number databases, and to monitor aggregate class parameters or individual student progress.

The report forecasted the performance of future personal computers at about "today's medium-sized computers (i.e., 1 MIPS) at an average price of \$2000 by 1989." Most of these predictions have come true in about the time forecasted, although the hardware is faster and cheaper (in constant 1978 dollars) than forecasted. The report recognized the power and importance of decentralization and networking, about which it says: "The recommendation to establish the MIT network is the heart of the MIT plan for information processing and communications. . . ." The ability to make these recommendations with confidence was a direct consequence of the LCS's research on distributed computing proposed to the Defense Advanced Research Projects Agency (DARPA) in 1976 and started in 1977.

Specific recommendations of the 1979 report were to

- establish a campuswide network;
- establish ten regional centers (of computation) within MIT;
- acquire new resources of five medium-scale computers and 400 terminals;
- initiate experiments in education, office automation, graphics, personal computers, computerized classrooms, mixed media, and library use;
- establish a standing faculty committee for information processing; and
- establish a "Czar of Information" at MIT to coordinate communications and computing.

The recommendation of establishing the "czar of information" was implemented after Athena was started, with the appointment of Professor James Bruce of the Electrical Engineering and Computer Science department to this position (later this position was elevated to Vice President of Information Systems). With this one exception, the report did not lead directly to action. However, the problems and concerns continued, and the report identified formally for the first time the need to take action.

(Much later, most of the committee's recommendations were carried out because of pressure from the faculty, largely within the framework of Athena. The incremental cost of carrying out these recommendations for the first five years starting in 1980 originally was estimated at \$2.6 million. When the Athena project did start in earnest in 1983, the actual incremental cost for the first five years was about $70 million. The cost increase in large measure represented the premium required to obtain a leading-edge system.)

Initiating Action

The deficiencies of MIT's instructional computing environment became increasingly apparent in the early 1980s, when the initial wave of personal computers began to make computing use for nonnumerical tasks much more common. Various academic departments, particularly within the School of Engineering, began to recognize the shortage of instructionally oriented computing in their annual reports and highlighted the potential benefits that computing might have for improving the quality of MIT's undergraduate education.

In 1982, Gerald Wilson, Dean of the School of Engineering, took a personal interest in this problem and added his considerable influence toward developing a solution. Wilson recognized the pressing need for improvements in the educational use of computers at MIT. Dertouzos and Joel Moses, Head of the Electrical Engineering and Computer Science department, were the other two members primarily responsible for shaping the vision of the project and getting it started.

Wilson had given up hope that anything would be done at the Institute level and decided to proceed with a program for the School of Engineering. His objective was to provide a first-class computational environment for undergraduate engineering students, who had no access to computers unless they were taking computer science subjects that specifically provided system access.

Wilson convened a committee to meet on long-range planning on Cape Cod in October 1982. Moses had done considerable work in putting together a position statement and recommendation on the use of computers in education at MIT. He was allocated 30 minutes at 8:00 P.M. to present the report, but discussion became so spirited that it continued for three hours and involved all the participants. The intense interest was fueled by announcement of the agreement between Carnegie-Mellon University and IBM for development and support of the Andrew system the previous week. The major recommendation of the meeting was to move forward on educational computing.

Wilson called another highly important meeting in November 1982 in Concord between Digital and MIT. Digital was represented by Gordon Bell (Vice President of Engineering) and Sam Fuller. Wilson made it clear at that meeting that MIT wanted an educational system, not a general purpose system to support all campus computing. At the meeting Dertouzos and Moses agreed to draft a proposal for potential sponsors, which was later accepted by Digital and IBM virtually unchanged. At this meeting the concept of "coherence," which was to become so important later, was first developed. Dertouzos and Moses sat in Dertouzos' car where they discussed alternatives for implementing coherence.

As a result of the Cape Cod meeting and subsequent work, Wilson assembled an ad hoc group of faculty members in late 1982. This group worked to identify the types of applications various faculty members wanted and to establish the requirements for an instructionally oriented computational environment that would serve instructional needs in the 1990s. The most significant findings of the group were:

1. An extremely large and diverse set of potential applications of computing existed in the MIT undergraduate curriculum. These ideas involved increasing the use of computing not as surrogate for traditional teaching modes, but rather to expand the scope and depth of the curriculum. Ideas included use of computer-aided design tools, the development of "expert tutors" that would provide hints and help in solving problems normally posed to students, expansion of the role of numerical solution methods within the curriculum, use of digital data acquisition and processing within undergraduate laboratories, and the use of simulations to allow students to explore complex mathematical models of physical and social systems.

2. The computational needs of the applications the MIT faculty envisioned would exceed the power of the then–current generation of personal computers. These applications required better graphics, more memory and computing power, and intermachine communication facilities, which were much more characteristic of engineering and scientific workstations just recently introduced into the market.

3. Faculty who developed or used computer applications as part of their teaching faced many barriers. One of the most vexing was the extreme diversity of operating systems in use on the campus. Faculty would often have to rewrite their applications almost completely as they moved from one computer system to another. In addition, as there was no common computer system on cam-

pus, faculty would often have to teach students how to use the operating system, the text editor, and related utilities. This necessity either reduced precious teaching time for the subject matter or increased the workload for the students, or both. The plethora of computing environments on campus also reduced program and data sharing across departments. Software developed by one faculty member was rarely of use to others; instead, faculty members were reinventing each others' work again and again.

These observations led to the recommendation that MIT undertake a large-scale program to explore the value of an ubiquitous, common computing environment. The group concluded that MIT needed to develop the resources that would free the faculty to explore the use of computing in undergraduate education on an unprecedented scale. In addition, the faculty needed a common computing environment that provided high performance, was accessible throughout the campus, and allowed a high degree of source code compatibility across diverse hardware platforms.

Wilson took this proposal to the Academic Council and presented it to all deans of the Institute. Interest varied from small to none, some stating outright that computers did not have a role in education.

The Vision

The initial concept of what was to become project Athena was to implement a next generation networked workstation computing system for educational use. The system ideally would be "coherent" and campuswide. It emerged from the 1978 Dertouzos report and was later articulated by Edward Balkovich of Digital [Balkovich 85]. In fact, the project (unwittingly) advanced the state of the art by two generations in a single step.

The existing state of the art in educational computing was time-sharing, an approach widely utilized in colleges and universities by the early 1980s. The next generation, as it turned out, was the stand-alone personal computer, typified by the IBM PC, the Apple II, and the Apple Macintosh. MIT briefly examined this alternative but rejected it as not meeting the Institute's needs.

The second generation beyond time-sharing was the network of workstations. From the beginning, MIT believed that networking was very important to make the system coherent and to unify the campus. An initial set of some 3000 workstations would be owned by the Institute and would be deployed in rooms with general access around the campus. These Institute-owned workstations would provide access for students on campus and would meet the needs for specialized workstations. Later, when the price of workstations was reduced to the target level of $3000 through advances in technology, workstations would be sold to students and faculty members through the campus Microcomputer Center. The goal was for every student and faculty member eventually to have a workstation. Because there were about 9000 students and about 1000 faculty members, the system had to be able to accommodate some 10,000 workstations.

A later policy (not part of the original vision) was to make all system software generally available to the academic and industrial community at no cost. Although MIT retains ownership of the software, it allows unlimited use and reproduction without cost if its copyright statement is retained in the source code. The first popular package to come under this policy was the X Window System. People on any of the common networks (including ARPAnet and CSNET) were able to copy source and binary code at literally no cost. People who wanted a tape were charged a nominal fee for the tape and its preparation, but not for the contents of the tape. The same policy was later applied to Athena system software and software tools as they became available.

The applications and instructional software could not be made freely available as a matter of policy because the faculty developers retained partial ownership in the code. The purchase of these packages was to be negotiated on an individual basis.

A vision of what was needed was coming into focus. To take the next step, which was not long in coming, resources of considerable magnitude had to be found. Meanwhile, an important event happened at another campus.

Project Andrew at Carnegie-Mellon University

A year before the Athena vision began to become firm at MIT, the Andrew system at Carnegie-Mellon University (CMU) had evolved as its vision of a next generation educational computing system [Morris 88].

An important event leading to the implementation of a campus-wide computing system at CMU was the creation in 1981 of the Task Force for the Future of Computing appointed by President Cyert and chaired by Allen Newell. The resulting report [Newell 82] recommended a conscious strategy of decentralizing CMU's computing facilities. Each department was encouraged to develop its own facilities for research computation in contrast to the then-existing large centrally managed time-sharing service. The report recommended the development of a campuswide local area network that would serve as the integrating mechanism for the department-oriented computation systems. The task force foresaw a vastly increased computational facility as a major aid to the quality and quantity of education delivered. Universal computer literacy was established as an important goal for CMU, and easy access to highly reliable computation was identified as crucial to the primary mission of CMU. However, the task force pointed out that the use of computing on campus would be diverse in nature because of widely differing needs by departments, and that use would be highly uneven.

In 1982 CMU developed a specification for a workstation that required

- 1 million pixels;
- 1 megabyte of main memory; and
- 1 MIPS.

This CMU specification gave rise to the name "3 M" workstation. The target price for this workstation was $3000. CMU requested proposals from computer manufacturers to help develop and support this system, which they named "Andrew," after Andrew Carnegie and Andrew Mellon. (Recent advances in hardware technology have now advanced the "3 M" model to the "60 M" model, with 27 MIPS of processor speed, 32 M bytes of main memory, and (still) 1 million pixels of display resolution.)

The Andrew system was created out of the vision established by the Newell report, and is now one of the largest and most successful advanced campus computing systems. Currently, all incoming freshmen at CMU participate in a computer skills workshop to learn Unix and the Andrew system.

Digital had many and long-term ties to CMU. Many of its top technical people had spent time there, either as students or on the faculty. These included Gordon Bell, then Vice President of

Engineering, Samuel Fuller, Vice President of Research, and William Strecker, then chief architect of the VAX system and later Vice President of Distributed System Software Development. John McCredie, later Director of External Research for Digital, had been Vice Provost for Information Services at CMU. Digital submitted a relatively generous proposal to CMU for the Andrew system. Thus it came as something of a shock when CMU selected IBM as its exclusive partner for the project.

Not long after CMU selected IBM for Andrew, MIT opened discussions with several vendors regarding its envisioned system. If there is one school with which Digital has closer ties than CMU, it is MIT. Kenneth Olsen, founder and president of Digital, graduated from MIT and worked in its Lincoln Lab. Olsen is also a life member of the MIT Corporation (its "Board of Trustees"). Digital had sold the first products it developed to MIT. The institute became an important customer, and a strong 35-year relationship developed between Digital and MIT. Following Digital's failure to win a role in the Andrew contract, Fuller was determined to find a suitable university partner to work with on what workstation systems should become. The MIT Athena proposal came at the right time.

The objectives of Andrew and Athena were quite similar: the support of educational computation, especially for undergraduates. This computational support was intended for all students, not just science and engineering. The means for meeting these objectives were also rather similar. In both cases the plan was to deploy workstations interconnected by a campuswide network. A number of workstations would be public, in workstation rooms with general access. However, the largest number of workstations would be owned by students and faculty. The CMU plan was to require all students to purchase workstations.

Obtaining Sponsors

MIT clearly lacked the financial resources to meet its computing goals without major outside assistance, so it sought computer manufacturer sponsors. MIT generated a list of potential sponsors, including its long-term partners Digital and IBM. Dertouzos led the MIT team that negotiated with potential sponsors. In late 1982 Lou Branscomb of IBM attended a joint IBM–MIT research meeting and heard Dertouzos report on the growing MIT/Digital potential and the prevalent MIT view that IBM would not support the project because it was supporting Andrew at CMU. Branscomb indicated that this did not have to be the case: that CMU could be viewed as doing system development and that MIT could focus on educational applications. In parallel in October 1982, Alan Weis of IBM contacted Professor Jerome Saltzer of MIT to say that IBM was interested in pursuing a project at MIT similar to Andrew. Although others at IBM opposed entry into Athena, Herb Schorr and Ralph Gomory supported the idea and were instrumental in IBM's ultimate decision to join the project.

Late in December 1982, the MIT team met with the top management of IBM at Armonk, New York, to obtain a briefing on product plans and to discuss a relationship for the educational computing initiative. At about the same time, Gordon Bell, Vice President of Engineering at Digital, contacted MIT and proposed a similar joint initiative.

Fuller had numerous meetings with Dertouzos to develop a rough outline of a proposal that would be acceptable to both Digital and MIT. Fuller took the proposal to the Operations Committee (the highest level committee in Digital), where he argued the case for funding the MIT project. He also went looking for one or two other comparable university projects that could be funded, convinced that 1982–1983 was critical as universities began moving to workstations. Without such a university relationship Digital had no solid position in this major move. In the months before and after May 1983, Fuller more than anyone else at Digital worked to get a project of this magnitude off to a productive start. He spent considerable time reviewing system alternatives, calling and attending meetings at MIT, and initiating early activities. He spent much more effort on getting this project started than on any other university project before or since.

The early approach was much more limited than the system that later developed. The initial concept was that the system be limited to the School of Engineering and obtained from a single vendor. The system was seen as a turnkey procurement from the vendor. It later turned out that a staff of more than 70 was needed to develop, deploy, and operate the Athena system. Fortunately, MIT had extensive experience in developing and operating large systems. MULTICS had been a much larger project than the system proposed, employing up to 75 professional programmers for seven years.

Dertouzos and Moses developed a white paper on educational computing in December 1982, which was to be submitted as a proposal to potential sponsors. The paper, which summarized many of the earlier discussions, also broke new ground in several areas. The major issues addressed were

- educational aspects of the system, including analysis, synthesis, and instrumentation as elements in the education process;
- design of the system, describing the campus communication system and the network of workstations and servers;
- coherence, defined to include operating system, network protocols, programming languages, data formats, and intercommunications data; and
- schedule and cost.

The educational, technical, and coherence aspects of the system described were relatively close to those ultimately implemented. The cost to MIT was also accurately estimated. The schedule was overoptimistic by one year (it took six instead of five), and the hardware cost was overoptimistic by perhaps a factor of 2. However, neither of the potential sponsors had workstation or communications equipment that met the needs of the project at the time the paper was written.

The proposal was sent officially to a number of potential sponsors, including Digital and IBM, on January 5, 1983. At that time, the concept was that only one vendor would be selected to provide the system. The response to the proposal was far more than the vendor selection committee expected. Instead of the two to four responses expected, nearly a dozen companies replied with generous grant offers. Overall, more than $100 million was offered for the project. The unexpectedly large response immediately caused MIT to consider a far larger and more aggressive system.

Digital proposed an initial system using graphics terminals (VAXstation 100s) and ASCII terminals on VAX 750 minicomputers, to be followed by up to 2000 personal computers by 1984–1985. Other support elements included onsite software engineer support, free maintenance, and cash donations.

IBM initially proposed an approach that consisted of adding a 32-bit microprocessor card to a personal computer and porting Unix to that system. After pursuing that plan for nearly a year, IBM abandoned it because by then it did not fit IBM's other workstation product plans. IBM switched to a plan of supplying 160 PC/ATs with the Xenix operating system, a Unix look-alike. The attempt to deploy Xenix on the first few PCs made clear a problem that had not been previously considered: that Unix in any form is not well suited to mass distribution as it "comes out of the box," because it requires a large amount of setup and tailoring for each system. Therefore the PCs were deployed using DOS, which could be mass distributed on floppies. Meanwhile, the lessons learned from working with Xenix were transferred to the main effort of recasting Berkeley Unix so that many systems could be deployed and managed by a small staff. Although the PCs did not run Unix, their use provided valuable experience relevant to deploying networked workstations and in managing the distribution of software to them.

IBM later considered an initial system using 200 Adventure (laboratory) workstations, to be followed in 1984–1985 by advanced workstations. This strategy was later replaced by a PC/RT approach. One faction within IBM wanted a relatively small program (under $6 million), because most of their objectives would be met by Andrew at CMU. Another faction wanted a $20 million program with up to 2000 workstations.

Intensive discussions took place between MIT and Digital, and between MIT and IBM, over the next month.

Even at this early time, concern was expressed among senior faculty and administration members at MIT that introducing computing into education would detract from the quality of teaching, because students would confuse mathematical models with reality and become further removed from the physical world. Concerns also were raised about the cost to MIT. These and similar concerns continue to the present. At that point, however, two major issues came to the forefront at MIT:

- Should there be one vendor or two?
- Should the system be confined to the School of Engineering (its primary advocate) or extended to the entire Institute?

They were vigorously debated during February and March 1983, while negotiations were being carried out with potential sponsors.

The argument over the number of vendors was: Selecting two would avoid alienating one of MIT's two long-time supporters and would double the resources available, but would complicate obtaining coherence. The argument over the system's scope was: An Engineering School system would be simpler, but an Institute-wide system would avoid a "hodgepodge of incompatible tools with no common base from which we can build."

The debate on these two issues continued through March 1983.

Wilson had been a strong proponent of limiting the system to Engineering and using only one vendor. His reasons were that limiting the scope would allow the program to move much faster and would provide a much more focused solution. However, after consultation with others and considerable analysis, he released a paper on March 1, 1983, recommending that the two-vendor approach be used for an Institute-wide system. He went on to recommend that Unix be used, supporting FORTRAN, C, and LISP "completely transparent to the user as to whether he or she is using IBM or DEC hardware." Nine days later, Dertouzos (who was attending a meeting in Italy) independently released a memo recommending the two-vendor approach and Institute-wide deployment.

Although both Digital and IBM expressed preference for the single-sponsor approach, the Wilson committee elected to accept both as sponsors. Digital would be responsible for supporting the School of Engineering, and IBM would be responsible for supporting the rest of MIT. Both Digital and IBM finally were convinced to accept this arrangement (after some complaints), ultimately agreeing that the multivendor approach would significantly benefit MIT and both vendors. The Wilson committee also decided to make the system Institute-wide, to achieve commonality in the educational approach for all students.

These recommendations were forwarded by Wilson to MIT President Paul Gray. The recommendation was reviewed by a subcommittee of The (MIT) Corporation, the highest level policy-setting group within MIT. This subcommittee agreed that the system should be Institute-wide, not just for the School of Engineering. Because Digital had already made commitments to the School of Engineering, the subcommittee decided that Digital would supply workstations for the School of Engineering and that IBM would supply workstations for the rest of the Institute. This decision was later to prove unnecessary; Digital and IBM equipment was mixed in all schools depending on technical requirements and products available, not by vendor.

A Coherence/Technical Committee, chaired by Professor Moses, was established in June 1983 to determine the technical direction of the project. Coherence was an extremely ambitious goal, because no one had ever before solved the problems of getting all applications to run on subsystems of such great incompatibility. The early meetings determined that the software environment should be based on Unix, Emacs, Scribe, C, FORTRAN, and LISP. The approach was to establish a standard environment that was to be the same on all hardware platforms (described in detail in Chapter 5). Ultimately, this approach was to prove extremely successful.

One of the most difficult problems in any project is selecting the name. All manner of Greek, Hebraic, and other names were proposed but rejected. Ultimately, Professor Chris Chrysostomidis's wife proposed Athena, the Greek goddess of wisdom, which met with strong acceptance and was approved. Subsequently, Michael Dertouzos purchased a number of brass owls (also a symbol of wisdom) in a flea market in Athens and brought them back for the participants in the process. One of the brass owls was used as the model for the Athena logo, and the tradition of using names of Greek deities for elements of the Athena system has continued to the present.

Commitment to the Project

MIT executed bilateral arrangements with Digital and IBM. These arrangements were simultaneously announced to the news media amid great fanfare in May 1983 as Project Athena. The partners were committed to the project!

The Athena academic–industrial partnership was one of the first of its type. IBM and Digital provided extensive grants of hardware, maintenance, staff support, and software. The value of these grants for the first five years (with hardware valued at list prices) was approximately $50 million. MIT undertook a major fund-raising campaign for $20 million to fund curriculum development and the MIT portion of the Athena staff, bringing the total to $70 million. In addition, space renovation expenses associated with installing Athena facilities around the campus, the costs of networking the campus, and overhead expenses were borne by MIT. However, the project took longer and cost more than the original estimate. After an eight-year development, in June 1991, about $100 million had been spent. The combined resources of MIT and its industrial partners make it the largest educational initiative ever undertaken at MIT, and clearly one of the largest academic computing efforts in the world.

All intellectual property created by Athena is owned by the Institute, including the work of industrial staff residents at MIT. All of the Athena work is done in the traditional university style of open research with the intent of making the results available to all interested parties.

Because the project at that point was seen as largely off the shelf with minimal development, expectations of early installation and use were high. Highly visible press announcements were made by MIT, along with Digital and IBM. The initial press release that fanned expectations is reproduced in its entirety in Appendix VI. The magnitude of anticipated benefits of the project were widely described in person and in the media. Some faculty members believed that within a few weeks they each would have a fully functional workstation on their desks and that students would have universal access to this new and wonderful tool. Athena was off and running, but the seeds of problems soon to emerge had already been planted.

T W O

From Vision to Reality

As with every large project, the initial euphoria of getting funding for Athena soon gave way to the harsh realities of implementation. The vision of a single campus system that would serve all students— from Electrical Engineering to Music Appreciation—was based on the use of workstations. However, neither vendor had one that was shipping as product. Although the commitment was to a "coherent" system, in which any program could run at any workstation, the way to achieving that coherence had not been demonstrated, and the two vendor architectures were highly incompatible. Similarly, methods for managing 10,000 user accounts in a workstation environment, to say nothing about the logistics of deploying thousands of workstations or software to support them, had not been developed.

These risks were known at the start of the project. Much more dangerous in any project are the unknown or unrecognized risks, which certainly was the case with Athena. The major unrecognized risk was the chasm between what the users and developers expected could be done and what the available technology could support. MIT and the two sponsors believed without question that the technology available at that time would allow project implementation in a few weeks or months and that the resulting system would provide the network transparency and functionality desired by the users. The users believed, based on the information released and imagining the kinds of functionality that they would like to have, that in a few weeks a new and powerful tool would be available for their use. In fact the technology available at the time prevented the system from ever meeting the initial expectations, and only through a major four-year development effort could the difference between expectations and reality be reduced to a manageable size.

Major Goals and Strategies

The central goal of Athena was to explore the application of a unified network of high-performance computer workstations within the MIT curriculum. Achieving it required efforts directed toward three major subgoals:

1. fostering and supporting innovative uses of computing in education by the MIT faculty;
2. designing and implementing a new computing environment to serve MIT's educational needs well into the 1990s; and
3. constructing and operating a computational facility distributed across the MIT campus of sufficient scale to make educational computing an accessible utility.

The main strategy adopted to meet the first subgoal of encouraging the innovative uses of computing in the MIT curriculum was to draw on the traditional source of innovation within the university: the faculty. Athena explicitly adopted a "bottom up" approach to educational computing applications, allowing interested faculty members to exercise wide discretion in how computation would be used in the curriculum.

The centerpiece of this strategy was to provide the financial, technical, and computational resources that the faculty needed to explore ways of using Athena in the various subjects taught. Athena operated an internal grant program in which faculty members and students could request funding and access to computer resources for educational projects. Faculty/student committees reviewed these proposals biannually.

An important part of the vision of the system was "coherence." *Coherence* in this context meant that Athena should act as a unifying mechanism on campus, providing communication and facilitating the sharing of all kinds of information, including programs and data. In a narrower sense it meant uniformity of user interface, applications software, and software development environment independent of the type of hardware being used. One purpose of coherence was to reduce the amount of development, documentation, and training necessary. Another was to minimize the support cost necessary for the MIT-developed software.

The workstation requirements were

- 1 million instructions per second (1 MIPS);
- 1 million pixels;
- main memory adequate to run Berkeley Unix;
- hard disk of 40 MB;
- local area network interface (Ethernet or token ring); and
- mouse.

The 1-million pixel requirement was established to provide adequate resolution for visualization of complex diagrams, schematics, and other graphic-intensive representations. It was also based on the belief that a windowing system would soon be forthcoming, which would require something approaching 1 million pixels. The initial estimate for the main memory requirement of Unix was 1 MB. By 1990 this requirement had risen to 6 MB and was still rising. The hard disk is used primarily as a swapping store to minimize paging traffic. Relatively little system code and no private files are left on the hard disk between sessions in order to maintain integrity.

Affordability was interpreted to mean that the steady-state operating cost should not exceed 5 percent of tuition. The operating cost of the system includes

- operation and maintenance of MIT-owned servers and networks;
- training;
- software development;
- software maintenance;
- documentation; and
- consulting.

Strategic Decisions

The project team spent considerable time late in 1983 and early in 1984 reviewing other large educational computing systems, including Dartmouth, CMU, Berkeley, Cornell, Stanford, and Stevens. The team also held discussions with staff members of the LCS. These sessions were to prove important in evolving the ultimate design of Athena.

Project management made a number of strategic decisions that dictated the course of development. Some of these decisions were made explicitly, some implicitly. Many limited the developmental effort required to implement the system, as inability to maintain schedules ran head on into considerable pressure to meet the expectations of potential users. The strategic decisions included the following.

- The project was set up outside the established campus computing organization. The reasons were to create a new educational computing group, to facilitate the hiring of needed skills, and to allow the new project to move quickly without upsetting ongoing campus computing activities.
- The concept of coherence was emphasized, providing a single, homogeneous computing environment that would minimize development, training, and support costs. This single, homogeneous environment would meet most, but not all, of the educational computing needs.
- The number of operating systems, languages, and application packages should be minimized.
- Relatively powerful hardware and software modules with good growth capability were preferred over simpler packages that might be easier to use in the short term but which did not have growth capability. Thus Unix was picked over DOS, "C" was picked over Basic, and workstations were picked over PCs.
- The operating system had to be available on both the Digital and IBM workstations in order to maintain coherency. DOS and Unix were the contenders. Because DOS lacked the features necessary to support the multitasking capability required of the system, Unix (specifically Berkeley Unix) was selected. Berkeley Unix was not available from either Digital or IBM. The version for Digital hardware was available from Berkeley, and IBM ported a special version of Berkeley Unix within its Academic Computing Information Systems organization for the RT/PC workstation.
- Management of the system would be centralized in Athena, rather than being decentralized to the departments.
- The system should be deployed quickly, so that work on instructional software could be started early.
- To maximize the speed with which workstations could be deployed, they should be put in public areas with access open to

all. There would be some department deployment, but that was not a strategic goal.

- Athena would be used initially for undergraduate computing but not graduate computing or research. This decision was made because undergraduates had the least access to computers, whereas graduate students often had access to the computers used in their research work. When significant numbers of workstations were available, the plan was to extend the use of the system to graduate students and researchers (who wanted it). The assumption was that partitioning use in this way would be possible to a reasonable extent.

Once the system was available, the teaching faculty would be expected to turn their considerable energies toward developing instructional software and make "a thousand flowers bloom."

Start-Up

With commitment to the vision in place and two major vendors signed up, implementation began. Implementation involved three major phases:

- installation of a relatively conventional time-sharing system during 1983–1985;
- installation of the workstation network during 1985–1988; and
- improvement of the stability and reliability of the system and a significant increase in the number of installed workstations during and after 1988.

At first the project shared offices with the Information System group. Meetings were immediately started with the faculty to determine system needs and requirements. The previous experience with MULTICS had a major influence on attitudes. MULTICS had mixed development and production activities on the same system. As a result the system was not as stable as desired by the people using it as a production system and not as flexible as desired by people carrying out research and development. Many long discussions ensued on how to balance stability and development in the Athena project. The Computer Science department advocated an active research program, with emphasis on experimenting with problems of scale. Those intending to use the system for pedagogical purposes opposed research and experimentation because it would lead to instability. The advocates of instructional use won; their views were adopted as policy, and the Computer Science people left the project.

Early management of the project was by committee. The composition of the committee was very fluid, however, so consistent progress was difficult. In October 1983, Dertouzos released a memo identifying the project's management problems, including lack of visible structure, inadequate communication with Computer Science, lack of a technical plan, lack of credible leadership, and tension over the technical approach.

These concerns led to a demand for a full-time project leader. Steve Lerman, a Professor of Civil Engineering specializing in transportation, who had been an early leader in development of the project's vision and implementation, agreed to be its leader. He was appointed Project Director in December 1983, and led the project through its first five, very difficult years.

When Athena began, there were perhaps fewer than 20 Unix systems on the MIT campus, which made staffing of the project relatively difficult. Those involved in the project saw the software task as primarily one of installing and using a standard Unix system. (Later events revealed many problems with conventional time-sharing Unix when it is used in a large workstation network. These shortcomings required 2–3 years of intensive software development to correct.)

In order to get some computing power in the hands of students and faculty quickly, the project committee decided to deploy a relatively conventional time-sharing system based on 50 VAX 11/750s. This time-sharing system would provide computational resources to the students and faculty while the workstation system was being completed and deployed. It would also get them used to Unix and would buy time for Athena to hire a staff and create the infrastructure necessary to develop and support the workstation system.

Each 750 typically had four VT100 (ASCII) terminals and two VAXstation 100 graphics terminals attached to it. Each system had 4 M bytes of main memory and about 750 M bytes of mass storage. Groups (called *clusters*) of 750s were installed in five buildings. The machines that supported the terminals were called *client systems*. Each cluster also had a *server* system, which was used for backup and had nearly 200 M bytes of mass storage and a TU78 tape unit.

Digital was determined to move quickly and generously in support of Athena to maintain its position as a major player. The Digital effort was led by Edward Balkovich of the External Research Program, working closely with Samuel Fuller. Digital and MIT reached conceptual agreement on the equipment and software needed, and large amounts of time-sharing hardware were shipped by Digital to Athena in the summer of 1983.

In keeping with the tradition of Greek names for Athena system components, the time-sharing systems had the names of Zeus, Hera, Hades, Athena (all in one building), Apollo, Aphrodite, Artemis (all in another building), and Charon (assigned to SIPB). Other system names were Paris, Priam, Jason, Theseus, Helen, Castor, Pollux, Odysseus, Agamemnon, and Orpheus.

The instructional software for any individual course was supported initially on only one or two of the time-sharing systems, so a student taking a course could use only the system(s) that supported that particular course. At a later stage, the student could log onto the correct system from any terminal in the same cluster.

Students not enrolled in a class that used Athena were limited to using the cluster in the Student Center. One reason for this policy was to intentionally skew the heavy load of general use away from systems being used as critical parts of courses. The Student Center cluster often was very busy while other clusters were virtually idle. However, the lack of a network file system precluded any other arrangement. This problem intensified when workstations arrived, because the software treated each workstation as a main frame and the fraction of systems that supported any particular course became smaller.

The initial version of Unix installed was a test version of Berkeley 4.2. Unfortunately, this operating system was not very stable (not surprising since it was a test system). The Scribe text formatter and the Emacs editor from CCA were standard on every system. The systems were booted from the 10 M byte removable RLO2 disk, with the remainder of the software then copied over the net.

Installed during the last half of 1983 through 1984, the time-sharing system steadily increased in capability. The entire system was developed, installed, and made operational by the spring of 1985, a little less than two years after the start of the project.

During this time period, the importance and magnitude of the site planning task became evident. Site preparation (power, air conditioning, and lighting) proved to be quite expensive and took considerable time. As with most colleges and universities, space at MIT was in very short supply, and Athena often could get only low-quality space that required extensive renovation.

Trying to put computers and modern networking in buildings 75 years old proved to be relatively difficult; drilling holes through several inches of concrete, for example, took considerable time. The management task also was difficult, involving many decisions and tasks—and several different campus organizations, each of which had different (and often conflicting) priorities.

Overcoming Early Shortcomings

By early in 1984 the many shortcomings of the standard Unix in a workstation network environment were obvious. Several projects were started to correct these deficiencies in the belief that a few additions to the system could make it viable. These projects included work on a

- distributed file system;
- remote procedure call (RPC);
- authentication server; and
- window system.

As the shortcomings of Unix became increasingly visible, the need for better technical direction of the project became evident. Faculty leaders determined that Professor Jerome Saltzer was the best person for the job, on the basis of his personal capability and his many years of system experience on MULTICS. He was convinced to join the project in late 1984.

After a detailed review of the current status of the project and the nature of the task that lay ahead, Saltzer initiated a design of the complete system. Equally important, he stopped some software projects, relying on the industry to provide acceptable solutions. Digital was made generally responsible for the system software, and IBM was made generally responsible for applications software. Reevaluation of priorities resulted in termination of the distributed file system and the RPC and emphasized the authentication server. Steve Miller of Digital and Cliff Neuman of MIT began work on the authentication server in earnest in the spring of 1985.

The first nonvendor software installed on Athena and available to users was the On-line Consulting system (*olc*), installed in the spring of 1985. This software was developed by the system consultants to improve the answering of questions from users. Over the years it became highly popular and successful, eventually answering some 12,000 questions per semester.

This period of time also was productively spent in building an organizational infrastructure. An organization usually develops a definite "culture," and Athena was no exception. Among the important resources of the project were the students hired in considerable numbers during the summer. The students who worked in system development were called "watchmakers." The name, coined by Dave Grubbs, was taken from characters in *Mote in God's Eye* by Niven and Pournelle. The "watchmakers" in the book were tiny people who would fix things when no one else was looking. The students who worked in operations were called "droogs," the name selected by Alix Vasilatos from the movie *Clockwork Orange*. A third group, called "gremlins," was assigned to "cluster patrol" to make sure that all of the workstations and printers are operational.

Arrival of Workstations

The first workstations began to arrive late in 1984 (VAXstation Is). Their delivery forced the first serious consideration of the requirements of a workstation system. The project staff quickly configured an initial system, and installed the initial workstations early in 1985 for the staff's use. The first public workstation cluster opened in March 1985. Testing and improvement of this system continued through the summer of 1985, and the initial deployment of workstations for student use followed that fall. Deployment continued aggressively, and, as workstations became more plentiful, use of the time-sharing system dropped off.

The new system software developed for the workstation environment ultimately corrected the problems encountered with the time-sharing systems. A student could sit at any workstation and get immediate access to all files and system services, independent of location. All sessions were authenticated, and equipment could be easily added, moved, or removed from the system.

The Crunch

All large projects go through roughly the same stages. The first stage is "wild enthusiasm," which Athena experienced during 1983 as the project obtained significant vendor support and funding commitments for five years. The second stage is "disillusionment," which occurs when the true magnitude of the task and the difficulties in accomplishing it become evident. The onset of the second stage for Athena was relatively slow, because the shortcomings of Unix in a distributed workstation environment became evident only gradually during 1984. But when workstations began arriving in 1985, the project staff was forced to face the issue of Unix shortcomings in the workstation environment.

Another problem was deployment. During 1985, after workstation deployment training was complete, the time required for installation of a workstation was about eight hours. This included the time to obtain the hardware from the warehouse, deliver it to the installation site, unpack it, configure it, connect it to the net, and load the software. Although the goal was to install three workstations per day, the best that the team could manage was about one workstation per day. This meant that the deployment fell further and further behind. (Later, better training, tools, and installation procedures reduced this time to less than 30 minutes.)

A serious problem also developed in the system file area. The plan from the beginning was to support files by means of a distributed file system, and development of such a file system was initiated early in the project. When Saltzer joined the project, he initiated a review of development status and its relation to resources available. He also reviewed the efforts underway at CMU to develop its distributed file system. After considering the magnitude of the effort required and priorities of other needs, he decided that Athena should acquire a distributed file system rather than developing one. He therefore terminated its internal development, much to the dismay of advocates of the project.

The initial plan called for using an existing distributed file system: LCS's Remote Virtual Disk or RVD. Besides its availability, the package could support a large number of users per file server because most of the processing was done by the requesting workstation. This approach worked quite well for system binaries, which were inherently hardware specific, and continues to be used today, although with many enhancements. For private files, RVD presented serious problems, because it depended heavily on specific machine data representation. Thus private files were not network transparent and would be accessible only on the system type on which they were created.

About this time, Sun Microsystems developed a proprietary distributed file system called the Network File System (NFS) and had shipped a few copies of it. Saltzer and other staff members reviewed the specifications for NFS and decided that it would meet most of Athena's needs for private files. Saltzer terminated work on the Athena distributed file system in the spring of 1985, to await the public release of NFS by Sun. Unfortunately, public release was delayed, bringing into question whether Sun could complete the release and MIT could complete the legal negotiations regarding the use of source code in time for full-scale deployment of the workstation system in the fall of 1987. Although licensing negotiation took most of a year, luck was with the project. The public release was completed in time and NFS was included in the initial full-scale deployment of workstations.

The greatest efforts by far were those required to develop software to correct the Unix shortcomings in supporting distributed systems and to develop user interfaces for the nonexpert. The nature of the system that resulted from this development is described in detail in Chapters 5 and 6. Software development to correct these problems continued at a rapid rate during 1986, so much so that the faculty and users began to complain about the constantly changing system interfaces and the resulting unreliability of the system. The fact that the system was constantly improving in functionality was not of real interest when it came at the price of unreliability. Because of the changing application programming interfaces, software (developed by faculty members at great cost in time and effort) that worked perfectly the previous semester often would no longer work the next. Needless to say, this situation caused many rather strong complaints.

At that point, the project team realized that it faced a decision having serious consequences. One option was to slow development to provide more system stability and reliability. The advantage of this approach was that it would respond to user demands for more stability and reliability in the system. The disadvantages were that it would further delay a project that was already seriously late and that it would seriously prolong the period of instability. The other option was to "go for broke," and install the needed changes as quickly as possible. The benefit of this approach was that it would get the period of instability and unreliability over sooner. The drawbacks were that it would fail to respond to user complaints and that things would get worse before they got better. A major part of improving functionality was to be version 11 of the X Window System. This version was incompatible with version 10, and applications developed for version 10 would not run with version 11. If only version 10 were supported for another year, many more applications would be developed that would later have to be converted to version 11. Thus early installation of version 11 could minimize the number of applications that would have to be converted.

The second option also carried the risk of a major system failure. At MIT, as at other colleges, the start of fall semester cannot be delayed. If software development and testing were to fall behind schedule, the system might have so many bugs in it that it would be unusable at the beginning of the semester.

After carefully considering the risks and advantages and consulting with the faculty, project management decided to "go for broke." It was reasonably confident of the software development and testing schedule and felt that there was adequate time for recovery in case of delays. They decided to support X version 11 as the primary interface, but version 10 could be invoked for compatibility purposes. X version 11 was available only in field test form, so Athena mounted an intensive testing program to stabilize it as much as possible.

The system development and release engineering groups were increased in size. Starting from a base of about 10 full-time equivalent people, they hired several more full-time staff. The bulk of the buildup, however, was with part-time student staff. An effort was made to hire every qualified student who could be located, and the head count of people in the groups went from 10 to about 40. The use of students proved to be very effective. Their quality and quantity of work exceeded expectations, even though they worked strange hours and broke most of the "conventional wisdom" management rules.

The increased staff allowed the mounting of a major development effort during the fall of 1986 and winter of 1987. Testing started in the spring and continued into the summer of 1987. Things went well considering the magnitude of the task, but there was some inevitable schedule slippage. As usual, the schedule slippage was offset by reducing testing. In a system of this size, problems of scale become evident only under heavy load testing. With Athena, adequate load testing the system to support 10,000 users with a staff of two dozen part-time testers was impossible; reduced testing time made the potential problems loom even larger. Moreover, because of the strict limitations on budget typical in the university environment, this buildup of system software staff caused some serious shortages in other project areas, such as user services.

The Gamble Pays Off

Labor Day 1987 arrived and fall semester started. The system looked relatively good, but the many unknowns due to the reduced testing period caused considerable anxiety. In the first few days of the term, several thousand students arrived and logged in, about 1000 for the first time. Many bugs and load-related problems immediately became evident but were fixed quickly. As the load built up over the first few days, the system exhibited many signs of stress, but it held together and performed acceptably. Bug fixing continued at a high rate as problems became evident, and performance continued to improve. Athena management had won the major gamble that it had taken.

The benefits expected also paid off. The applications programming interface stabilized, as did the user interface. All new applications were written for X version 11, minimizing the number of applications that had to be converted. Over the next year, the system continued to be stable and increasingly reliable. As a consequence, the start of fall semester 1988 was very smooth, with no major problems.

Earlier analysis had shown that users greatly preferred the workstation over the terminal. As more workstations became available, terminal and time-sharing usage dropped off substantially. Therefore in the fall of 1987 the time-sharing service was terminated, and the minicomputers supporting the time-sharing system were converted to file servers for the workstations. The cutover was very smooth, and few complained about the time-sharing system being turned off.

Because money was a finite resource and because of a big staff buildup to meet the needs of the start of fall semester, an adjustment had to be made. It took the form of a significant staff reduction in the spring of 1988, which as always, was relatively painful for all involved.

Over the next year, the emphasis changed from system development to productivity aids and deployment. Applications such as MATLAB were installed, greatly helping both users and application developers.

Late in 1988, Bond University in Australia requested that the Athena distributed software system be made available to them. A team of people was trained on the system, and it was installed in February 1989. Thus Bond became the first external university to use the Athena system. Installations at Digital, the University of Massachusetts, North Carolina State University, Iowa State University, and IBM were to follow.

All Students Receive Accounts

Prior to September 1989, the policy had been that only undergraduate students received Athena accounts. Exceptions were made for graduate students who had a special need, such as taking a course using Athena or developing software for Athena. The exceptions were relatively generous, and about one fourth (1100) of the graduate students had received Athena accounts. Early in 1989 Athena management decided to add all graduate students to the system that fall. This decision required a significant increase in the number of workstations.

Because of the lack of available floor space, project staff worked closely with the MIT departments to find additional space to install "department clusters." Although controlled and managed by the individual departments, these clusters serve as public workstations for small communities of users. Existing workstation clusters received additional units to the extent possible with the space available, and some new clusters were created. A major deployment push took place during the second week in September 1989 when nearly 130 workstations were installed in a three-day period. This high rate of installation was possible only because of the great improvement in tools and procedures developed in response to past problems.

All graduate students were given accounts on Athena with the opening of MIT in September 1989. Many of the load factors (for example, the number of new accounts generated per day) on the system doubled with the addition of the graduate students. However, response time remained acceptable and the system required no changes. Once all the graduate students were added to the system, faculty interest in the system increased substantially. Many more requests for workstations were received from departments, with the intent of making computing much more of an integral part of teaching and student interaction.

By the summer of 1990 the Athena system was fully functional, stable, reasonably reliable, and performed adequately. Maintenance continues, and the industry experience that it takes as many people to maintain a system as it does to develop it initially has proven to be the case with Athena.

Summary

The following is a summary of the important events in Athena development.

1978	Perceived lack of instructional computing resources
Early 1982	Athena concept developed
Early 1983	Discussions with potential sponsors
May 1983	Agreements finalized with Digital and IBM
May 1983	Project announced
September 1983	First Digital hardware arrives
December 1983	Steve Lerman appointed Director
March 1984	First Athena facility opens with time-sharing and some PC/ATs
November 1984	First workstations arrive
January 1985	All undergraduates receive accounts
March 1985	First public workstation cluster opens
September 1986	First production use of X version 10
September 1987	Time-sharing phased out, resulting in pure workstation environment
September 1987	X 11 put into production
September 1988	Earll Murman appointed Director
February 1989	Athena installed at Bond University—first external use
June 1989	Open Software Foundation grant to test and extend *Motif*
September 1989	All graduate students received accounts
December 1989	Athena installed at the University of Massachusetts/Amherst
January 1990	1000th workstation installed

Pedagogy

THREE

Athena as an Instructional System

As stated in the Preface, the purpose of Athena is to improve the quality of education at MIT. More specifically, Athena was planned to improve the quality of education in nonprogramming courses. Programming classes at MIT already had good access to computers, and Athena was not needed in that regard. Athena was not intended to reduce the cost of education; the MIT priority is quality, not low cost. Therefore, in the final analysis, Athena must be judged on its success in improving the quality of education at MIT, independent of its success as a computational system. Unfortunately, there is no general agreement on the criteria for educational success.

In this chapter we describe the use of Athena specifically in education at MIT and then review some of the more successful instructional projects that use Athena. Considerably more information is available in a 1989 MIT report [Avril 89]. We do not discuss the role of the multimedia workstation in instruction here, because we describe it in Chapter 7.

Background

Academic computing may be divided into three main segments: administration, research, and education. Historically, computing for these three segments was provided by large time-sharing systems. Many universities have uncoupled administrative computing from research or educational computing for security reasons, but until recently they still used the common technology of time-sharing. More recently, the price and performance of workstations and personal computers have made them attractive for educational computing.

In the early 1980s, when MIT began to give serious attention to upgrading its computing facility, many other academic institutions were doing the same thing. Various approaches were tried, including

- time-sharing;
- microcomputer labs;
- privately owned (but not required) microcomputers;
- privately owned (required) microcomputers; and
- institution-owned workstations.

Many colleges and universities, perhaps following the lead of Dartmouth, had been using time-sharing for years. Unfortunately, time-sharing systems required a large up-front capital investment and a large bureaucracy to operate.

Microcomputers, in the form of personal computers or workstations, were clearly very attractive. Entry cost was both low and modular, and minimal bureaucracy was involved. Indeed, a department could set up a microcomputer lab with no outside help (or interference). In some cases, the cost burden was shifted largely to the students by encouraging or requiring them to purchase microcomputer systems.

The required use of microcomputer systems on a widespread basis in higher education seems to have been implemented first at Clarkson College in 1983. That year, IBM-compatible personal computers built by Zenith Data Systems were issued to every incoming freshman as part of tuition. By 1986, all students had computers and about 4500 were in use. All software, much of which was developed at Clarkson, was provided at no extra cost, in many cases through software vending machines. College databases, including course catalogs, were made available through the personal computers. Thus students are able to plan course schedules up to four semesters in advance. Communication is provided using TCP/IP on NYSERnet, the New York State educational network system. Because every student has a personal computer, the faculty can take their availability for granted, and the students use them extensively both inside and outside class. Large-screen projection is accomplished by using light valve overlays on overhead projectors.

Drexel was another early user of personal computers, requiring every student to purchase an Apple Macintosh. Drexel accepted development of instructional software by faculty members as evidence of scholarly accomplishment.

Purchase was encouraged at other institutions, including Carnegie-Mellon University (IBM PCs) and Stevens Institute (Digital Pro 350s). Purchase was often encouraged through discounts and sales programs (for example, Apple Macintoshes at Dartmouth). A significant advantage of personal computers, in addition to cost, was the availability of personal productivity software, which was much better than software available for either time-sharing or workstation systems.

Even after computer access became available to the students, computer use in the classroom was relatively rare. More commonly, the student used the computer for personal productivity (word processing and spreadsheets) or for working homework problems. In a few instances, the instructor made software available for the particular course. This instructional software was normally on floppy disks, but in a few cases it could be down-line loaded over the network (e.g., at Dartmouth). In networked environments, access was often provided to mail, shared printers, library services, file transfer, and public bulletin boards.

Enter Workstations

Workstations have historically been far more powerful than personal computers. They have much larger memories, networking capability, and 1 million pixels on 19-inch screens, compared to personal computers with 300,000 pixels on a 14-inch screen. Workstations also tend to use Unix, which is functionally more powerful than DOS or proprietary operating systems used on personal computers. However, cost is a serious obstacle to the use of workstations for education. Workstations are commonly used for research, where cost is much less important. Only a few institutions, including MIT, have installed workstations for education on a broad scale—and then only if subsidized by the manufacturers.

Several categories of software must be considered in educational computing, including

- system software, such as Unix, DOS, X Window System, and compilers;

- personal productivity software, such as spreadsheets and word processing;
- instructional software, such as for teaching chemistry or physics;
- tools, such as database management systems and graphics drawing packages; and
- applications software, such as laboratory data management, data presentation, matrix manipulation, and statistical analysis.

At the time Athena was started, very little instructional software was available for personal computers—and essentially none at all for workstations. Thus institutions had to develop their own. Since then, instructional software has been developed faster for personal computers than for workstations, although in many instances the instructional software available for workstations is much more sophisticated.

The Computer's Role in Education

Computers have been used in higher education since soon after their invention with varying degrees of success. Although they have failed to live up to claims or expectations for improved quality, quantity, or cost of education, computers are now used at all levels in education. The many pedagogical models for using computers in teaching include the following.

- *"Skill and drill" exercises.* These are repetitive problems presented to the student to encourage memorization of basic facts and skills. This method is often used in the lower grades for routine drill in arithmetic and spelling.
- *Programmed instruction.* In this approach a page or so of material is presented to the student, and then several questions are asked. Depending on the answers to the questions, the student may be presented with new material, the same material again, or remedial material. Athena does not use this approach.
- *General information delivery system.* The computer can be used as a general purpose information retrieval and presentation system, drawing information from public databases, bibliographic services, on-line library services, and stored documentation. This capability gives the student rapid and efficient access to a wide variety of information services. Athena provides some access to some of these services and has all user documentation on-line.

- *Communications system.* The computer offers rapid communication among students, professors, lab instructors, and consultants. This capability can greatly improve learning efficiency. Athena provides this function through electronic mail and the *turnin* program, which provides for the electronic submission, grading, and return of homework and greatly speeds up the learning cycle. Experience has shown that electronic mail encourages students to help each other. The Athena *On-line Consultant* program provides communication between users and consultants on system questions. Late in 1989 this program was expanded to include question answering on course-specific information.
- *Tutoring.* Some research projects have shown that the computer can act as a "tutor" by delivering customized instruction to the student, based on the student's existing skill level and mastery of the material. In some instances natural language has been used to answer specific questions submitted by the student. Athena has not been applied in this way.
- *Simulation.* The computer can simulate complex systems and thus reveal the relationships among subsystems to provide better insight. Athena uses this approach extensively.
- *Laboratory instrumentation.* The computer can be an integral part of a laboratory experiment: gathering, manipulating, reducing, and presenting the data. This use prepares the student for similar systems in industry and commerce, where computer-controlled instrumentation is common. This model is used in Athena.
- *"Virtual laboratory."* This approach is a generalization of computer simulation. However, rather than having the ability to simulate only one specific system, the virtual laboratory allows the student to construct a simulation of a wide variety of systems using generalized objects. An example is a virtual physics laboratory, where the student constructs experiments using "objects" such as frictionless planes, massless pulleys, and rigid structures. Athena is moving toward use of this model.
- *Blackboard replacement.* The computer together with a large-screen display can present impromptu information in the classroom that the instructor would otherwise draw on a blackboard. With the computer, powerful paint and drawing programs can be used, along with prestored images, which present more complex and higher quality images than could be drawn by hand. In addition, animation, charts and graphs of several varieties, output of simulation, and video can be presented, which simply are

not possible to do by hand. Athena uses large-screen projection in the classroom for these functions.

■ *Recreation.* Recreation can be used as a powerful motivator to learn specific disciplines. With Athena, all users must acquire at least a minimal knowledge of Unix and Athena-supported applications software, such as editors and text formatters, in order to use the system. At the beginning of each semester, a series of minicourses provide students with a minimal capability in system use. Students are then allowed to use the system to play computer games. The experience with Athena has been that students learn a great deal about the system from creating, modifying, and playing computer games, so recreation is viewed as a legitimate part of the educational process.

The University of Illinois and Control Data Corporation funded and developed the Plato project—a large initiative in using computers for educational purposes. Students use terminals supported by large time-sharing systems. Installation of the terminals anticipated the multimedia workstations of today by offering not only text, but also graphics and image overlays from a rear-screen slide projector. The pedagogical model used in Plato is usually programmed instruction. However, it also includes mechanisms for instruction management, that is, to automatically keep track of test scores and course grades and to compute averages, deviations, and class completion information.

Although educational software was available during the first few years of Athena, it did not meet project needs. Some of it ran only on the personal computer, much of it was not available in source code (required to customize it to the Athena environment), and the rest could not be fully integrated with courses. As a result, the project staff soon realized that nearly all of the instructional software would have to be written by the faculty. The requirements for the instructional software were that it should be implemented in a set of modules that could be integrated into a system, be easily modified, be usable with projection in the classroom and be usable on workstations in a lab or for homework. The staff recognized the need for a method of software distribution that could disseminate and support software at an affordable price to students and faculty members alike.

The pedagogical models used largely (but not exclusively) at MIT rely heavily on simulation, analysis, and computer-aided design. Instructors make little or no use of the programmed instruction model. Thus, when teaching fluid dynamics, the instructor uses a simulation of a wind tunnel, rather than presenting a page of static information to the student. Many instructors use computers in their courses, and results indicate that computer use is more successful when it is closely integrated with classroom activity.

Instructional software is stored in the network file system in "course lockers." These can be attached to the user directory as read-only files by executing the *attach* command to make them appear to be local to the user's workstation.

Learning Problems

A major problem at most colleges and universities before the use of computers in education—including MIT before Athena—was that disciplines were taught using pencil and paper. This technology limited the kinds of pedagogical approaches possible. Those that can be used with pencil and paper generally use "clean" problems with closed-form analytic solutions, which is the only kind the students learn to solve. However, when students graduate and enter the industrial and commercial world, they find that the problems are relatively "messy" and that computer-aided techniques are used. The result can be a major discrepancy between what the student learns in school and what the graduate needs to know to be successful on the job. With Athena, computer-aided design techniques can be used in the classroom, and many instructors have begun using them. This approach reduces the gap between what the students are taught and what they need to know.

An early concern of the MIT faculty was that Athena might further separate the student from the physical world, rather than support the faculty objective of increasing exposure of the student to the physical world. However, pencil and paper technology also does not encourage or facilitate contact with the physical world. The use of workstations and simulations can approximate this contact and, in addition, can allow students to work on experiments that are either too costly or too dangerous to be done in a conventional lab.

A closely related problem is that of dealing with large amounts of data. Typically, many current problems in the industrial and commercial world do not lend themselves well to analytical approaches, requiring, instead, extensive data gathering and data manipulation.

When students attempt to solve these problems in an academic setting without proper computational resources, they often become so overwhelmed by the mass of data to be handled that they lose sight of the educational objectives of the task. Also, dealing manually with large amounts of data is time-consuming, limiting the number and types of problems that students can solve during the semester. With proper computational resources students can deal with large amounts of data efficiently. They can therefore use their time to best advantage, use techniques that they will need in the workplace, solve more problems, and understand better the instructional objectives of the problems.

Without adequate computer support, teaching design is relatively difficult and sometimes is made artificially simple to make it tractable. Therefore instructors tend to teach analysis, because it is better supported by available tools. Proper computer support, including computer-aided design tools, encourages instructors to teach realistic design techniques in addition to analysis and thereby cover the discipline more completely.

Two closely related problems in education are the difficulty that many students have in visualizing abstract concepts, in general, and the difficulty in translating formulas into intuition, in particular. Use of the computer can attack both problems. Many of the concepts required in science and engineering are difficult for the student to comprehend initially. This comprehension can be obtained more quickly through the use of simulation, animation, and graphic representation than by presentation of an abstract symbolic representation of the concept. For example, a student can grasp the meaning of a solution to a differential equation more easily if it is presented in graphic form than if it is simply presented in analytic form. Similarly, the equations representing fluid flow can be more easily translated into intuition if the various parts of the equation can be related to the physical world through simulation, animation, and graphics.

Students are able to solve more complex problems and examine "what if" questions by using Athena. Observation of the use of Athena suggests that students like to explore a discipline through simulation and that they gain considerable intuition and understanding of the discipline from such exploration. They are also able to proceed at their own pace, thus promoting individualized instruction.

Teaching with Personal Productivity Software

Perhaps the most common way to use computers in education is as personal productivity tools with generic software—a method widely used at MIT. Indeed, word processing is the most common use of Athena, which causes some to question whether doing word processing on workstations is an appropriate use of the system. Personal productivity software often used on Athena includes

- *Scribe,* a text formatter;
- *Gnu Emacs,* a screen editor;
- *MatLab,* a matrix manipulation and data presentation package;
- *Hoops,* an object-oriented graphics drawing package;
- *LaTEX,* a text formatter;
- *20/20,* a spreadsheet;
- *Macsyma,* a symbolic mathematical manipulation system;
- *NAG,* a package of numerical algorithm subroutines; and
- *RS/1,* a laboratory data management and presentation system.

At present, Athena staff tries to negotiate for a systemwide or sitewide software license whenever possible, so the software can be quite expensive. As resources permit, more personal productivity software is being obtained.

Developing and Using Instructional Courseware

Faculty members who wanted to use Athena as an integral part of their courses could obtain funding and hardware from the Athena resource allocation committees (see Chapter 9). The faculty member would develop the pedagogical concept and lay out the general functionality of the software. Students or professional staff hired for the task usually did the actual programming, although in some instances the programming was part of a thesis project.

Funding was made available for the first five years of Athena (1983–1988). Project grants ranged from $5000 to about $1 million, and, overall, 125 projects were funded. As might be expected, the majority of the proposals and funded projects were from the School of Engineering, because at that time about 60 percent of the MIT students (although only 30 percent of the faculty) were in engineering. However, a significant number of proposals and funded projects came from the other schools, including Science, Architecture and Planning, and Humanities and Social Sciences. Indeed, many of the more innovative uses of Athena in education came from the non-engineering disciplines, including the multimedia workstation, which came largely from language instruction.

Of the 125 projects funded, about one third resulted in software that is used regularly in courses, about one third resulted in nothing useful, and the rest fell somewhere in between. In retrospect, funding fewer projects at higher levels might have been better. The reasons for nonsuccess included underestimating the size of the task (often by a large amount), using an inappropriate pedagogical model, difficulties with the system, difficulty in obtaining necessary skills for programming (Unix, C, X Window System, human interface design), and declining interest on the part of the faculty member.

An applications development group was formed within the Athena project to assist course developers and to provide consulting in X windows and human interface design and implementation. At its peak it had 7–8 people, but the demand for consultation was much larger than the group could handle.

A serious concern on the part of younger, untenured faculty members is that work on instructional software does not appear to assist them in obtaining promotion and tenure. Departments do not have a good mechanism for evaluating original contributions made in instructional software, relative to more traditional original contributions in research.

At MIT Athena is generally used in the following ways for education:

- classroom demonstrations;
- electronic classroom sessions;
- homework problems;
- laboratory sessions;
- personal productivity aids; and
- submission and return of homework assignments.

For classroom demonstration, the instructor uses a large-screen projector to project the image on the workstation screen. Light valve projectors can give a 1 million pixel, bright image about eight feet by ten feet in size. This display provides an "electronic blackboard" capability. The instructor explains the concepts in the discipline with the aid of the system, using text, graphics, and animation, perhaps with a simulation of the physical or mathematical system. Students can use the same software used in the classroom to solve homework problems. This capability is especially true of simulation and computer-aided design software.

The most successful projects have yielded significant educational benefits. Among these courses are

- scientific and engineering writing;
- fluid dynamics (Aero-astro);
- statics (Civil Engineering);
- thermodynamics (Mechanical Engineering);
- physiology (Health, Sciences, and Technology; Electrical Engineering);
- membrane simulation (Electrical Engineering);
- special relativity (Physics); and
- infrared spectroscopy (Chemistry).

Athena Writing Project

One of the instructional software projects in which the system became an integral part of the course was the Athena Writing Project, led by Professors James Paradis and Ed Barrett [Paradis 88]. The purpose of the project was to develop an integrated classroom system for teaching courses in Scientific and Engineering Writing and Expository Writing. Paradis and Barrett teach these courses as a team to about 15 upper division students each semester. The method allows a fallback to conventional pencil and paper teaching if the workstation system fails. Individuals responsible for developing system improvements attend all classes. The classes are open, and observers are encouraged to attend.

The components of the system (called the *electronic on-line system,* or EOS) include computerized tools for editing, annotating, presenting, and filing elements of course writing activities. A closely related aspect of the project is the "electronic seminar room," or lab, where workstations can be used interactively in the course. The committee for writing instructions and computers guided this part of the project. Begun in 1983, this activity is quite successful and the system and software get better each semester.

The approach taken was to design a system that would support the standard classroom pedagogical process in an organic manner. Rather than try to create a piecemeal system around some existing packages, the system was designed from scratch. End-to-end support is provided for the course. That is, all aspects of the course, not just a few selected functions, are uniformly supported by the system. Although the tools developed are presently not widely available, eventually such tools will be commonplace. Thus the students need to learn writing in the context of electronic tools.

The major elements of the system are as follows.

- *Text editor.* *Emacs* is used as the text editor to retain compatibility with the text editor used in other parts of the Athena system. The text formatter used is Scribe, as is common throughout the campus. The *ez* editor from the Andrew project at CMU is now being tested; it provides What You See Is What You Get (WYSIWYG) capability.

- *Annotator.* The annotator provides the capability of adding on-line comments to a paper by using marginal notes, comments, corrections, highlighting of text, flagging of common errors, and long comments. The metaphor used corresponds to the familiar pencil and paper method.

- *Presenter.* The presentation system allows the sharing of information in the classroom through the use of the large-screen display or on workstations. The shared information generally consists of model text files, comparisons of student papers, in-class writing, and revisions.

- *File exchange.* The student can submit text files electronically to the instructor for grading and comment. The instructor can return the resulting annotated files electronically to the student. A complete revision history can be kept and retrieved as necessary. The program that accomplishes this electronic communication is called *turnin.* A command line interface performs the functions of

  turnin—submit a file to the grader;

  pickup—retrieve files annotated by grader;

  put/get—real time exchange of files in the electronic classroom;

  take—obtain electronic handouts; and

  grade—allows grader to obtain files, view, annotate, and return.

A graphic menu-driven user interface is now being tested. On-line help is available for writing tutorial and reference materials. Students can access the reference material both inside and outside the classroom.

Electronic Seminar Room

The best environment in which to teach a course with workstation support is a specially designed "electronic seminar room." Such a room was constructed as part of the writing project, and, based on the problems and shortcomings encountered, a much better "ideal" room has been designed.

The ideal electronic seminar room that has evolved is a classroom equipped with a screen at the front, controlled from the instructor's workstation. Each student has an individual workstation. All workstations are networked so that material on one can be instantly shown on others or on the large screen. At times, the students focus on their own workstations (for example, doing a writing exercise in class). At other times, they will watch the large screen for expository material or view material from another student's screen.

Athena Writing Project Experience

The system as it exists is relatively complex to use, and training is required for both students and instructors. The sheer volume of information can also be a problem. Text files are currently stored on-line for the duration of the semester plus one month; then the files are put on tape.

Evaluation indicates that students feel comfortable using the workstations both in and out of the classroom. They believe that this technology gives them an important advantage in learning the subject. Requiring students to carry out writing assignments in class has improved productivity and effectively related theory to practice. The individual workstations allow students to concentrate on individual in-class writing assignments in a timely manner and enable the instructors to work with each individual on a regular basis. The instant feedback provides strong reinforcement to eliminate errors and to follow correct procedures.

On-line evaluation of homework is much faster than conventional methods and encourages instructors to provide both more extensive and more specific comments. Papers are electronically composed, turned in, annotated, and revised, often several times. The time between submission of homework and its return with annotations and grades is usually less than one day.

In spite of some definite limitations, the electronic seminar room is viewed as successful and is being used by some 20 instructors. Two more electronic seminar rooms are being developed. The electronic *turnin* program is being used by 18–20 instructors, not all of whom use the electronic classroom.

Fluid Dynamics

Late in 1983, a group of 12 professors from the Fluids Division of the Aeronautics and Astronautics Department spent two days in a retreat at the MIT Endicott House developing a strategy for using Athena's facilities. The department has about 300 undergraduate students and all are required to take at least some coursework in fluid dynamics. This discipline has long been difficult for students to grasp when taught by traditional means. The faculty members decided to explore the uses of Athena workstations in the teaching of fluid dynamics and agreed that each would develop one of the modules required for the course.

Pedagogical Objectives and Methods

The pedagogical approach taken was to augment and enhance traditional methods using the graphics and computational power of the workstation, rather than trying to automate existing techniques. Of particular interest was the opportunity to use the interactivity of the system. The system was to be developed so that students would not need to know programming. The specific pedagogical objectives [Murman 87] were

- enhancement of existing material in areas where understanding traditionally has been difficult, including dimensional analysis, kinematic concepts of convective systems, and kinetic theory of gases;
- application of existing material through hands-on experiments; and
- replacement of some existing material through the use of modern computational approaches to the study of subsonic flow and boundary layers.

To achieve these objectives, those working on the project developed an approach based primarily on simulation of physical systems (such as a wind tunnel), also called the *virtual laboratory* approach. Implementation was based on modules, wherein a module is a program related to a set of closely related concepts. The participants designed modules to be used as part of a lecture, for homework problems (worked outside of class), and for self-study. Of particular importance, the module designs had to be integral parts of the teaching approach and closely coupled to classroom methodology. One or more faculty members developed the general approach for each module, based on the topic, flow of information, and concepts to be communicated. Once the general approach was developed, undergraduates developed the programs with help from the Athena staff.

The modules were organized by technical topic, not by course. A module might be used in a fundamentals course initially, and then perhaps a year or two later the same module might be used to teach an advanced version of the same topic.

Implementation

The software was written mainly in FORTRAN 77, with some written in C. Because the designers clearly understood the importance of the human interface they devoted considerable effort to its design and implementation.

Project Athena purchased and supported a commercially available user interface generation package called BLOX. It provided a graphics subroutine library, menus, icons, screen layout, and on-line help. A significant benefit of BLOX was that it provided an applications interface that could be ported to X11. The project staff decided to standardize on BLOX, because it allowed the department to standardize the "look and feel" of the human interfaces across the modules.

A total of 25 modules, collectively referred to as the TODOR system (named after the famous aerodynamicist Professor Theodore von Karman), have been implemented. The implementation approach taken relied heavily on menus, graphics, and animation. Most input is with the mouse. The designers expended considerable effort to standardize the user interface and make it friendly, error-free, and highly interactive. Overall, the efforts of 14 instructors, 39 undergraduate students, and two full-time programmers went into the development of TODOR. Details of the implementation are given in Murman's 1987 report.

When the modules are used for problem sets or take-home exams, the students are usually required to obtain results from the module and then combine them with other analyses to complete the assignment. To make sure that the student understands the underlying methodology, the instructor often requires a solution by hand first. Then the student can use the computer version to explore many more cases than could be done by manual methods. In this way, the software can be used for design problems rather than being limited to analysis.

Results

Workstations have characteristics quite different from the traditional teaching materials of books, blackboards, and pencils and paper, thus complementing them well. An important area of difference is in the degree of interactivity allowed. A student can view a book or even listen to a lecture in a rather passive way, but the interactive nature of the workstation demands attention and active participation.

The ability to run electronic experiments and to generate realistic data seems to help students internalize theory. In a real sense, theory interpolates experimental data. Another important characteristic of workstations is the ability to provide animation. This feature appears to have a significant advantage in explaining difficult and abstract concepts. Animation is especially useful when combined with interaction, so that the student can run a number of cases to see how the experiment progresses. The multiple means of providing visualization can also be important. Data can be provided in tabular, graphic, and animated form simultaneously. Inputs can be shown at the same time as outputs.

About 250 students use the TODOR software each year. Both faculty members and students have stated (in surveys) that Athena has significantly improved the quality and quantity of course material taught. In the classroom, the faculty has found that the ability to generate graphic displays and to show simultaneity of events has added significantly to lecture effectiveness.

The use of Athena with problem sets and take-home exams has been "an unqualified success" in the words of Professor Leon Trilling of the MIT faculty, who interviewed a group of students. The problems assigned are more realistic than those possible with purely analytic approaches, and they are more comparable to on-the-job assignments than were previous problem sets.

A major drawback to the expanded use of Athena in this department is the extraordinary effort required to develop the software, most of which is devoted to the human interface. Module design and development require a high level of expertise. Typical module implementation required a year of development and $20,000 to become operational. Use of the modules shows areas of needed improvements, and development typically continues for years.

TODOR is now being made available to the general engineering community through a low-cost licensing arrangement, and some 20 licenses have been purchased so far. TUDOR won an Educom/ NCRIPTAL (National Center for Research to Improve Postsecondary Teaching and Learning) best engineering software award in 1989.

Civil Engineering

The GROWLTIGER program [Slater 87] is a structural analysis and design package for two-dimensional mechanical structures, such as bridges or buildings. It provides an interactive environment for experimenting with the design of structures and feedback to the student on the behavior of the resulting structure. Professor John Slater designed the program and implemented it with the help of graduate students. The package provides interactive input and editing of the geometry and material characteristics of the structure. Its output provides a graphic display of deformation relative to the original structure, as well as bending moments, shears, mode shapes, and natural frequencies. GROWLTIGER is intended for use by students of entry-level courses through graduate school.

The structure is defined to GROWLTIGER as a set of nodes, which are connected by members. The members are straight structural elements, such as bars or beams, which start and end at nodes. The members may be constructed of any material and have any prismatic cross section. They may be connected to the nodes by either momentless pins (without torque) or by moment-resisting rigid-frame connections. Several prestored truss types are available in the system. Loads may be expressed as nodal loads, member loads, and support settlements; any self-consistent set of units may be used. The analytic approach assumes linear elastic displacement.

The results of the analysis may be displayed graphically to scale, or they may be printed in numeric or graphic form. A steel design module and tutor are also available for use in association with the analytic procedure.

To use the system, the student defines a structure to the system interactively. The steps in defining the structure include specifying the

- system of units;
- location of the nodes;
- start and end nodes of each member and type of connection (pin or rigid);
- node displacement boundary conditions;
- nodal and member loads;
- support settlements;
- material properties and unit system;
- cross-sectional properties and unit system; and
- data file name.

The nodal boundary conditions can be fixed, pinned, roller, slider, frame truss, or free. The graphic presentation includes the conventional symbol used for each of these conditions. It also allows presentation of several output functions simultaneously (for example, geometry, loads, deformation, shear, and bending).

GROWLTIGER uses the X Window System, as does all Athena software. The graphic output appears in the main window of the display. Several control buttons surround the main window, allowing the user to control the display. The user may pan and zoom on the structure, as well as plot dimensions, draw coordinate grids, and activate hardcopy. A button to control panning is located in each corner of the main window. Along the top of the main window are buttons to control zoom in/out, restore, percent, clip box, grid on, dimension on, redraw, and print. Menus are used extensively in GROWLTIGER, and no programming knowledge is required.

Thermodynamics

The Computer Aided Thermodynamics (CAT) package was developed by Professors Gilberto Russo and Joseph Smith of the Mechanical Engineering Department to assist in teaching classical thermodynamics [Russo 86]. CAT is designed to solve a wide range of thermodynamic problems, using a single set of basic algorithms and a single set of boundary conditions. The boundary conditions imposed on all problems are those of closed, isolated systems in which no mass, energy, or entropy crosses the boundary. A front end to the basic algorithm module is used to communicate with the user, both for accepting input and editing instructions and for displaying the problem structure and results.

CAT system components are

- graphic symbolic language to enter the problem;
- a compiler to generate equations;
- numerical solution generator; and
- user interface for output.

CAT is written in FORTRAN 77. The source code is about 1 M byte in size, and the binaries are about 500 K bytes.

Thermodynamic systems are displayed as ordered meshes of interconnected elements representing the physics of the problem. The individual elements, such as piston, fluid, or thermal capacity, are available in an element library. Arbitrary levels of complexity can be obtained by adding elements to the mesh.

Thermodynamic elements are modeled independently of any particular problem. They are represented by sets of equations that determine the behavior of the element in terms of its equilibrium state equations and derived quantities relative to its local frame of reference. Elements are of two types: storage and interconnection. Storage elements are used to model parts of the system whose energy varies. Interconnection elements model the interaction between storage elements, with each element modeling one interaction.

The CAT screen is divided into functional areas for model construction, system prompts, menus, and icons, including symbols for elements. The user defines the problem to the system by creating a mesh of elements (from the library of elements), using the mouse. The mesh of elements is represented graphically. When the mesh is complete, the system prompts the user for the initial conditions. The program then generates the solution from the physical properties and initial conditions by solving the set of simultaneous equations. Output is in tabular form or in various standard graphic forms—on the screen or on hardcopy.

CAT is important, because it changed the basic approach to teaching thermodynamics. It represents more than a change in presentation methods; it changed basic methodology.

Physiology

Cardiovascular physiology has been taught at MIT for several years with the aid of a mathematical model using lumped parameter differential equations. More recently, an interactive course module was developed [Davis 88] as part of Athena, with X Windows and the X Toolkit in a workstation environment.

Human physiology is a difficult discipline to teach effectively because of the complex interaction of the physical processes in a three-dimensional environment. The faculty desired a modeling system in which students could introduce common abnormal conditions in the cardiovascular system by suitably modifying the parameters of the system. The students could then observe the resulting deviations in the observable parameters of pressure and flow. This process would help the student understand the relationship of pathological conditions in the patient and the resulting symptoms. The student could also study the relationship of corrective measures and the resulting change in symptoms.

The model relates changes in blood pressure, volume, and flow through six cardiovascular body compartments. Each compartment is modeled by parameters for hydraulic capacitance, resistance, and zero pressure volume. The parameters may be varied as a function of time to model the properties of the heart. The overall simulation is modeled as a hydraulic system with valves, reservoirs, pipes, and capacitance devices. The model is implemented as a set of six differential equations for six nodal points that is solved by the Runge–Kutta method. The model provides pressure, volume, and flow rates at each of the nodes as the functions of time. The model operates in real time, simulating a real subject. The instructor may set the parameters of the subject to model specific case histories. The model has been validated by comparison with laboratory measurements.

The major improvement in simulation for the workstation environment was the addition of a relatively sophisticated, user friendly human interface. The human interface approach makes extensive use of graphics and menus, with the mouse used as the primary input device. In operation, the mathematical model runs continuously, sending a stream of results to the human interface as a real subject would. The user can then control the human interface to select the parameters of interest to be displayed.

The user is presented with a primary graphic display of the system with its six nodes. The user edits the model parameters by first selecting the node of interest with the mouse and then the component within that node. The user may also select parameters and axes to be plotted. Variables can be plotted as a function of time or as functions of each other.

The top-level human interface uses a row of command buttons at the top of the screen over the primary graphic display. The user may plot a maximum of three dependent variables simultaneously. If the independent variable is time, the system simulates a scrolling strip chart. When the user requests multiple simultaneous charts, the system displays them in a tiled arrangement so that they do not obscure each other. The user, however, may then control size and location.

The cardiovascular simulator is now being used in a Quantitative Physiology course. The system has received generally favorable reviews in terms of meeting its pedagogical objectives.

Membrane Simulation

The Hodgkin–Huxley model, which won the 1963 Nobel prize, consists of a set of coupled nonlinear algebraic and ordinary differential equations that describe the electrical characteristics of the membrane of the giant axon of the squid. Professor Thomas Weiss of the Electrical Engineering and Computer Science Department developed software [Avril 89] that allows users to explore this model of nerve-cell membrane response to electrical stimulation for different environmental variables, such as the temperature and concentrations of ions. The user may manipulate the electrical stimulus, model parameters, and environmental variables and observe the responses using powerful graphic tools. This program simplifies the model, allowing membrane study by undergraduate students in such diverse disciplines as biology, engineering, mathematics, and physics.

The principles involved underlie our understanding of the electrical properties of all electrically excitable cells, such as nerve and muscle cells. The model explains the generation of "action potentials" used by cells to transmit nerve messages, initiate mechanical contractions, and trigger chemical secretions. Because the model is complex, it was rarely taught in a way that allows students to acquire an understanding of electrical excitability. This program overcomes that problem by giving students direct access to the model and an ability to explore it by performing simulation experiments. A reasonable starting parameter set encourages initial exploration and supports gradual learning. Later, students may explore all the parameters and observe results. These results appear in clear, complete form and can be saved, compared with other results, and included in documents. By making this process accessible to students, the software encourages deeper understanding of electrical excitability and is a useful method for teaching students how to formulate and execute a research project. This software won a Best Engineering Software award in the 1990 Educom/NCRIPTAL competition.

Physics—Special Relativity

The teaching of the theory of Special Relativity in physics presents a considerable challenge, because most of its consequences are counterintuitive. To assist in the teaching of this subject, a module set [Taylor 86] has been created as part of Athena, using the "modeling toolkit" (or "microworlds") pedagogical approach. Its designers implemented the module set differently from most other Athena modules, that is, on stand-alone personal computers rather than on networked Athena workstations.

The following modules were developed for this subject.

- *Visual Appearance*. This program presents a simple graphic representation of a landscape as seen by an observer moving at relativistic speed. The landscape consists of a large cube, a small cube, a pyramid, and a "skyscraper." At high simulated speeds, these figures are distorted according to the laws of relativity. The operator may accelerate, decelerate, turn right and left, and change altitude.

- *Spacetime*. This program presents four different graphic representations of the same data. The first is a "position versus velocity" display of objects, including a shuttle, clocks, rods, and light flashes on a highway. The second is a "position versus time" view of a spacetime diagram. The third shows events and world lines of objects that move along the highway. The user places objects and events on the highway and on the spacetime diagram. The user may then step time forward or backward, assume the viewpoint of an object on the highway, or transform the spacetime diagram from one frame of reference to another. The fourth representation is a table of numerical values on events and objects that can be annotated by the user.

■ *Collision*. This program simulates relativistic collisions in two dimensions. It provides three displays of the information. This first is an input table, on which the user may enter known quantities about each incoming and outgoing particle or relations among them. The program then attempts to complete the table. The second is a display of the resulting interactions as an animated movie. The third is a display of energy versus momentum for each particle.

The programs are distributed on diskettes to students and are executed on personal computers in labs.

Results

The instructor evaluated extensively the value that students placed on the modules. Although the students responded that all of the modules were useful, there was a definite correlation between the amount of interactivity and the value given a module. Those programs that were mostly demonstration (such as VisualAppearance) were of value the first time they were shown but had little value after that. The programs with much more interaction, such as Spacetime and Collision were perceived to have much more value. A primary value of the programs as reported by the students was the ability to help them visualize the consequences of the algebraic formulation of the model.

Both students and faculty members had been concerned that use of computers would allow the students to blindly plug in values to solve problems without understanding of the theory behind the solution. To minimize this problem, instructors administered no more than one third of the exercises and none of the tests on the computer. As Taylor states, "Computers are used to reduce the usual pathological dependency on algebraic models of the subject, not to encourage dependency on the computer models of the subject!"

Other important lessons were learned about the use of computers in higher education. To motivate students to use the programs, instructors must assign, collect, and grade problems requiring their use. Moreover, instructors should require students to hand in a printout of the displays and results with the problem sets.

Algebra and graphics can work together synergistically. The specific solutions displayed must be complemented by the general algebraic solution. That is, the graphic information must be supported by numeric information. As Taylor states, the learning of a new concept becomes a three-step process. The first is visualizing the phenomenon in the setting of a specific case, then viewing animations and alternative representations of the specific case. The second is developing the analytic formulation of the general problem. The third is demonstrating that the analytic formulation gives the same answer as the specific case. Thus the rigor and generality of the analytic solution is combined with the visual representation of specific cases. The resulting mutual reinforcement of the two approaches substantially improves the learning experience.

As with the other modules developed for Athena, this module set required a significant investment of resources and far in excess of that originally estimated. Also, based on use and feedback, the program evolved and improved over a period of several years.

The faculty members who worked on the project stated that "developing the programs changes the developers more than using the programs changes the users." The process of developing the programs significantly enlarged the participants' view of the subject and made thinking about the subject much more visual—to the extent that transformed both their professional life and view of the subject. Other faculty developers have reported similar experiences. This program won a prize as "the Best Physics and Best Tool Software" awarded by Educom in October 1988.

Chemistry—Infrared Spectroscopy

Laboratory experiments can be a significant drain on student time. In some cases, the students can be overwhelmed by the mass of data to be gathered, computed, and compared to theory. Simply dealing with the mass of data could cause the student to lose sight of the educational objectives of the course. For these reasons, Professors Jeffrey Steinfeld and Keith Nelson led the effort to develop a personal computer-based laboratory data management system for an Advanced Chemistry Laboratory course.

One package in this system is Peakfinder, which was programmed by Simpson Garfinkel, an undergraduate in Chemistry and Computer Science. Peakfinder accepts data from the infrared spectrometer, scans the data, and finds the peaks. Students assign values to the peaks, and the program records the values and the distances between them. The program then computes the parameters of the quantum mechanical equations to compare theoretical and experimental results. Peakfinder also provides data needed to compute bond lengths and to generate a spectrum from a model based on values provided by the student.

Computer use has significantly reduced the time students spend collecting and analyzing data (intellectually trivial tasks) and has improved the quality of term papers. Student response to the use of computers for this task is "overwhelmingly positive" [Turkle 88].

Athena Laboratory Data System

All good ideas, including coherence, can be carried too far. Development of the Laboratory Data System is an example of such an attempt; thus this development is an important contrast to the success of the course systems described.

The Laboratory Data System [Milgram 87] was developed by Professor Jerome Milgram of the Ocean Engineering Department for use in a number of different laboratory courses with widely differing requirements. In general, it was to provide signal capture and analog-to-digital conversion for several channels simultaneously, with sampling rates of a few tens of kilosamples per second. A typical example is the instrumentation of a towing tank for measuring forces on a ship hull as a function of several analog variables. Initial development concentrated on a coherent system approach based on workstations and Unix. In the end, the developers could not make this approach work. The version of Unix that was available simply did not have sufficient real time control to reach the desired sampling rates. The system was also very expensive because of its workstation base.

The developers finally realized that this effort was an example of pushing coherence too far. The workstation-based approach was finally abandoned in favor of a personal computer–based system using DOS. The resulting system easily reached the desired sampling rates, was relatively simple to use, and could make use of a wide variety of add-in sampling and conversion boards that are available for the PC bus. The system is widely used and highly successful.

The Athena laboratory computer is a standard XT or AT microcomputer with a hard disk, a Hercules graphics card, 640 K bytes of memory, and an 8087 math coprocessor. In addition it contains laboratory interfacing hardware and software. Software includes DOS, FORTRAN, EMACS, UnkelScope (a third-party laboratory data management system), SLIP (a set of simple laboratory interfacing programs), and graphics drivers.

The SLIP programs are a set of subroutines that allow the user to sample the output of one or several A/D converters, write the data to a disk file, and draw a graph of the data versus time on the screen. The analog input channel accepts an input signal between +10 volts and −10 volts and provides an output of +2048 to −2048 counts. The maximum single channel data rate is 40,000 samples per second, and the maximum multichannel data rate is 28,000 samples per second for the combined channels. The user provides input parameters of

- sampling frequency;
- number of data points (5000 maximum);
- channel number; and
- file name for output.

The UnkelScope program is much the same for data capture but has added features. The input parameters can be stored and loaded from a file, and more flexibility in viewing the output data on the screen is available. This program provides far more functionality for manipulating the output, including calibration corrections, more flexible plotting, applying high pass, low pass, and band pass digital filters, computing the power spectral density, integration, differentiation, and a number of other functions.

Courses Using Special Software

Courses using Athena with special instructional software are listed in the following table, along with the software utilized. The table was prepared by Naomi Schmidt of the Athena staff and is used with her permission.

Subjects Using Athena

Subject Name	Software
Civil Engineering	
Introduction to Computers and Engineering Problem Solving	c;turnin/pickup;olta
Behavior of Physical Systems	growltiger★
Computer Models of Physical and Engineering Systems	c
Numerical Modeling of Physical Systems	FORTRAN;c
Engineering Geology	Geology Tutor★

Mechanical Engineering

Methods of Engineering Analysis	NAG
Elementary Programming and Machine Computation	FORTRAN;turnin/pickup
Control Systems Principles	clascon★;visdycon★
Advanced System Dynamics and Control	matrixx;simnon
Multivariable Control Systems	matrixx;simnon
Computer Aided Engineering	sgi_graphics_library
Analysis and Design of Digital Control Systems	Matlab;simnon;visdycon★
Advanced Fluid Mechanics	nekton^2
Computational Fluid Dynamics	nekton^2
Thermodynamics	CAT★
Convective Heat and Mass Transfer	nekton^2
Measurement and Instrumentation	TEX
Project Laboratory	FORTRAN
Design Projects	sc
Advanced Engineering Design	opt2★
Designing Smart Machines	Matlab;simnon;visdycon★
Quantitative Physiology; Cells and Tissues	channel★;cmt★; diffuse★;hh★;rwalk★
Artificial Intelligence in Design and Manufacturing	FMS.simulator★;asset★

Materials Science

Polymer Engineering	feap★;prep★;post★;mesh★
Mechanics of Materials	feap★;prep★;post★;mesh★
Structure of Solids	crystal structure★
Transport Phenomena in Materials Engineering	c;FORTRAN; own_software★

Electrical Engineering and Computer Science

Quantitative Physiology; Cells and Tissues	channel★;cmt★; diffuse★;hh★;rwalk★
Quantitative Physiology; Organ Transport Systems	cardiovascular_simulator★
Artificial Intelligence	lisp
Computer Graphics	tgif★
Probabilistic Systems Analysis	LAS★;own_software★
Introductory Digital Systems Laboratory	fsm★;osc★;kmap★
Laboratory in Software Engineering	clu^2
Introduction to Dynamic System	Matlab
Multivariable Control Systems	matrixx;simnon
Dynamic System	Matlab
Introduction to Optimization	opt2★
Numerical Simulation of Large Scale Circuits	simlab
Discrete-Time Signal Processing	Matlab
Two-dimensional Signal and Image Processing	under development

Applied Probability	LAS★
Programming Languages	scheme[2]
Dataflow Architecture and Languages	scheme[2]
Natural Language and Computer Representation of Knowledge	lisp
Dielectric Physics and Electrical Insulation	under development

Biology

Metazoan Cell Biology	video courseware★

Physics

Computational Physics	FORTRAN
Observational Techniques of Optical Astronomy	observe★;starchart★

Chemical Engineering

Introduction to Computer Methods	FORTRAN;c;pplot★
Integrated Chemical Engineering	batchfrac★

Earth, Atmosphere, and Planetary Sciences

Chaos and Complexity	sine★;logistic★; maplog★;henon★;dist★
Observational Techniques of Optical Astronomy	observe★;starchart★
Planetary Science	own_software★

Ocean Engineering

Computer-Aided Hydrostatics and Hull Surface Definition	ducksoup★;numint★; mouseloft★;shcp★
Introduction to Ocean Science and Technology	Matlab
Marine Hydrodynamics	hydro★
Hydrofoils and Propellers	todor★
Principles of Naval Ship Design	asset★;tss86★;shcp★;smp★
Numerical Methods with Applications to Marine Problems	turnin/pickup;FORTRAN
Management of Marine Systems	own_software★
Mechanical Vibrations	NAG

Economics

Engineering Aspects of Economic Analysis	asses★
Econometrics	sst★
Economic Structures of Cities	sst★

Aero–Astro

Aerodynamics	todor★
Numerical Fluid Dynamics	FORTRAN;grafic[2]
Advanced Computational Fluid Dynamics	FORTRAN;grafic[2]
Aerodynamics of Flight Vehicles	todor★
Molecular Gas Dynamics of Space and Reentry	todor★
Principles of Automatic Control	clascon★

Algorithms for Function Minimization and Optimal Control	Matlab
Rocket Propulsion	todor★

Political Science

Political Science Laboratory	sst★
Debates and Arguments	gmats★;scheme[2];c
Conflict and Its Resolution	gmats★

Mathematics

Calculus	LAS★
Differential Equations	1803★
Numerical Methods of Applied Mathematics	unknown
Topics in Numerical Analysis	Matlab

Humanities

French II	A la rencontre do Philippe★;Direction Paris★
Spanish III	No recuerdo★
Scientific and Engineering Writing	turnin/pickup

Nuclear Engineering

Advanced Engineering of Nuclear Reactors	thermit★
Modeling and Simulation	macsyma;c;FORTRAN
Interactions of Radiation with Matter	unknown

Health Sciences and Technology

Cardiovascular Pathophysiology	cvssm★
Quantitative Physiology; Cells and Tissues	channel★;cmt★; diffuse★;hh★;rwalk★
Medical Image Processing	image_processing software

Notes:

1. This list includes those courses that use Athena for purposes other than simple word processing. These include problem sets, programming languages, distribution and collection of course materials, modeling and visualization aids, etc. Some of the software packages are third-party packages, others were written at Athena and are general resources, and still others were written with a particular subject in mind. In the last category are some packages that were written for one subject but found useful in other subjects or even other departments.
2. The symbol ★ following the name of a software package denotes courseware developed at MIT by faculty for use on Athena.
3. The symbol [2] denotes software developed at MIT on another platform and then ported to Athena.
4. The designation own_software means that the software package does not have a name known to the Athena staff and was developed specifically for that subject, residing in a course locker or file system.
5. LAS is the Lecture Authoring System, which is a general authoring system being developed in the hope that it will eventually be used across the curriculum.
6. turnin/pickup and olta were developed by the Athena staff as general utilities for use in an educational environment. The first is for electronic submission and sharing of files, and the latter is an On-Line TA program which is parallel to the Athena On-Line Consultant system.

Lessons Learned

The projection of workstation images as an integral part of classroom activity proved to be very effective in communicating new ideas and explaining difficult principles. It also proved to be an effective way to allow students and instructors to interact in real time, greatly increasing productivity. One difficulty is that, if the equipment does not work, major disruptions can occur in the class. In the early days of Athena, numerous equipment and system problems seriously curtailed use of the workstations in the classroom. Although most of these problems have been solved, having a backup mechanism, perhaps videotape, is always important.

The value of networking has been demonstrated clearly, with the writing course as a concrete example. Networking greatly improved communication between the students and the faculty members, with a resulting increase in the quality and quantity of material taught. The concept of a "course locker" proved to be an economical way of storing software in the system so that it is universally accessible.

Teaching a course and using teaching materials such as instructional software involves personal preference and choice. Therefore the instructional software must be flexible enough to be integrated easily and uniquely with other teaching materials and information by every instructor.

The cost and skill levels required to develop instructional software have proven to be far greater than first assumed, raising a serious barrier to development of large amounts of such software. Far better developmental tools are required, perhaps in the form of authoring environments. In particular, experience has shown that, on average, 50 percent and in some cases as much as 90 percent of the labor required is for developing good human interfaces. Improving the efficiency of developing such interfaces is a key to increasing the amount of quality instructional software. These improvements can only come from better tools. A mechanism to distribute and support this software is also crucial.

Difficulty that both students and faculty members had with learning the Unix user interface (C shell and system application programs, such as emacs, in the case of Athena) proved to be a barrier to use of the system. Ideally, users should interact with a menu and graphic shell rather than with the Unix command language. Perhaps some of the new developments by industrial consortia (Open Software Foundation and Unix International) will provide the needed improvements.

The team approach to the development of instructional software is often much more successful than for each individual to develop his or her own. The team can be organized around a discipline or department and can more readily assemble the people and skills needed to develop high-quality software. Comments by colleagues, even about preliminary versions, can be very helpful in improving software.

Instructional software often evolves over several semesters. The experience gained in using the software provides valuable insight into how to do it better. Producing the "perfect" software package the first time around is impossible and not necessary, but persistence and continuity can lead to a final product that will relate well to lectures and problem sets.

Many faculty members who have developed instructional modules report that this experience changed not only the way that they teach the material, but also that it led to fundamental changes in the way they view the discipline (e.g., thermodynamics and special relativity). This result, of course, was one of the original objectives of introducing computers in education, and must be considered as a success.

Remaining Concerns

Although there have been numerous clear successes in improving the quality of education with Athena, there also have been failures. The reasons for these failures requires more analysis, because the proper use of computers in education is far from understood. There is a lack of general agreement in this area by the MIT faculty, in particular. Many faculty members believe in a core of "sacred" aspects of the educational process, which should not be computerized. Doing so, they feel, would mean loss of contact with the physical world and loss of understanding of the theory behind the ability to "deliver numbers." These concerns are described in Turkel's evaluation [Turkel 88].

The computer will continue to make inroads into those areas of education that are amenable to computation as techniques are improved. Indeed, educators must move beyond the excessive dependence on analytic models that characterizes current science and engineering education. Equally important, however, is preventing loss of the physical experience and understanding of the theory behind the numbers. For these and other reasons a consensus must be developed on the appropriate use of computers in higher education. Only then can far more and better educational software be developed, used, and shared.

FOUR

Athena and
the Faculty

One of the more difficult areas in Athena development was the relationship of the project to the faculty. The primary reasons were conflicting goals and poor communication. Even though the project leaders were faculty members the requirements of the project led to polarization between participants and nonparticipants. The history and nature of the relationship between Athena and the faculty was studied and documented in detail [Turkel 88].

Concept versus Reality

Recall that the initial concept had been to obtain the system from a single vendor using off-the-shelf operating systems. The installation of the system was thought to be virtually a turnkey deployment that could be done relatively quickly and inexpensively. The model of computing popular at that time was time-sharing, and indeed the time-sharing technology was mature enough that systems could be deployed routinely with minimal system software development. Because details of the system were not available, faculty members assumed that it would meet their diverse objectives.

Proponents seriously underestimated the degree to which time-sharing operating systems were inappropriate to the workstation environment. As described earlier, time-sharing operating systems do not work well in a workstation environment, because workstations

69

violate many of the fundamental assumptions that time-sharing systems are based on.

The combination of these problems caused serious underestimation of the size and cost of system development. As planning for deployment proceeded, the impact of the system's shortcomings gradually emerged over a period of about two years. Unfortunately, the budget did not allow for an adequate system development effort. Even if the true magnitude of the task had been understood with perfect foresight, it is still unlikely that enough money could have been obtained. Although the hardware grants for the system were relatively generous, little cash was available to fund people.

As a result the system was

- late by two years;
- not a panacea, because it met a midrange of computing needs but did not support features such as color or 3-D which were critical to some applications;
- initially lacking in productivity aids, such as plotting tools, WYSIWYG editors, statistical analysis packages, and paint programs; and
- lacking in software development tools, such as graphics, human interface development aids, and courseware development systems that were available on stand-alone systems costing much less.

Another problem was that both vendors were late with workstation hardware. This further delayed system development and consumed valuable staff time that could not easily be spared. Also, both vendors were used to a time-sharing, text-oriented environment and had little software available that was not oriented to monospaced text on terminals.

Many of the strategic decisions described in Chapter 2 caused tension between the project and the faculty, partly because of poor communication and partly because of differing goals. Whereas the faculty wanted the system operational immediately (and thought they had been promised that), the project team first had to develop the infrastructure and then the system. Whereas the faculty wanted a system customized to each professor's needs, the project team wanted a "one size fits all" approach to minimize cost. Whereas the faculty wanted something simple immediately, the project team wanted a system with growth potential and longevity. Thus, although each of the strategic decisions was justified as being important to the success of the project (and in retrospect, they probably were the right decisions), each also had undesirable side effects on relations with the faculty.

Effects of Strategic Decisions

Although the Athena approach emphasized homogeneity to maximize sharing and to control cost, departmental computing approaches varied greatly. Some of these differences reflected the diverse orientations and experiences of faculty members, others their perceived needs and priorities. For example, some departments wanted color, 3-D, and high-performance processing; others did not. One consequence of these differences was the view that Athena was trying to impose its model of computing on all faculty members—whether it fit or not. The faculty also felt that Athena should meet all instructional needs. Although Athena did not claim to do this, in practice it was the primary source of funding, and its existence made difficult the obtaining of funding from other sources.

Unix was picked over DOS, because it had functionality that was important in the workstation environment. Subsequently, the ease of developing instructional applications with DOS has made it more popular in the educational software field than had been foreseen. Its shortcomings in networking and shared resource environments have been partially overcome, although much of the development with DOS has been in a stand-alone environment. Although many faculty members accepted the system as defined by Athena, many others wanted something else, often for ease of development and use or compatibility with other software packages. Some faculty wanted to use DOS instead of Unix because of

- its ease of use;
- its popularity in instructional computing;
- the large amount of application software available for it; and
- the large market for instructional software created at MIT that existed at other colleges.

Some wanted to use Basic rather than C. Most departments also had their favorite application packages, such as those for statistical analysis and graphics. Later, many wanted to use Macintoshes rather than workstations to get access to its high-quality and easy-to-use application software.

Centralization of system control in the project meant less departmental control. The departments had traditionally been the source of planning, control, guidance, and resource allocation. As is usually the case at MIT, attitudes toward centralization of control varied greatly among the schools. Departments that had their own computer facilities before Athena tended to react negatively to the loss of control to an outside central authority. This reaction was especially strong in departments that lost computer facilities because of the creation of Athena. Departments that had no prior departmental computing facilities generally felt that a centrally managed facility was better than none and did not react as strongly to central control.

A particular case in point was the allocation of resources for the development of instructional software. Resource allocation committees were established, one for Digital equipment and one for IBM equipment. The committees solicited proposals directly from the faculty and allocated resources to the faculty. Although departmental support for a proposal was felt to be important, the departments were not involved in resource allocation to any significant degree.

Initially, the project staff selected the locations of the public clusters. Later, during the extension phase of the project, departmental support was acknowledged to be much more important. Thereafter the Athena staff solicited departmental input and support for the installation of departmental clusters and development systems. The department also became the source of resources for instructional software development and for pedagogical and discipline guidance.

Developmental Issues

The instructional software effort started relatively early in the schedule. Unfortunately, the system was not yet stable, and developmental tools were relatively primitive. Thus the people who tried hardest to meet the objectives of Athena bore the brunt of the problems. By the time the system had stabilized and the tools had improved, the funds for instructional software development had been largely exhausted.

Although Athena management assumed that undergraduate instructional computing could be partitioned from other campus computing, in practice it proved somewhat difficult. Graduate students often took courses that required the use of Athena, or they were involved in software development for Athena. In both cases it was necessary to provide graduate students with Athena accounts. Also, the teaching faculty often integrated research and education, more so than at most other colleges and universities, making the partitioning of computing between the two difficult for them. Thus at times Athena seemed to be put in the role of imposing artificial (and unwelcome) constraints on faculty members in the way that they chose to do their work.

Development of instructional software was much more demanding than the Athena staff or the faculty had realized or were prepared for. There were few, if any, models of success. Plato, the major previous initiative in instructional computing, did not seem appropriate for MIT. The various pedagogical models for instructional computing were poorly understood, and there were no accessible centers of expertise in this area. Although the basic computational parts of the instructional software could be developed in a relatively straightforward manner, development of an acceptable human interface could vastly increase the total effort required. Estimates made by faculty members suggested that 100 to 200 hours of software development effort were required for each hour of use of the software in the classroom. This huge resource requirement, together with the lack of adequate developmental tools, created significant barriers to the use of Athena by the faculty.

Another developmental problem was, and still is, the standard of success at MIT: research leadership in the discipline of the department. Time spent developing instructional software was time not spent doing research. Thus nontenured faculty members had little, if any, incentive to work on instructional software. Doing so took significant amounts of time away from research that would lead to tenure. Yet, many of the faculty members most interested in instructional software development were nontenured. Even if tenured faculty devoted enough time to instructional software development to do it well, they were seen as diverging from department objectives.

Many faculty members had significant basic concerns about the proper role of computing in education. Some thought that students and instructors might substitute computing for thinking or that computing might come between student and instructor. Others were concerned that computing might detract from the theoretic and analytic aspects of the discipline being taught. Although the faculty as a whole held a broad spectrum of opinions about the role of computers in education, a substantial correlation of opinions about this subject arose by school. In some schools the faculty members held a predominately negative opinion about using computers in education, but in others schools a predominately positive opinion existed.

The Turnaround

The system had a few strong supporters among the faculty from the beginning, but, over time, this number grew slowly despite the many delays and problems. However, many faculty members maintained a negative attitude or questioned the value of the system. Attitudes began to change from negative to neutral by the fall of 1988, as the system began to deliver on its commitments and access to workstations became easier. With the start of the 1989 fall semester, the attitude of many of the faculty clearly changed from negative and critical to positive and helpful. Requests flooded in for departmental clusters, faculty workstations, and additional software.

The following are possible reasons for these changes.

- All graduate students were put on the system. They may have influenced the faculty more than the undergraduates. In any case, the faculty no longer had to worry about who had accounts and who did not.
- New priorities had been in place for a year. With completion of system development late in 1988, the new priorities emphasized faculty involvement, department clusters, and improved faculty communication.
- The system had been reasonably stable and reliable for a year.
- A few "success stories" about improvements in education began to emerge, showing that significant education benefits were possible [Avril 89].
- Athena hired a second faculty liaison person to fix problems, respond to faculty requests, and improve communication.
- A faculty newsletter was started to foster better communication between Athena and the faculty.
- The first students who had never known life at MIT without Athena were graduating.

Outlook for the Future

At present, relations between Athena staff and the faculty have improved significantly. The project addressed most of the faculty's early concerns once the initial crunch of system development was over. The initiatives that addressed the concerns of the faculty included a much greater emphasis on working with departments and improving developmental tools.

At the beginning of the project, the need to get the basic system running as soon as possible precluded the possibility of supporting other hardware platforms. Because of the enduring and growing popularity of varied approaches—and because the immediate pressure is off the project's system software group—the Athena staff is now looking at technical approaches for incorporating DOS, MAC/OS, and various application packages into the Athena environment, thus responding directly to faculty requests.

Many of the earlier problems, such as instability and unreliability, have now been solved, leading to improved Athena–faculty relations. The faculty is also in a much better position to understand what Athena can and cannot do and to set expectations and plan realistically. Perhaps the best indicator of the new phase of Athena–faculty relationships is that many departments have installed departmental clusters or requested Athena workstations for all interested faculty as a matter of policy.

Technology

FIVE

Athena as a
Distributed System

Initial work on Athena dealt with system requirements. Some of those established were generic to campus computing in general, whereas others were unique to MIT. In order to meet the needs of instructional computing on campus, the following requirements relative to distributed systems were identified.

- *Scalability*. The system must scale to support 10,000 workstations or more.
- *Reliability*. The system must be available continuously, 24 hours per day, even though equipment failures occur frequently in a system this size.
- *Support public workstations*. Any user may use any workstation.
- *Security*. The system services must be secure even though the workstations are not.
- *Heterogeneity*. The system must support a variety of hardware platforms.
- *Coherency*. All system applications software must run on all workstations.
- *Affordability*. The cost to own and operate the system must not exceed five percent of tuition on a sustained basis.

The support of public workstations is necessary because workstations are presently too expensive for purchase by individuals. The plan is to allow (but not require) the purchase of workstations by individuals when they become affordable.

An early concern was that the system's size might make it too complex. Therefore a policy of eliminating needless complexity was followed throughout the project.

Definitions

We define a *user* as a human who uses a subsystem (e.g., workstation), program, or service. A *client* is a user or a program acting for a user. A *server* is a provider of services or resources. A *service* is a set of actions to be performed.

An object is referenced by its *name*. The object is located by its address or (more generally) by its path. A *binding* of the name to the object occurs when the name is associated with the address. Often part of the address is contained in a context of the name. Some systems use an address for a name. Although this approach may simplify system development, it can cause problems in binding a name to a different object. *Resolving* a name means identifying the address related to a name.

Coherence refers to the ability of two distinct hardware architectures to compile and run the same software. *Interoperability* is the ability of two subsystems to cooperate in the execution of a single task. For example, two subsystems supporting the X Window System can cooperate on a single task as client and server, because they support the same network protocol. *Fault tolerant* refers to the ability of a system to continue to operate in spite of the failure of a subsystem, possibly with degraded performance.

Security has two major aspects: authentication and authorization. *Authentication* is determining the identity of the user. *Authorization* is determining whether the user has legitimate access to the requested resources.

Models of Distributed Systems

Many different models of distributed systems have been proposed for computer systems in general. One extreme might be called the "main frame" model. In it each workstation or other node in the distributed system can exchange files with other nodes, subject to security restrictions, but nodes cannot work together in any other manner. All resource allocation, security access, and functional access are handled at the node level.

If a user of such a distributed system wants access to a printer on another node, the user must log into that node, gain security authorization on that node, move the file to be printed to that node, and then issue the print command. A major benefit of the main frame model is that presently available time-sharing operating systems (such as Unix) support it and can be used to implement it with minimal development.

Another extreme might be called the "unified" distributed system. In this model, all nodes in the distributed system are considered part of one logically unified system. Resource allocation, security, and access to function are handled at the system or network level, not at the node level.

If a user of such a distributed system wants to do the same print function, the user would simply issue the print command, logical printer name (if not the default), and file name. By logging in on the local workstation the user becomes logged into all services provided anywhere in the distributed system, and all resources in the entire system are accessible transparently. The major benefit of the unified model is that it automates much of the user control that must be supplied manually in the main frame model. Indeed, the unified model has most of the characteristics of one main frame in the mainframe model.

Although the main frame model would have been easier to implement, it would have had serious drawbacks in the Athena distributed system environment. One of these drawbacks is system security. The main frame model maintains system security by preventing users from obtaining access to the kernel of the operating system. In the Athena environment, users can gain access to the kernel of the workstation by either obtaining the superuser password or by booting their own operating system from removable media. Thus workstation integrity cannot be ensured. As users can corrupt the kernel of the operating system, they can (for example) masquerade as others or as a system service. The user can also "infect" the workstation with a Trojan horse, virus, worm, or other undesirable code. Of course, the user can monitor all Ethernet messages on the local net.

The main frame model also assumes that users are known to a particular machine. User files exist on that machine, and mail is sent to the user on that machine. However, in the Athena environment, the objective was to let any student use any workstation, so neither of those characteristics was desirable. Instead, the objective was to provide mail and file access as network services, accessible from any workstation and independent of location.

Access to these network services (described later) has security implications. If user files or the system software were stored on a public workstation, the previous users could have damaged (or deleted) files. They could have corrupted the operating system, perhaps by inserting a Trojan horse that would capture passwords of subsequent users. As any user can use any workstation, the concept of sending mail to a machine is not suitable for the Athena environment. Instead, the objective is to send mail to "username" using a network service and to allow mail to be read, written, and filed from any workstation.

The main frame model also had undesirable support implications. The classical support model for main frames is a system manager per system. At a scale of 10,000 systems (workstations), this level of support clearly was not appropriate. Athena's ultimate objective is to have one "system manager" per 1000 workstations, which would result in vast improvement over conventional approaches. (Presently, nine operations programmers support 1000 workstations.)

Existing Distributed Operating Systems

Several other distributed operating system projects have addressed requirements that are similar in some respects to Athena's. These projects include Amoeba [Tannenbaum 85], Andrew [Morris 88], Dash [Anderson 87], Eden [Black 85], Emerald [Jul 88], Grapevine [Birrell 82], HCS [Notkin 89], ISIS [Birman 85], Locus [Walker 83], Mach [Rashid 86], Sprite [Ousterhout 88], and V [Cheriton 88]. Although Amoeba and Grapevine are designed for larger environments than a single campus, they have addressed many of the same issues that Athena has.

Amoeba is designed to run in both a local and extended network environment. A typical local environment might consist of, say, 16 processors connected to a pool of several tens of workstations. Beyond that, multiple Amoeba sites can be interconnected through a wide area network to form a single system. The research focuses on the use and management of the processor set in addition to communications and protection. An extended system currently interconnects local Amoeba systems in a wide area network through several countries in Western Europe.

Andrew is a system for support of instructional and research computing at Carnegie-Mellon University, with objectives very similar to Athena's. Both systems support some 1000 midrange workstations in a Unix and Ethernet environment, with plans for growth to 10,000 workstations. Both assume that the user has complete control over workstation functions, with a central mechanism controlling and supporting network services. A distributed file system, called the Andrew File System (AFS), was developed and is now being used as the basis of a nationwide file system experiment. The AFS file space is separated into two parts: local and shared space. The local space is accessible to the user (generally on a local disk) but not publicly shared. The shared space can exist anywhere in the network and is publicly accessible.

In contrast to these systems, Dash is designed for very large future hardware installations and systems. It is designed for far faster and cheaper processors and networks, to be implemented by the thousands to millions, with worldwide dimensions.

Eden is an object-oriented operating system based on a single remote procedure call mechanism. It has a single, uniform, system-wide namespace spanning multiple machines. An object is a set of processes that is referenced by capabilities and can migrate freely among systems. All objects have a data part, which includes short- and long-term data. Objects can checkpoint autonomously. Eden is a unified distributed system, as described earlier.

Grapevine is an older system designed for extended geographic distribution. It supports message delivery, resource location (naming), authentication, and access control services. The primary use of Grapevine is delivering mail. It has rapidly come to be used throughout the Xerox internet, with nodes located in clusters around the world. Resources are accessed within the local cluster, but access is allowed to any other Grapevine system in the Xerox internet. Grapevine consists of about 1500 users and 17 servers in 50 local area networks.

The objective of HCS is to integrate different hardware/software combinations into a single system. It is based on heterogeneous communications protocols, including TCP/IP, and uses a single global name space for the entire heterogeneous environment along with remote procedure calls. The network services supported are remote computation, mailing, and filing.

ISIS provides a network environment for developing relatively sophisticated distributed applications under Unix. The ISIS environment provides multiple processes at distributed nodes, fault tolerance, coordination of processes, automated recovery, and dynamic reconfiguration. It also provides serialization to ensure predictability of results. The ISIS toolkit uses a subroutine call style of interface and functions as a networkwide meta–operating system. ISIS provides a novel "virtual consistency" property for applications to coordinate actions of cooperative processes.

Locus is a distributed operating system that supports transparent access to data through a networkwide file system. It permits automatic replication of storage and transparent distributed process execution. Locus also provides for automatic replication of resources to meet reliability requirements and can degrade gracefully with network and node failures. Locus is another example of a unified distributed system.

Mach provides support for both tightly and loosely coupled general-purpose multiprocessors. It also supports transparent remote file access between autonomous systems. It has large, sparse, virtual address spaces, copy-on-write virtual copy operations, and memory mapped files. Multiple threads of control are provided within a single address space. Large amounts of information can be transferred by the interprocess communications facility by using copy-on-write techniques. Mach has a binary applications program interface compatible with Berkeley Unix 4.3.

Sprite is an operating system that supports multiprocessing (multithreaded kernel), process migration, and distributed files. The user level facilities are identical to BSD Unix. All files and I/O devices are uniformly accessible to all systems, and they appear as a single shared hierarchy. There are no private partitions to manage, and devices and files can be accessed remotely. Complete Unix file semantics are provided, including locking and consistent access. Remote procedure calls are used for file management, and extensive file caching is done to improve performance.

V is a testbed for distributed system research. The four logical parts are: the distributed Unix kernel; the service modules; the runtime support libraries; and the added user-level commands. It manages a cluster of workstations and servers, providing the resources and information-sharing facilities of a conventional single machine.

At the beginning of Athena, these and other distributed operating systems were reviewed. None was found to be suitable for Athena, often because they were in the early stages of research.

Athena's Unique Aspects

Athena differs from the distributed systems described in various ways. A comprehensive analysis of these differences is beyond our scope here, but we can describe some of the more important differences.

Amoeba provides support for processor server back ends supporting workstation front ends over a network using a capabilities-based operating system. The operating system supports distributed processing by network processors that are assigned to tasks dynamically as processing load requires. Athena performs all processing on the local workstation as a default. The user can initiate remote execution manually through the X Window System.

Athena and Andrew are similar in scope and objectives, but their developers approached the problem with different priorities. Andrew felt that the issue of a distributed file system was so important that it needed to develop its own (AFS). Andrew also developed a number of end user application packages, such as compound document editors. Athena also thought that the distributed file problem was very important and therefore believed that industry would solve the problem—thus the use of Sun NFS. Athena concentrated on distributed services and did little with end user services. The Andrew and Athena implementations complement each other quite well: Andrew is using the Athena windowing system (X) and authentication service (Kerberos), and Athena is using the Andrew compound document editor (*ez*) and instructional authoring environment (*cT*).

Eden is object-oriented and allows processes to migrate freely among processors. Athena uses conventional subroutines and does not support process migration.

Athena and Grapevine have relatively similar architectures. Both build on existing operating systems, and both provide distributed services of mail, naming, and authentication on dedicated servers. One difference is that Grapevine provides access control, whereas Athena uses Unix access control. Athena supports the additional distributed services of file access, notification, printing, and service management.

Like HCS, Athena supports a systemwide name space and provides distributed services. In contrast, Athena uses a single operating system programming and user interface.

The Locus architecture was studied carefully by the Athena designers early in the project. They used several of its design concepts, and the fact that it was operational on 17 main frames interconnected by local area network established confidence that the approach worked. Locus is a distributed operating system that provides a high degree of network transparency. Files and programs can both be moved dynamically with no effect on correct operation or naming. Local and remote resources are accessed in a uniform manner. Locus also provides reliable operation. Reliable facilities include replicated file storage and automatic recovery from various subsystem and network failures. In these areas, Athena and Locus are quite similar. A major difference is that the Locus distributed file system puts all files in a single tree, whereas Athena has about 10,000 file roots, to obtain flexibility and reliability.

Mach is the kernel of a distributed operating system on which a variety of programming interfaces can be built. In contrast Athena took the Berkeley programming and user interface as a standard and developed a relatively clean layer of distributed services on it.

Like Athena, Sprite provides a "single system image" and both have network files. The design points are different, with Sprite designed for tens to hundreds of workstations and Athena for thousands of workstations. Athena is independent of the operating system and can use any distributed file system, but Sprite requires the same operating system on all workstations and has an integral file system. Sprite uses the file system instead of a name server.

The V system provides a "software backplane" that supports network transparent address spaces, lightweight processes, and interprocess communication. Athena provides none of these capabilities, but instead uses standard Unix. Both systems support distributed file servers and print servers.

Issues in Distributed Systems

Several issues arise immediately in the design of a distributed system. Among the most important are naming, authentication, and compatibility.

Naming

A name service converts a logical name into a physical address by an algorithm, a table lookup, or a combination of the two. The purpose of a name service is to decouple the logical support of a function (such as printing) from the physical implementation of that function. This decoupling makes changing the configuration of a system far easier. Changing the logical-to-physical mapping, not all of the code that references the function, is the only modification required.

System objects that can be named include hosts, printers, services, files, and users. Factors affecting the design of name servers include the number of object types, number of objects, frequency of queries, requirements for reliability, and frequency of update.

The simplest implementation of a name server is by means of a centralized service. If that is inappropriate for reasons of network bandwidth, distance, reliability, or load, the service can be distributed. If implementation is by means of a database, the usual methods of data distribution, including replication or partitioning, may be used.

A replicated database is created in multiple copies. Replication has the advantage of providing good performance and reliability, but update is difficult because of synchronization requirements. Replication also uses considerable storage.

In partitioning, the database is split into multiple, disjoint databases. Some means must be provided to identify the correct partition holding the data of interest. This can be done through a directory or with a broadcast search. The advantage of a partitioned database is that only one copy of the data exists, thus saving storage and simplifying update. One drawback is that the correct partition must be found for the access, and in some cases multiple partitions must be accessed to resolve the name. Another drawback is that it is less reliable than replicated systems.

Most of these systems use a combination of replication and partitioning to achieve a balance between performance and storage requirements. Most name servers also use caching of frequently used names.

Scalability

Design approaches that work well with a few nodes in a distributed system may not be usable with many nodes. For example, broadcast protocols work well for small numbers of nodes but not for large numbers. Techniques such as putting complete system configuration lists on every workstation (storage intensive), or making all workstation software configurations different (labor intensive), are not usable for even moderately large configurations (e.g., 100 workstations).

Security

Two issues must be considered in security design for distributed systems: authentication and authorization. On a distributed system of more than a few dozen workstations, the root password cannot be different on each workstation because the support task quickly becomes unmanageable. Therefore Athena made all root passwords the same and known to all users (it is "mrroot").

For user passwords, Unix systems store encrypted passwords for all users on each workstation. Maintaining passwords for users of 100 or more workstations is very difficult and completely impractical in a large network. Thus the replicated database approach to authorization does not work well in large systems and suffers from the usual problems of replicated databases. A natural alternative is to provide a centralized password checking service. However, in order to access remote services, passwords must be sent over the net, which makes the system vulnerable to eavesdroppers who can steal passwords. It is also vulnerable to availability failures.

A solution to the problems associated with sending passwords over the net is to encrypt the passwords. Two approaches have been developed to implement encryption-based authentication: public key cryptography and key distribution servers.

With public key cryptography, encryption keys come in pairs. Each key in the pair is used to decrypt messages encrypted in the other key. Therefore one key of the pair can be given to the servers and the other (secret) key can be given to the user. The user uses the secret key to become authenticated.

A key distribution server can be used to assign secure keys to be used between a user and a server. This approach works well in large systems but requires a third party. The method generally utilizes private keys and a trusted third party.

Authorization can be handled in many ways. One is to delegate the function to the servers and implement it by access control lists showing membership in groups [Birrell 82]. Another is to use capabilities implemented as a bit pattern passed to the server, showing that the user is authorized to perform a particular operation [Mullender 87]. Capabilities are usually encrypted to prevent forgery.

Compatibility

Various levels of system compatibility are possible, including the binary level, execution level, and protocol level. In binary compatibility, all processors execute the same binary instruction repertoire and are compatible at the binary level with differences only in performance and input/output. Emerald and VAX systems exhibit this level of compatibility. Although greatly simplifying system development, it restricts the source and architecture of systems greatly and is not often used in large systems for this reason.

A more common level is to provide system compatibility at the next level up; the execution abstraction (called "coherence" in Athena). A common execution level abstraction exists if the same source code can be compiled and executed properly on the two systems. Andrew and Athena both support the Unix execution abstraction for the hardware platforms (VAXstation, DECstation, and PC/RT for Athena).

The least restrictive form of compatibility is one that achieves interoperability by requiring all system components to support a common set of protocols. The X Window System [Scheifler 86] is an example of this level of compatibility. The protocol level of compatibility allows a distributed system to be based on common protocols for essential system services, such as file access, naming, and authentication. Athena supports this level of abstraction as well. The execution abstraction could be given up and diverse operating systems could still be supported within Athena through the protocol compatibility.

Athena addresses the issue of application data coherence in several ways. The X Window System provides separate network connections for the two different byte orders. Each type of workstation accesses its own type of data representation separately. Data coherence is also provided by NFS so that different workstation architectures can share the same directory hierarchy. FTP performs translations from the machine character set to the network standard and back again. Hesiod and Kerberos use only ASCII text to guarantee coherence to all clients.

The Athena Model of Distributed Systems

The distributed systems model for Athena has three major components: workstations, network, and servers. The Athena approach is to implement a set of network services to replace equivalent time-sharing services, in essence converting the time-sharing model of Unix into a distributed operating system.

The network is invisible to the user. All services appear to be local and are available to the user with only a single submission of a password at log in. The actual delivery of the services is physically distributed over the system and communicated to the user over the network transparently.

In concept, any operating system can be used on components (workstations or servers) in Athena. To achieve interoperability with the other system components (and to gain access to the distributed services) the components need only support the Athena protocols for authentication service, name service, file access, and print service.

In order to minimize development cost, the protocols to date have been implemented mainly in Unix on all hardware platforms (some have also been done in DOS). A side benefit of supporting only Unix is minimal training and support cost. The computational model seen by the users, therefore, is Unix.

To meet the project's objectives, Athena management adopted a strategy consisting of the following elements.

- *Scalability.* Partitioned network, centralized servers, identical workstation software.
- *Reliability.* Redundancy of all system elements required for operation.
- *Support public workstations.* Deployment of public clusters.
- *Security.* Development of a trusted third-party authentication facility.
- *Heterogeneity.* Standard interfaces to workstations.
- *Coherency.* The same operating system used on all workstations.
- *System management.* Tools developed to allow dynamic change of the system configuration through the use of a service management system.
- *Affordability.* Centralized operations, development, and maintenance; development of software tools to allow remote installation and maintenance.

Scalability

The designers improved scalability by minimizing the demands on scarce resources in three areas: network bandwidth, mass storage, and labor. The campus network [Schiller 88] design included a backbone of optical fiber and a token ring protocol running at 10 Mbits/sec. Network routers are attached to the backbone, with each router supporting one or more Ethernets configured as IP subnets. Because of the routers, traffic local to a subnet does not load the backbone. This approach gives a good measure of growth capability, because, as more workstations are added, more Ethernet subnets can be added to the backbone.

Athena workstations are dataless nodes; i.e., all workstations have local hard disks that are used to reduce paging traffic on the net. System software file service is replicated on all subnets, so communication traffic for loading of system software remains local to a subnet.

To minimize mass storage, files that would normally be replicated on a per-workstation basis are centralized. These include password files and most configuration files. Services provided by network servers also are centralized.

To minimize labor requirements, all workstations are anonymous and interchangeable. They all have the same root password and the same software configuration. The only unique items are the workstation name and net address. Initial loading and subsequent updates of the software are done over the net.

Reliability

For improved reliability, no systems other than network routers are attached to the backbone. This approach limits the number and types of problems that can bring the entire net down. A closely related benefit is that one organization has complete responsibility for the network, so that maintenance and upgrade decisions can be made in one place. All other systems are attached to the Ethernet subnets.

As a general rule, a hardware failure may prevent the updating of master files for, say, adding new user accounts or changing the hardware configuration. However, the system can continue to operate. Those subsystems whose failure would stop system operation, such as authentication service, name service, or access to system software, are replicated with automatic cutover. However, some types of failures, such as failure of private file server, can still deny service to a subset of users. Methods of eliminating these vulnerabilities are being studied.

Workstation Clusters

Clusters of workstations are provided in about 40 locations around the campus. They are located so that students do not have to walk more than about 5–10 minutes to get to a workstation. In addition to the clusters for student use, several clusters are dedicated to development of departmental instructional software. Any user can log into any workstation and gain immediate access to private files and environments.

Public workstations have no retained state between sessions. Therefore the operations staff can reload the system at any time with no adverse consequences. By default, the workstations refuse remote services, such as remote log in or remote command execution, to minimize the response time impact to the workstation user caused by others who might log in. Private workstations, generally used by faculty members and project staff, retain state between sessions.

Security

The system's designers assumed that the security of the workstations could not be maintained. To obtain system security with insecure workstations after log in, Athena developed an authentication service called Kerberos.

The Kerberos authentication server [Steiner 88] is a trusted, third-party, private key, network authentication system that validates the identity of individuals to network servers. Kerberos is named after the three-headed dog that was the servant of Pluto in Greek mythology. He guarded the gates of the underworld and received immortality. Kerberos is based on the model developed by Needham and Schroeder [Needham 78]. Each user and network server has an encryption key known only to it and the Kerberos authentication server. Timestamps have been added to that model to help detect and prevent replay. Kerberos operates without imposing any additional burden on the user as a part of the normal log-in or service request process.

Kerberos establishes authentication by securely making and distributing a session key for each server–client instance. The particular server then has the responsibility to use the key in a manner consistent with its own authentication policy. The server may elect to (1) not use authentication, (2) use authentication on the first request only, (3) use authentication on all transactions, or (4) authenticate and encrypt all transmissions.

Heterogeneity

Because the two major project sponsors have incompatible workstation products, the system must support at least two incompatible workstation platforms. In addition, each vendor has supplied multiple generations of hardware, which are not always compatible. The following minimum workstation requirements were imposed to bound heterogeneity and thereby bound the range of hardware for which instructional courseware must be developed:

- Ethernet interface;
- 1 million instructions per second processing speed;
- 1 million pixel display (monochrome);
- local hard disk of at least 40 MByte;
- 4 Mbytes of main memory; and
- pointer device (mouse).

More recently, personal computers using Unix are also supported.

Interoperability and Coherency

Athena supports both interoperability and coherency. In particular, the X Window System provides both, although its main contribution at Athena is in coherence because most applications run on the same system as the display. As with the X Window System, the subsystems in Athena interoperate by using a number of common network protocols. Unix and C provide a high level of coherence so that the same application source code, and most of the system source code, can be compiled and executed on all workstations regardless of architecture. Coherence at Athena includes standardization of three lower level interfaces [Balkovich 85a]. They are

- network service, or system interface between the applications and the operating system;

- application programming interface, or the interface between applications; and
- user interface, or the interface presented by applications to the users.

To obtain system coherence, Athena used the same operating system and the same communications protocols on all hardware platforms. Operating system options considered were MS-DOS and Unix. Athena selected Unix because of its functional power and multitasking capability. It provides the same virtual machine interface to applications on all workstations. Some 85–90 percent of the source code for the operating system is common to all workstation types. Essentially all source code is common for applications. Separate binaries (compiled from the same sources) are supported for all workstation types. To obtain communications coherence, Athena selected TCP/IP to implement the same virtual network interface to all applications.

Application coherence is a much more difficult problem. It has been approached in part by supporting a small number of languages on Athena. Presently supported languages are C, Lisp, and FORTRAN.

Another part of the coherence requirement is met by using a standard windowing system. The X Window System was developed at the MIT Laboratory for Computer Science and Athena to meet this need. The X system provides a network-transparent, device-independent, vendor-neutral windowing environment. Unix has an abstract, machine-independent interface to most of the operating system, except to the display. Thus portability does not extend to display-oriented programs. With the use of the X System, an abstract, machine-independent interface that provided machine independence by recompiling became available.

The user interfaces for the various types of workstations are as identical as the keyboards and mouses will allow. The X System was developed to provide application coherence to the human interface. However, X solved only part of this difficult problem. Recently, the Motif human interface development environment from Open Software Foundation has been installed to provide a more powerful level of abstraction in obtaining user interface coherence.

Similarly, current standard applications—including a 2-D drawing package (GKS), a text editor (*Gnu EMACS*), a spreadsheet, a laboratory data management system, and a document formatter—have been adopted.

As the different workstation architectures support different floating point and byte orders, the system must handle these differences in a method transparent to the user. Each workstation knows its own system type, and separate sets of program binaries are stored for each. Text file formats are the same for all hardware platforms. When binary data are accessed, each workstation type accesses its own type based on data from the name server.

Affordability

From the beginning, the system designers recognized that any support approach whereby the labor requirement scaled normally with the number of workstations was likely to be too expensive. To achieve affordability, Athena management decided to use centralized system management and support, even though the hardware was distributed. Experience with the system indicates that this decision significantly reduced support costs and improved service quality, compared to distributed management and support. (However, distributed management can solve political and organizational problems better than the centralized approach can.) Although labor cost still varies linearly with the number of workstations in the Athena system, the coefficient of scale is much smaller.

Athena System Design

The Athena system design views the entire hardware complex of (up to 10,000) workstations, file servers, communications servers, and printers as a single, unified, distributed system (as described earlier). Figure 5.1 shows a block diagram of the system, which is network-oriented. The software configuration of all workstations attached to the network is identical. Workstations communicate with a variety of network servers that provide services to the users. Because all services provided are network services, they are available to all users without regard to location. These network services include

- name service;
- file service;

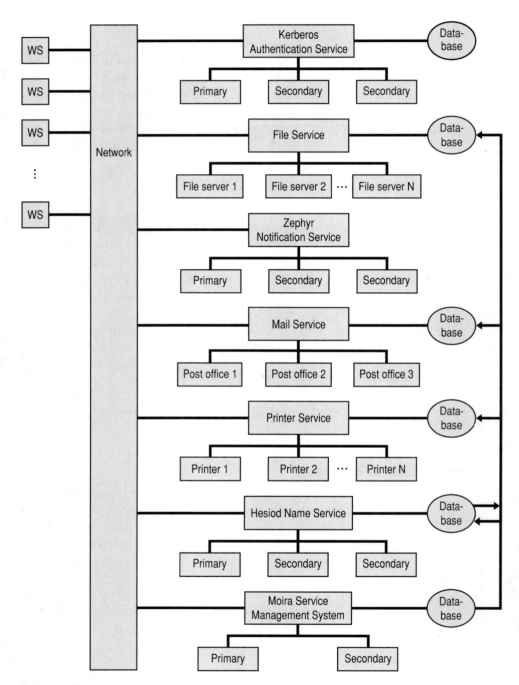

Figure 5.1   Athena system block diagram.

- printing;
- mail;
- real time notification;
- service management;
- authentication; and
- installation and update.

Files that would normally be provided for the entire system at every workstation are centralized, with a small number of copies to provide fail-safe capability and improved performance.

Service Management

Configuration management of large numbers of workstations and servers is labor intensive and cannot be done effectively by manual means. Therefore Athena developed a service management system, called Moira after the Greek word for fate [Levine 87 and Rosenstein 88], to automate much of the routine management task. Greek mythology identified three fates represented by the women Klotho, Lachesis, and Atropos, whose names appear in the Moira code as major modules. Moira includes a central database of system control and configuration information, tools for manipulating that information, and tools for updating the services to maintain conformance with the database. Types of information stored in Moira include disk quotas, all hardware configuration files, allocation of individuals to post offices, and access control lists. The centralized database has proven to be both effective and economical, because each piece of data is stored only once, is easily updated, and is subject to fine-grained access control.

Name Service

In time-sharing systems, object names typically are resolved into addresses by using configuration files. These files tend to be relatively static and reside in each node. However, this static approach is not appropriate for workstation networks; a more dynamic reconfiguration method is needed. Also, per-system configuration files are somewhat wasteful of storage if replicated on all workstations. However, the primary benefit of a name server is to maintain consistency of configuration files. This benefit increases with the size of the system because both the rate of change and number of copies increase with overall system size.

The purpose of the Athena name server, called Hesiod [Dyer 88], is to allow centralized, dynamic linkage between names and objects. Hesiod is named after the Greek farmer and poet who was the scribe for the gods and was the only one allowed to chisel names in stone. As an example of Hesiod usage, Postscript printing for building E40 third floor might initially be provided by a printer named NIL at address PS.MIT.EDU. If at some later time this service were moved to a different printer at address LQP.MIT.EDU, updating a configuration file on each of 10,000 workstations to reflect the change would not be feasible. Instead, the name server provides a single, centralized location for the configuration file for all workstations, thus providing significant savings in storage and allowing system configuration changes with minimal staff.

Hesiod includes the Berkeley bind name server [Bloom 86] with some extensions. It provides information on users, location of users' private files, mail delivery addresses, and locations for network services such as authentication and printing. The central system database (maintained by the Moira service management system) updates Hesiod every few hours, which in effect represents a fast front end to the Moira database.

Authentication Service

System software (except for the kernel) is not kept on the workstations, which function as dataless nodes. When a user logs in, new system software is down-loaded from a secure network file server, thus ensuring a validated initial operating system.

When the user logs out, a program called *toehold* "deactivates" the workstation. All attached file systems are detached, all temporary storage areas are cleaned out, and the window system is terminated. No network connections (for example, to external file servers) are retained. Several other housekeeping activities are performed, such as destroying any tokens of authenticity created for the previous user. Finally, the next log in is solicited by a "Press any key" prompt. If a new system library is loaded onto a server while the workstation is deactivated, it will be used at the next log in; this deactivation/activation cycle provides en masse software update of the nonresident portion of the system.

When the key depression is received, *toehold* executes a shell script that attaches the system libraries from the read–only file server (described in the next section) and starts the X Window System. A log–in window then is activated for the user and log in is solicited.

Log in proceeds with the user submitting user name and password, and the Kerberos authentication server authenticates the user in a transparent manner. Information about the user is obtained from the Hesiod name server. The user home directory is then attached from the appropriate file server. The Zephyr real time notification service is activated and a Zephyr windowgram client is started. Log in continues with the usual execution of the log-in files.

Kerberos authenticates the identity of the user to the desired service in a fully transparent manner through the use of encrypted "electronic credentials." Kerberos establishes identity (authentication) only and does not become involved in the decision of whether an individual is allowed to use a specific service (authorization). Server mechanisms (Unix or other) are used for authorization.

Two types of credentials are generated by Kerberos: *tickets* and *authenticators*. A ticket securely transmits the identity of an individual to a server for a temporary "session key." The authenticator contains additional information that can be compared by a server to the ticket to prove that the user presenting the ticket is the same one to whom the ticket was issued.

Athena File Service

Before describing the Athena file system, we need to present some background and definitions on distributed file systems in general. File systems are categorized in a number of ways. One way is to develop a taxonomy, such as the one shown in Figure 5.2. The highest categories in a file system hierarchy are remote versus local file systems. Local file systems can be handled by conventional time-sharing techniques and are relatively simple compared to remote file systems.

The data in remote (from the client) file systems can be divided into categories of centralized, partitioned, and replicated approaches. A *centralized* file system is one in which all the data are in one place. A *partitioned* file system is one in which the data are segmented into disjoint partitions, and each partition is stored on a system. A *replicated* file system is one in which duplicate copies of files are stored. In any particular system, these approaches are not mutually exclusive and may be used in combination. Each approach has strengths and

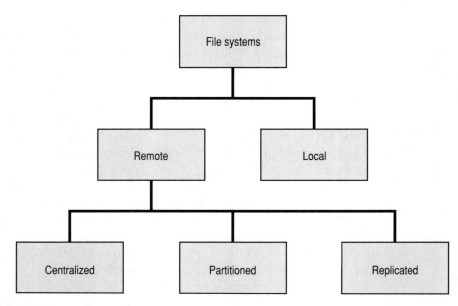

Figure 5.2   Taxonomy of file systems.

weaknesses, depending on relative rates of update and query, but a discussion of them is beyond our scope here.

Just as data can be supported in three ways, the directories in remote file systems can be handled by centralized, partitioned, or replicated techniques. The method of handling data need not be the same as the method of handling the directory. For example, the data can be partitioned and the directory centralized.

Athena workstations are dataless nodes supported by an extensive file service. Athena has three different network file services and in principle supports an arbitrary number of other file services. One service—the Remote Virtual Disk (RVD)—holds read-only files, such as system software libraries and some applications software. Another—the Network File System (NFS)—is used for read/write files. The third—the Andrew File System (AFS)—is also used for read/write files but is especially useful for files used for cooperative work.

The reason for using both NFS and RVD is that they have quite different characteristics and are used in different ways. NFS is used for shared access to writable private files and directories. These private NFS files are distributed across the subnets in a relatively uniform manner. The likelihood that users will be on the same subnet as their private files is relatively low—about 4 percent. Therefore nearly all private file accesses go across the backbone. Because these files are generally small and are accessed less frequently than system files, they can be accessed across the backbone network without excessive data transfer rate requirements. RVD is used for read-only shared system and courseware libraries. Therefore, the RVD files are replicated on every subnet. RVD does not provide file service (only disk block access service), so it can support many more clients per server.

By default, each user has an NFS file system with the same name as his or her username. This home directory is attached transparently at log in via the *.login* file. Additional file systems may be mounted upon user request via the *attach* command. File systems are named objects. The names are resolved to {location, type, mount point} by Hesiod. The user's ability to customize the namespace is an important capability.

Attach is a file system utility developed at Athena that provides a logical connection of a remote file to a local directory. *Attach* provides the capability for files (system or private) to be available at any workstation. Files are stored in "lockers"; that is, each Athena locker is an imported file system. Lockers are stored on network file servers distributed across the system, but they appear to be local to the user in a single, local file directory. The files must be attached to the workstation directory, but this is usually done in a transparent manner in the *.login* file.

Attach currently supports the file systems of NFS, RVD, Unix File System (UFS), and AFS. It therefore acts as the integrating mechanism for Athena's various file systems. The logical connection then allows access to remote files as though they were local.

Attach looks up the file-system name in Hesiod to get the file-system type, the server host, the default mount point in the user directory, and the mode (i.e., read-only, read/write). *Attach* then authenticates the user for the file system and creates the links from the user directory to the desired remote file.

Additional file systems may be mounted upon user request via the *attach* command. RVD and NFS file systems are named objects. The names are resolved to {location, type, mount point} by Hesiod. AFS files are always accessible with a fixed path name. Hesiod is used to translate from the short path name to the true path name.

Printing

Conventional time-sharing systems provide local printing. The use of this model in a workstation environment creates two problems: print queueing and printer configuration.

Unix normally queues the print file on the workstation, with no indication of whether the requested printer is accepting jobs. The possibility exists that if the user logs off, the next user may alter or delete the spooled file before it gets printed. The possibility also exists that the spooled file may never get printed because the printer is not accepting jobs. Finally, sending a print request to a particular named printer is an arbitrary limitation on the manner in which the print request is eventually serviced. Athena designers modified the *lpr* Berkeley print spooler to queue the print file at the remote print server. If the print server is not available, an immediate error message is generated.

The configuration problem is similar to the password problem. The file defining printer characteristics (the *printcap* file) would normally be stored statically on every workstation. Athena moved the *printcap* function to the Hesiod name server, permitting configuration control (logically) to be separated from print service location.

Early in 1989, Athena decided to go to a much better distributed print system than *lpr,* called *Palladium*. Test and evaluation began in September 1989. The system is scheduled to go into full production soon.

Electronic Mail

In a conventional Unix time-sharing system, users send mail to remote individuals using a mail address of *username@absolute-path-name,* or to local individuals using an address of simply *username* with the remainder of the address as a default. The Athena requirement that any user can use any workstation makes absolute path names inappropriate, because individuals are not limited to one system.

Figure 5.3 shows the approach developed by Athena, which combines the best of the local and remote approaches. All individuals are addressed as though they were local, without using a machine name. The mail is sent to a central *mail hub* and then to a "post office," where the mail is queued until the addressee decides to pick it up. When the mail is "picked up," it is transferred from the individual's post office (based on Hesiod information) to the private (NFS)

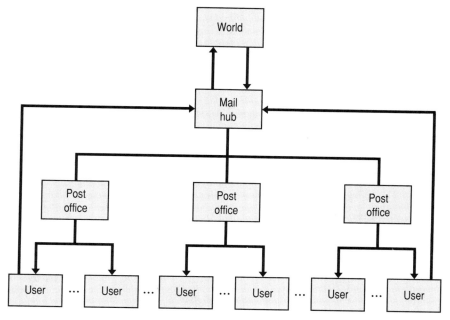

Figure 5.3 Athena network mail system.

mail file for that individual (also based on Hesiod information), who can then read, write, and edit mail from any workstation, as though it were actually local.

To accomplish this result, Athena uses the MH mail system [Rand 85]. An improved graphical front end has been added to MH (called XMH) based on the X Toolkit [Swick 88] so that all commands are entered through mouse selection of active objects instead of the command line interface. The Post Office Protocol [Rose 85] utilized by MH has been retained and is modified to require the use of the Kerberos authentication server. Multiple post office servers are provided as required for load management and reliability. The proper post office for each individual is selected using information in the Hesiod name server. All changes to MH to support a distributed system are transparent to the user, and the user utilizes the software as though it were on a single centralized time-sharing system.

In fact, the network mail system is a generic design that is independent of MH, which is only one of several mail interfaces that can be used. A popular alternative is *rmail,* which comes with *gnuemacs.* Although they are embedded in a distributed system environment, MH or *rmail* are unchanged from the standard distribution. The only change required is to adjust the Post Office Protocol library to use Hesiod and Kerberos.

Users outside Athena can also send mail to individuals within Athena as though it were a single, centralized system. They send mail to address *username@athena.mit.edu.* This mail goes to the mail hub and is distributed by the same mechanism as internal mail.

The mail hub also handles distribution lists within Athena. At present, some 400 mailing lists and 13,000 mail messages per day cross the hub. Three post office servers supporting the 10,000 users handle these 13,000 messages.

Real Time Notification

Occasionally, real time notification is useful, as when new mail has arrived or when a file server is going to be taken out of service temporarily. Such notification is easily accomplished on a centralized time-sharing system, because the identity of all individuals logged in is available in a single location. Notification is much more difficult in a distributed system, because no central file exists to hold this information, nor can the workstation report of this information be trusted blindly.

To meet this need, Athena developed a real time notification service called Zephyr [Della Fera 88], after the Greek god who provided the gentle, warm, west wind upon command of Aeolus. Using this system, one person can send a message to another immediately by using a single command and without knowing the location of the recipient (or even whether that person is logged in). Zephyr searches the active workstations to locate the recipient, and, if he or she is logged in, it creates a pop-up window immediately with the message. A user can select classes of Zephyr messages of interest and suppress the rest. This capability operates within the constraints of privacy and permission.

On-Line Consulting

An on-line consulting system *olc* [Coppeto 89] permits users to direct questions to consultants or other expert users logged in elsewhere on the network. A key feature is the "topics" idea, whereby *olc* finds a resident expert willing to answer a question. A set of stock answers is maintained for quick response to common questions. The user can get access to the answers through a menu system, and the consultants can return a standard answer electronically if appropriate. If the consultant is not available, questions are automatically queued. Answers are often returned by electronic mail if the questions are difficult or if the question remains unsolved when the user logs out.

The *olc* component was so successful in providing answers to questions about the system, that it was extended in the fall of 1989 to be the On-Line Teaching Assistant (*olta*). *Olta* is used to answer questions about course material in the same way that *olc* answers questions about the Athena system. Instructors are using *olta* experimentally in several courses.

Discuss

Discuss [Raeburn 89] is an electronic conferencing system that allows Athena users to communicate easily and effectively on specific subjects. The approach used is to support the "electronic meeting" model, and there are presently about 100 concurrent meetings in progress. *Discuss* is authenticated by Kerberos and uses Zephyr to send real time new transaction announcements. The system evolved from an earlier system called *Forum* supported on MULTICS.

System Software Development

To support coherence at the application programming interface, most of the source code for the operating environments is the same on the different workstation platforms. The source code is partitioned into a machine-independent section (e.g., the applications and most of the operating system) and a machine-dependent section to simplify the system build process.

Currently, the basic operating system software used on all Athena workstations and servers is UNIX, with machine-dependent software (e.g., device drivers) supplied by the manufacturers. The standard UNIX distribution is augmented by several third-party software packages and local Athena modifications and additions. To maintain control of the software configuration, all software is completely built from source code about once each year. Module updates are provided 3 or 4 times a year.

The new source code for the Athena distributed services is about 20 Mbytes [Davis 89]. The total amount of source code for the Athena system, including Unix, the Athena distributed services, and applications, amounts to 400 Mbytes. This source code is structured into a hierarchy of about 1300 *makefiles* and generates some 12,000 binary modules.

To control the amount of labor required and the quality of development, management, and support of this large amount of source code, the Athena staff developed or imported a number of software tools. These tools [Davis 89] include

- *Prot_sources,* to manage access privileges;
- *Track* (like *rdist* [Nachbar 86]), to manage distributed files; and
- *Maksrv,* a script set to convert workstation software to servers.

Prot_sources manages access privileges so that system builds are not aborted by lack of privileges for access, while also providing some measure of protection. It allows software developers to start a build at any time without using *root* access and its lack of protection. *Prot_sources* provides four categories of protection: writable, executable, locked, and unlocked. It traverses the 400 Mbytes of source code in about 1.5 hours, reporting on its actions as they occur.

Track creates a local file containing the update status of all of the distributed files used for the system build. After the local file is complete, the system build process can compare local copies to the update status contained in *track* instead of comparing against remote files, thus saving thousands of remote file accesses. Another more important use of *track* is for workstation software version update. Currently, *track* runs at the system level when someone types an "update_workstation" command, but the mechanism is in place to allow it to run automatically whenever a deactivating workstation notices that the version number of the workstation release is behind the version number of the central library release.

Ideally, all software update should be entirely automatic and should propagate to all workstations essentially simultaneously. Tools to do this at Athena are available for nonkernel code but not for kernel code. Currently, changes to the kernel require that each individual workstation be visited and the kernel loaded from a floppy disk (the "roller skate" approach). Work is proceeding to largely automate workstation kernel software update.

Server systems (e.g., printers, name servers) are built as modifications from a standard workstation system with *makesrv*. The workstation software is initially installed on servers. Building a server from a workstation then becomes a standard operation. *Makesrv* presently can build the server types of NFS, Hesiod, Kerberos, Moira, On-line Consulting, RVD, Zephyr, Discuss, and Printer.

SIX

Athena Tools and Distributed Services

———

In this chapter we discuss in more detail the tools and distributed services summarized in Chapter 5. We first describe the human interface work done at Athena, then the network that supports Athena's distributed system, and, finally, more details of Athena's distributed services.

Human Interface Development

Concerns about the nature of the human interface to both the operating system and applications on the Athena system existed almost from the beginning. The types of concerns for the two cases were very different.

Unix uses a command line input syntax that was developed for 10-character/second hardcopy terminals. In that environment, every keystroke was expensive for both input and output, so commands were very cryptic (e.g., "mv," "cp," and "ls"). In Athena the output is not 10 characters/second but about 50,000 characters/second. Nevertheless, users must still use the same cryptic syntax.

Although the Unix command structure has a very clean and consistent architecture, the implementation has a large number of inconsistencies and ambiguities. This drawback, together with the flat command structure, imposes a heavy memory burden on the user, which is made worse by cryptic mnemonics that have marginal relationship to the commands that they represent (such as "grep"). The "man" pages are of some help but are limited in effectiveness, because they are very lengthy, not provided in context, and can only be invoked if the user "almost" knows the answer anyway.

The human interface design for MIT applications is controlled completely by the implementers. The ability of implementers to develop good human interfaces varies widely. All application implementers faced the dual problems of the high skill level required and the labor-intensive nature of the task. Both problems were caused by the relatively primitive tools available for this purpose. The skills required included programming ability in C, X Window System, X Toolkit, and Unix.

X Window System

The X Window System [Scheifler 87] was the first step taken at Athena to implement better human interfaces. A major advantage of X was that it provided device independence, so that the same human interface could run on any Athena workstation independently of design. Athena was one of the earliest users of the X Window System and later the X Toolkit [Swick 88] in a production environment. Unless otherwise noted, all Athena operations described are done using the X Window System and X Toolkit.

Work on a windowing system had started early in 1984 as a joint project between Robert Scheifler of LCS and Jim Gettys of Digital/Athena. Scheifler needed a window system for the Argus project and Gettys needed one for Athena. Stanford University had developed the W window system for the V research operating system in 1980, and W was subsequently ported by Digital to the VAXstation 100. The W window system had good fundamental characteristics but needed major functional extensions and performance improvements. The new window system was sufficiently different that it needed a new name. This system became the X Window System, and it played a key role in attaining coherence for Athena. Development of improved tools for human interface implementation began with X at the lowest level and proceeded upward through increasingly powerful levels of abstraction over several years.

Athena began using X version 9 in a production environment in September 1985, and version 10 a year later. This operation satisfactorily provided the desired benefits of X to Athena and could have continued to do so for several years. However, intensive X development continued, producing X version 11 early in 1987. Because X version 11 was incompatible at the protocol level with version 10, conversion was required of all applications using X. X version 11 went into production in September 1987, but version 10 was also supported for compatibility. Although some bugs were discovered after the system went into full-scale production on the first day of fall semester, the number was manageable and the risk taken using field test software proved to be worth it.

Figure 6.1 shows a simplified schematic of the X Window System. Application programs interface with the toolkit or the X library of subroutines to create and manipulate windows and their contents.

Figure 6.1 Structure of the X Window System.

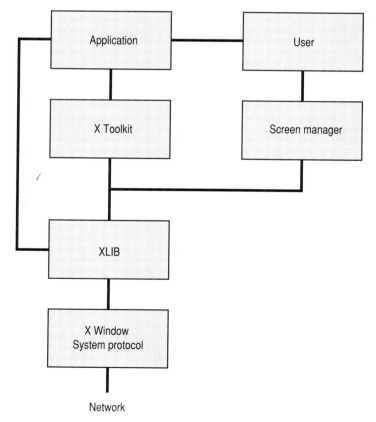

The user interfaces with the application to carry out the desired functions and with the screen manager to control the visibility and arrangement of objects on the display.

The development of X started with the protocol commands transmitted between the client and the server. In order to make it easier to generate the commands, the X library (XLIB) was created to provide a subroutine interface for command generation. As work on the X library was nearing completion, it became obvious that this interface was still at too low a level for development of human interfaces, so work on the X Toolkit was initiated in 1987. The design of the architecture for the X Toolkit was relatively difficult, so this work proceeded slowly at first. However, as soon as the X Toolkit was available, it became the preferred technology for implementing human interfaces.

By late in 1986, a few people with a background in human interface development had joined Athena, and efforts were started to define developmental objectives in this area for both Unix and applications. A graphic user interface that would shield novice users from the command line interface was desired for Unix. The application developers needed much more powerful tools and a style guide to provide easier development of human interfaces with better consistency across applications. Various research projects elsewhere had tried to develop a graphic user interface for Unix, but none had been successful. The development of better tools and a good style guide was clearly beyond the resources of the project. There seemed to be no way to improve the situation and to reach the desired goals. This bleak outlook changed for the better with the creation of the Open Software Foundation (OSF) and the *Motif* human interface development tools.

Enter Motif

Because of its close relationship with Athena, Digital developed the first commercial version of X under the name of DECwindows. Digital had the personnel and skills needed to develop a comprehensive set of tools in DECwindows, assigning more than 1000 software engineers to the project at the peak of development. Digital provided DECwindows to OSF to be part of the *Motif* product early in 1988.

Motif is a set of tools for developing human interfaces. It is layered on the X Window System and includes a toolkit for creating and presenting "widgets," a window manager, a User Interface Language (UIL), and a style guide. A *widget* is a human interface graphic object, such as a dialogue box, menu, or mouse-sensitive button. UIL is a grammar for statically describing the layout of widgets and eliminates a great deal of repetitive code. The style guide describes rules for designing good human interfaces in a consistent manner using the tools in *Motif*. These elements met a clear need in Athena for improved tools for development of human interfaces.

Soon after the formation of OSF, a relatively close relationship developed between the research department of OSF and Athena, resulting in large part from shared interests. Athena had built up a high degree of expertise in X and the X Toolkit. Athena also had a strong need to obtain more powerful tools for human interface development. Concurrently, the research department of OFS wanted to test *Motif* and its documentation thoroughly and to extend it to more powerful levels of functionality.

Because of the synergy between the goals of OSF and Athena, OSF provided a substantial research grant to Athena to test and extend *Motif* in the summer of 1989. Athena put together a task force of 17 trained students and gave them free rein to develop useful extensions to *Motif*. The students had a good idea of new features needed, having experienced the shortcomings of *Motif* when using it in application development. The OSF grant resulted in development of a large number of new "widgets" that were useful in application development. The effort also resulted in improved human interfaces for the following components.

- For Unix:

    xjobs—lists all jobs running and permits easy modification of state;

    lprint—easy print queueing of files and screens;

    xtar—simple method for backup and restoring files to/from removable media; and

    dbrowser—directory/ file browser/ file selector.

- For Athena services:

    webster—Webster's Dictionary;

    mmail—simple mail handler based on rmail;

    hotline—hardware problem reporting interface;

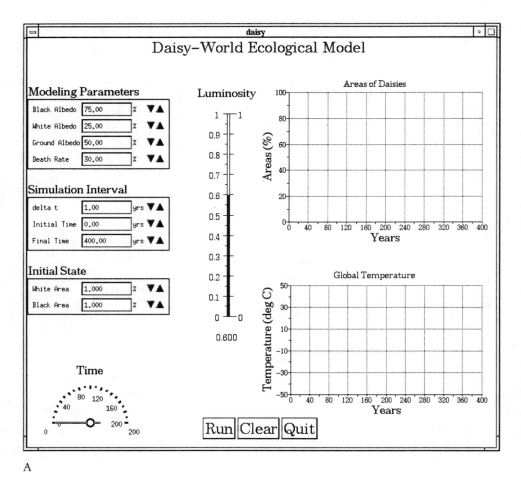

A

Figure 6.2   New *Motif* widgets developed at Athena.

olc—on-line consulting (also on-line teaching assistant);

help—on-line help system including on-line documentation delivery;

rolodX—personal Rolodex-style address book;

calendar—personal appointment calendar;

font chooser—font browser and tester;

Argus—intelligent mail filter;

TI—provides help and documentation browser for Emacs;

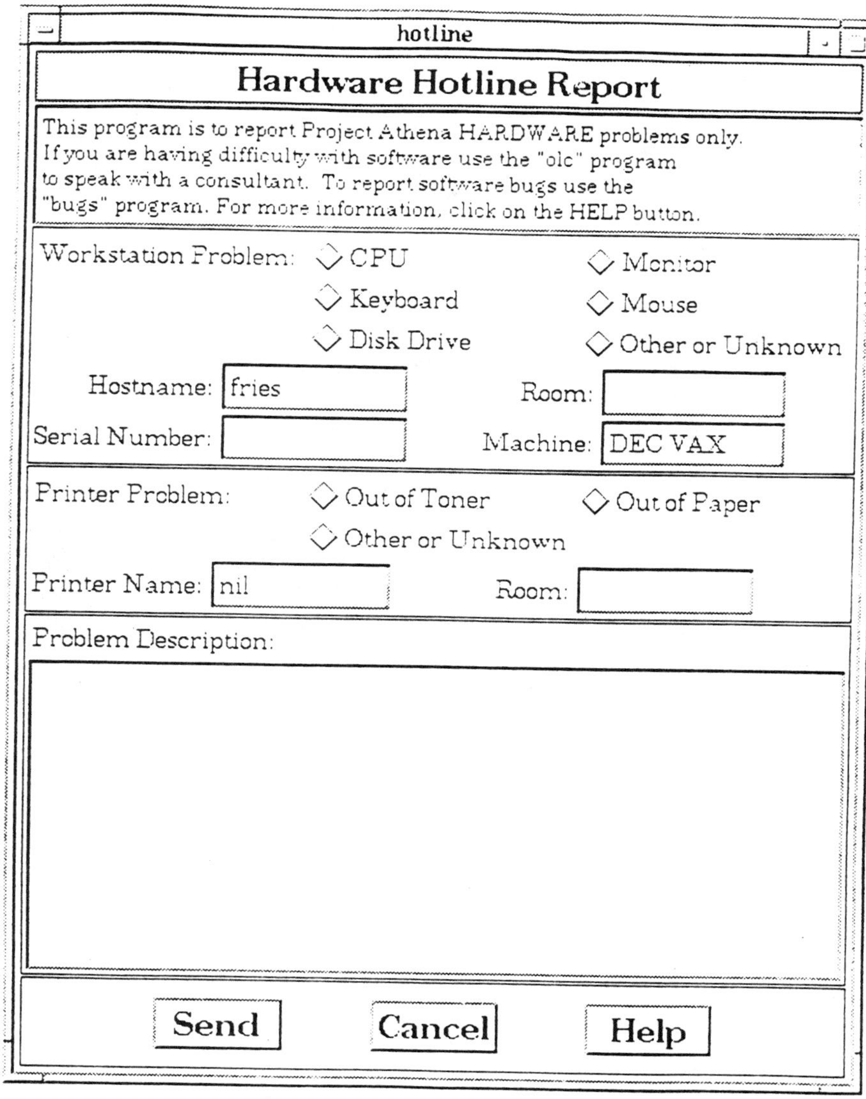

```
┌─────────────────────────────────────────────────────┐
│  ─ ║                    hotline                    · │ ─│
│ ┌───────────────────────────────────────────────────┐ │
│ │           Hardware Hotline Report                 │ │
│ ├───────────────────────────────────────────────────┤ │
│ │ This program is to report Project Athena HARDWARE problems only. │
│ │ If you are having difficulty with software use the "olc" program │
│ │ to speak with a consultant.  To report software bugs use the │
│ │ "bugs" program. For more information, click on the HELP button. │
```

Workstation Problem: ◇ CPU   ◇ Monitor
                       ◇ Keyboard   ◇ Mouse
                       ◇ Disk Drive   ◇ Other or Unknown

Hostname: `fries`   Room: _____

Serial Number: _____   Machine: `DEC VAX`

Printer Problem: ◇ Out of Toner   ◇ Out of Paper
                   ◇ Other or Unknown

Printer Name: `nil`   Room: _____

Problem Description:

[Send]   [Cancel]   [Help]

B

Figure 6.2 (Continued)

Project Athena's Toybox

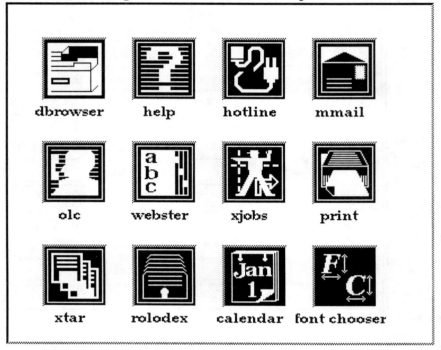

C

Figure 6.2   (Continued)

>*whatsup*—a distributed calendar public database; and
>
>*toybox*—easy access to selected *Motif* applications.

- For education:

>analog/digital sliding scales for input;
>
>analog/digital scales/gauges for output;
>
>*xim*—X image manipulator system; and
>
>*xmath*—function plotting.

Figure 6.2 shows examples of some of these new *Motif* front ends or widgets.

In parallel with development of the new widgets for *Motif,* two MIT faculty members were developing another, more general human interface tool under the name of the Lecture Authoring System (LAS) [Moriarty 89]. The goal of this effort was to develop a software package that would allow lecturers to prepare computer-based educational materials for classroom and student use without the need for programming. The package was designed to support interactive modeling and graphics in addition to the presentation of textual material. It not only met the design objectives, but also provided the following capabilities.

- The lecturer can create and modify an electronic presentation using an interactive graphical layout editor that approaches WYSIWYG (What You See Is What You Get) functionality.
- For any given application, the lecturer can design a number of screens, each of which can be subdivided into any number of windows. The lecturer has complete control over the size, placement, and content of the windows. Constraints and predefined functions can be applied to the modeling environment.

Figure 6.3   Modeling and graphing using the Lecture Authoring System.

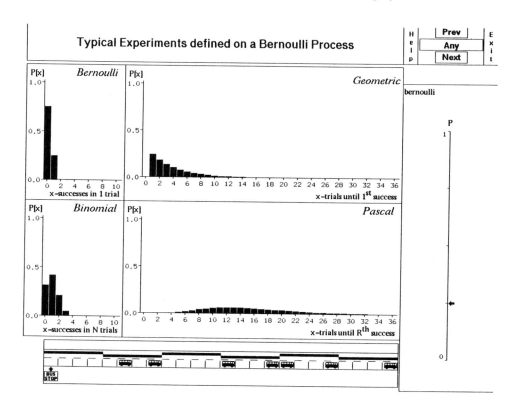

- The user can accomplish input and output by assigning I/O-sensitive control objects to the desired location on the window.
- The user can create new widget-like objects.
- The user can easily accomplish interobject interfacing (for example, between a modeling environment and a plotting object).

LAS is now being ported to *Motif.* Figure 6.3 shows an example of LAS modeling and graphic output.

New modules for windowing and human interface development, starting with the X Window System, have traditionally been created in a bottom–up manner. The reason is that the desired functionality is not known at the outset and learning/research is required. Now that the *Motif* package is available, attention is being devoted to the next higher level in the hierarchy. LAS appears to have the kind of functionality desired for this next level.

The Network

Although the network is transparent to Athena users, details of the design and implementation may be of interest to some of the readers who may be designing or modifying their own network systems. More detail is given in [Schiller 88].

Perhaps the earliest network at MIT was ChaosNet, developed by the Artificial Intelligence Laboratory (AIL). This network predated Ethernet and included both physical network technology and protocols. Use of ChaosNet grew over the years because of availability and the local base of expertise. Later, the LCS designed and implemented a token ring system. The ProNET-10 product developed by Proteon was based on this technology and is the system currently used by MIT for its campus spine.

These networks grew over the years and, in some cases, became quite large. However, they were typically maintained by researchers and students for research purposes and were not planned or developed to be generally available services. MIT created a campus network group to coordinate these activities. Initially this group was directed by Professor Fernando Corbato of the Electrical Engineering and Computer Science Department, and the network used Chaosnet protocols and hardware on a private cable that linked the LCS, the department, and the Plasma Fusion Center. In 1984 this group was expanded to install campuswide network systems and to deliver campuswide local area network data communications services on demand. Creation of this network was, in part, in response to the needs of Athena, which became its first major customer.

Although a number of alternatives existed for networking the campus, its topology severely limited the viable options. The campus is about 2 km long and about 1 km wide. This size precluded the use of a single Ethernet system and mandated a network of networks.

The approach chosen uses a "spine" or backbone, which visits most of the major buildings on campus. The technology choice for the spine was fiber optic token ring. The fiber optic technology was chosen for its excellent drive distance capability and electrical isolation. The spine is presently operated at 10 M bits/second but the cable is capable of operating up to 100 M bits/second.

The individual local area networks are attached to the spine. Ethernet at 10 M bits/second was chosen for the subnet technology, because it met the limited drive distance requirements and because interfaces are supported by a large number of manufacturers. The protocol supported on Ethernet is the DOD TCP/IP, the most common protocol used by the academic community. The only attachments to the spine are through gateways, each of which supports a few Ethernet subnets. This approach limited the number of types of equipment and software (to one of each) that are attached to the spine and that could bring down the entire network. Thus, if the gateways can be made reliable, the network becomes much more reliable. All of the computing devices, including main frames, servers, workstations, and printers are attached to one of the subnets.

The use of gateways (instead of, for example, bridges) has other advantages. The local traffic on a subnet is kept off the spine, thus greatly reducing the performance requirement of the spine. The gateways also act as "firewalls" preventing problems on a subnet (such as "message storms") from affecting the entire net. The use of subnets gave additional administrative flexibility in that subnets could be owned and administered either by departments or by the central network support organization.

Other types of subnets can be attached simply by providing the appropriate gateways. In 1987, MIT purchased a new telephone system, including installation of all new twisted pair cable. Cost analysis indicated that twisted pair local area network technology would be far less expensive than co-axial cable, especially since the additional twisted pair could be installed as part of the new telephone system at minimal incremental cost. Consequently, every telephone outlet has an associated outlet for future data system applications.

A number of protocols and services are used in Athena from within the Transmission Control Protocol (TCP)/Internet Protocol (IP) family, which ARPA and the defense industry developed and standardized. TCP is a host–to–host protocol, whereas IP is a protocol for communications between networks. IP transmits packets or datagrams as a connectionless communications service between nodes. TCP provides connection–oriented communications service on IP. The protocols and services included in the TCP/IP family include *telnet,* a remote terminal service, *file transfer protocol* (FTP), *simple mail transport protocol* (SMTP), and *simple network maintenance protocol* (SNMP). SNMP and other services use the *universal datagram protocol* (UDP). Figure 6.4 shows the relationship among these services and protocols.

The spine transmits IP packets from the source router to the destination router, where they are then transferred to the appropriate subnet. The MIT network group assigns each attachment to the subnet an IP address. Charges for attachment to the net are based on equipment class, with workstations being charged at the rate of $20 per month.

The first sections of the spine were installed late in 1984. The Athena time-sharing VAX 11/750s were initially used as routers. This approach did not work well administratively, as the people trying to run a reliable network were constantly at odds with the people trying to do operating system development work on the same

Figure 6.4 Relationships in the TCP/IP family.

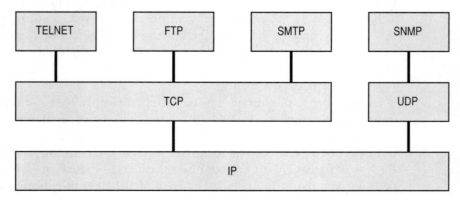

machines. The following year the original equipment was replaced with MicroVAX IIs to solve the administrative problem. (It was not a technical or a performance problem.) The initial software implementation used Unix, but it proved to be much too slow and unreliable. Subsequently, a stand-alone router software package called CGW, developed by LCS and modified by the network group, was installed in 1986.

In addition to greatly improved performance and reliability, CGW provided remote maintenance capability. This feature has proven to be very important, because the routers are physically distributed across campus. Earlier software required a physical visit to restart a failed system. With CGW, a software failure can be handled remotely.

On a large, far-flung campus, expecting that every good candidate location for a workstation will be initially accessible to the campus network is unrealistic. Requiring that workstation installation be limited to places that the network already serves was initially very restrictive in practice, but as the network expanded it became less of a problem.

The following three categories of communications are supported at MIT.

- *Tightly coupled.* This includes communications networks with a bandwidth of 1 Mb/sec or more. Technologies presently in use in this category include fiber optics token ring, token ring over copper cable, and Ethernet over co-axial cable and unshielded twisted pair. A few Applebus nets also are connected to the campus net through specialized routers.
- *Loosely coupled.* This includes Ethernets that are linked to routers on campus Ethernet networks through voice grade lines at bandwidths of 14.4 Kb/sec.
- *Modem connected.* This includes dial-up service at 1200 or 2400 baud. This class of service is used for remote terminal access to time-sharing.

Workstations can be both on campus and off campus. On-campus locations include offices, public areas, dormitories, and other student housing facilities. Off-campus locations include remote living groups (e.g., fraternities, sororities, and independent living groups).

This system of tightly and loosely coupled networks forms a single logical network with a single address space. Performance variations among links are large enough to require different modes of use. The subnets connected to the campus by low-speed links have their own local file servers to provide good access to local files. Access to remote (i.e., on-campus) files is provided but at a lower performance level.

By the end of 1987, the spine reached 27 locations on campus

Figure 6.5   NEARnet configuration diagram (courtesy of Dan Long, Bolt, Beranek, and Newman, Inc.).

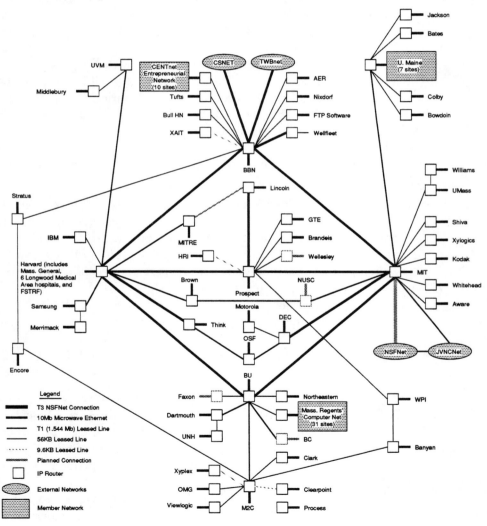

using 20 km of fiber. About 3000 computers are now being served by 22 routers.

More recently, MIT has joined the New England Academic and Research Network (NEARnet). This network links various colleges, research labs, government departments, and industrial/commercial organizations at speeds up to 1.5 Mb/sec. The area covered includes eastern Massachusetts with branch nodes in Maine and New Hampshire. NEARnet is a regional network of NFSnet (National Science Foundation Network). Figure 6.5 shows the current configuration of NEARnet.

Organizations currently supported on NEARnet include MIT, Boston University, Harvard, the Digital research lab in Cambridge, Open Software Foundation, Massachusetts Microelectronics Center, Lincoln Lab, Thinking Machines Corp., and BBN. NEARnet provides electronic mail, remote log in, and file transfer services by means of TCP/IP.

Network Services

The following material describes in more detail the network services supported by Athena. In some cases clarity requires simplified descriptions or omission of some details of important features.

Authentication

Kerberos [Steiner 88] is a trusted, third-party, private key, and key distribution service functioning as a network authentication service. Kerberos is based on the model developed by Needham and Schroeder [Needham 78], to which a globally synchronized time service was added. Key terms are defined as follows.

- *Principal.* Each network entity (user or server) that uses Kerberos is in some sense a client. To distinguish Kerberos clients from clients of other services we use the term *principal.*
- *Authentication.* Authentication is the process of establishing proof of identity, and the Kerberos service provides validation of the identity of one principal to another.
- *Trusted.* Each principal trusts a particular Kerberos service, and each potential network correspondent also trusts that same particular Kerberos service. Each principal has a key known only to it

and the Kerberos authentication server. It is important to note that the workstation being used by the user is not trusted as it can easily be compromised. Only Kerberos is trusted.

- *Third party.* Kerberos is a third party to any transaction between two principals separated by the network.
- *Private key.* As with all known security systems, encryption forms the basic technology for proof of identity. The ability to perform useful encryptions and decryptions is taken as proof of the principal's claimed identity. In the case of Kerberos, the encryption method is of the class *private key*. All encryption in Kerberos uses the National Institute of Standards and Technology Data Encryption Standard (DES) [NBS 77]. We use *key* as shorthand for *private key*.
- *Key distribution service.* Kerberos provides a method to move a private key safely through a hostile network environment, where safe means free from attacks of either "disclosure of message contents" or "message modification." In particular, the proof of a successful authentication interchange between principals is that, at the conclusion of the Kerberos portion of session initialization, both principals will hold a session key that has been securely generated and distributed by the Kerberos service.

Kerberos operates without imposing any additional burden on the user during normal use. Kerberos authenticates the identity of the user to the desired service in a fully transparent manner through the use of "electronic credentials." Kerberos establishes identity (authentication) only and does not become involved in deciding whether an individual is allowed to use a specific resource (authorization). The normal server or Unix mechanisms handle authorization.

Global time synchronization was added to help detect and prevent replay. All clocks in the system must be synchronized to within a few minutes. If the time in the request differs from that in the electronic credentials by more than a few minutes or is identical to one already received, the server assumes that a former request is being replayed and service is denied.

Secure transmission of a session key permits three levels of message security, from which the applications programmer may select, depending on specific needs. These levels (and the attacks they address) are

- authentication at service connection time (spurious association initiation);

- authentication of every message (message stream modification); and
- authentication and encryption for every message (release of message contents).

Because Athena hosts do not typically contain special hardware support for encryption, the third level is rarely used.

Kerberos uses two forms of electronic credentials for passing authentication information. The first of these is the ticket, which contains

- username;
- server name;
- user IP address;
- timestamp;
- lifetime of the ticket; and
- session key.

The ticket is used to pass the identity of the user securely between Kerberos and the server. It is valid for only a single user and single server. It is encrypted in the server key, so the user can pass it to the server without fear of compromise.

The other message type used for passing authentication information is the authenticator. The authenticator contains the

- username;
- IP address; and
- current time.

The authenticator is used for comparison against the ticket to validate that the user submitting the ticket is the same one to which the ticket was initially issued. The authenticator is encrypted in the session key included in the ticket. Kerberos is used three different ways in authentication:

- log in, to obtain the "ticket-granting ticket";
- first access, to get a service ticket; and
- authentication, for service delivery.

Log In The individual's identity is initially established at log-in time. The user submits a username to the workstation. The login program sends the username to the Kerberos server as a request for the authentication service. Kerberos looks up that username in its database. If an entry is found, it retrieves the user key (derived from the password), generates a session key, and encloses the session key in a ticket. The ticket is then encrypted in a key known only to the ticket-granting service and Kerberos. This encrypted ticket is appended to the session key for the ticket-granting service, and the entire message is then encrypted in the user key. This message is sent to the user's workstation. Note that the user key (derived from the password) is not sent over the net.

At the workstation the message is decrypted, using the password submitted by the user. If decryption is successful, the identity of the user is verified. In addition, the session key for the ticket-granting service is now available to the workstation because it is outside the ticket. At this point a "secret" is shared between the user workstation and the ticket-granting service: the ticket-granting service session key. This shared knowledge is the basis of authentication, as with any other service.

The ticket and session key are stored for later use. The password and derived user key are deleted. All tickets are deleted on log out.

Ticket-Granting Service   The ticket-granting service avoids the security problems associated with storing the client's plaintext key on the workstation, yet avoids the requirement that the user type the key for each new service connection. With a ticket-granting service, the user can obtain at log in a credential that will be useful for subsequent service requests. That credential is a sharply bounded security risk, representing a limited authority and a limited time from a single client site, but its possession also removes the otherwise onerous necessity of rekeying a password at the time of each service request. (One exception is that, if the user wishes to change the password, the old password must be entered again.)

After log in, the ticket-granting ticket held by the workstation has the (encrypted) session key for the ticket-granting service. This ticket can therefore be used to obtain tickets for other network services for the life of the ticket-granting ticket, generally eight hours. The procedure for getting other tickets from the ticket-granting service is the same as accessing other network services.

Authentication for Service Delivery   Initially, we assume that the user already has a ticket for the desired service. Figure 6.6 shows the nature of the transaction for a client requesting a service and providing proof of identity as part of the service request. The client prepares a message to the desired service, consisting of the ticket and an au-

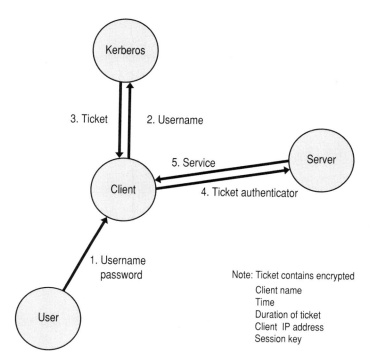

Figure 6.6 Kerberos service request.

thenticator. The authenticator is encrypted in the session key for that service received with the ticket and combined with the ticket. The client then forwards the ticket and authenticator to the service. The authenticator contains duplicate information to that inside the ticket.

The service decrypts the ticket with its private service key and recovers the session key. It uses the session key to decrypt the authenticator. It then verifies that the contents of the authenticator and the ticket match. If they match, the service and the client are each and jointly known to Kerberos, and the service can be satisfied that the client has the claimed identity. In addition, both the client and the server share a session key, unknown to all other principals on the network.

If the client wants to verify the identity of the service, say, prior to providing security-related data to that service, the client can request that the server provide something in return that accomplishes that goal. Although numerous methods are possible, the implementation used in Kerberos takes the timestamp from the ticket, adds 1, encrypts the result in the session key, and returns it to the client. The client, using its copy of session key, is able to verify that only a server in possession of the private service key could obtain the session key, and hence the server is its claimed identity, as well.

A ticket and its associated session key are valid for only one kind of network service (e.g., file access). Authenticated tickets for other types of services (e.g., printing) can be obtained from the ticket-granting service by the mechanism just described. If the user does not have a ticket for the desired service, he or she must obtain one. The client sends an in-the-clear request for a ticket for the desired service, an authenticator, and the ticket-granting ticket to the ticket-granting service. A ticket is returned to the client for the requested service, and operation proceeds as described.

Kerberos Database

Kerberos maintains a replicated database to ensure availability. Updates are made only to the master database; slave copies are read-only. The use of Kerberos for network authentication service, as described, requires only read access to the Kerberos database, and therefore slave copies are entirely satisfactory. To maintain synchronization of the master with the slaves, the master database is sent, in its entirety, to the slaves at regular intervals. The database is encrypted for transmission in a key that both the master and slave machines possess. Read/write transactions to the master are from administrators adding new users to the system and from users changing their passwords. The Kerberos servers must be physically secured.

Modifying Applications for Authentication

Modifying an application to incorporate authentication is quite easy and involves only a few lines of code. The application calls a subroutine that generates a message for the server desired. The application then sends that message to the server along with the service request. The server calls another library routine with the message as an argument that returns the decision about the user identity.

Application programs and servers that have been modified to use Kerberos include

- Berkeley "r" command series (*rlogin, rsh,* etc.);

- *lpr* line printing system;
- Post Office Protocol mail delivery;
- New user account generation;
- Password-changing service;
- *Zephyr* notification system;
- *Remote Virtual Disk* block server;
- *Andrew File System*;
- *Network File System*; and
- *Discuss* conferencing system.

The password-changing service is one of the few applications that uses the session key of a completely encrypted transaction. Kerberos became available for system users in September 1986.

Name Service

Various files must be maintained on any Unix system. These files include, for example, passwords, hardware configuration, communications, and system software. In a network of a few systems, simply replicating these files is feasible. This replication approach does not work well in larger networks, however, and is simply not feasible for networks of hundreds to thousands of workstation systems. Even if the storage cost were acceptable (which is unlikely), management of the replicated data quickly becomes impossible. Consider, for example, the task of maintaining the hardware configuration tables individually on 10,000 workstations in an environment of constantly changing hardware configuration.

Rather than replicating this information, Athena chose to retrieve it from a network name server called Hesiod [Dyer 88]. Other examples of network name servers are the Xerox Clearinghouse [Xerox 84], the Sun Yellow Pages [Sun 86], and Internet Domain Name Server [Mockapetris 87]. Hesiod is based on the Berkeley Internet Domain Name Server *bind*. Hesiod, through *bind,* provides a hierarchical name space with the ability to delegate authority to subsidiary name servers and to provide local caching. Hesiod uses a thin layer of code in front of *bind*, which extends the capability of *bind* to allow translations of logical names to strings.

The basic function of Hesiod is to provide a table lookup function on its database. In this regard it can be thought of as a *service-to-server* translation mechanism or a high speed front end to the Moira service management system. It does not perform any processing or interpretation of the data. It simply does the lookup, accepting as input one ASCII string and returning another. It is designed to retrieve quickly small amounts of data that change infrequently (less than one change per day per data item). A query can have multiple matches of the key in the database; when this situation occurs, all the matches are returned.

The maximum record length that can be exchanged by Hesiod and a client is 512 bytes, a limit of the UDP datagram protocol used for communications. If there are multiple matches, all matches must fit in the 512 byte limit. The Hesiod database is updated several times a day by the Moira system management server.

A query consists of two arguments: the name (of the object) and the type (of the object). Hesiod returns a network address of an object based on the arguments. The form of the name is a left–hand side and a right–hand side separated by an @ symbol, as represented by:

<left–hand–side>@<right–hand–side>

A set of library routines accepts the name and type as arguments and converts them to a fully qualified domain name that can be supplied to *bind*. The *bind* library is then called with the domain name as an argument, and a network address is returned.

A new object name or type can come into existence simply by being used by the system and supplied as an update to the database. No change in Hesiod is required, because it has no knowledge of the meaning of the data that it stores.

Valid (and actual) names include

- default–printer;
- default–printer@SIPB;
- @heracles.MIT.edu; and
- kerberos@Berkeley.MIT.edu.

Hesiod transforms such names into valid *bind* names. [Dyer 88] provides the algorithm for this transformation. Typical object names used in Athena include

- username;
- workstation name;
- fileserver name;
- printer name; and
- group name.

Typical Athena object types include

- cluster;
- pobox;
- filsys;
- password; and
- group.

Athena Uses of Hesiod

The *login* program uses the username as a name to find the password and group authorization information. *Login* also queries Hesiod to find which Kerberos server to use for authentication of that individual. *Login* then runs *attach* using the username to mount the user's home directory. *Login* uses Hesiod to obtain a "passwd" record, but that record contains neither password nor authorization information. It is merely the Unix name for a record that has the user telephone and office numbers, nickname, and the name of the shell to be used. This record is sometimes called the "finger" record, as it is displayed by the *finger* command.

The *attach* program uses Hesiod to find the file server for a given username, and then authenticates and attaches the files to the local directory for that individual. If the primary file server for an RVD server (which is replicated) is unavailable, Hesiod can point to the backup.

The network mail program queries Hesiod to find the post office for each individual. The *lpr* program queries Hesiod to find the net address of a printer logical name.

Given the workstation name, Hesiod provides the cluster name. Given the file system name, Hesiod provides the file server it exists on. Given a username, Hesiod finds which password and post office to use.

Current Hesiod Status

Hesiod currently supports a database of 3 Mbytes and 35,000 table entries. These include about 10,000 password entries, 10,000 group entries, 7000 file system entries, and 9000 post office entries. It is replicated in three servers to provide adequate performance and availability. Response time to a query is usually only a few milliseconds. The three copies are updated by the Moira server management system four times a day.

Service Management System

The purpose of the Moira service management system [Rosenstein 88] is to provide a single master copy of information about the Athena system and to distribute that information to specialized replicated subset copies around the system. Moira provides centralized data administration and update, which greatly reduces the labor required to maintain the system's data resources and therefore of the system itself.

Moira consists of a centralized database, a means of updating that database, and a means of distributing selected portions of the database to servers such as the Hesiod name server and mailing lists, access control lists, and group memberships. Moira provides update services for the following types of servers.

- Hesiod name server, to update the database. Each server requires nine separate files, but the files are identical on all servers.
- Network File System, to provide quota-based resource allocation and load balancing. Each NFS server requires two files, one in common and one unique.
- Mail, to allocate individual post office boxes to post office servers, and build the control file used on the central mail hub. The hub requires one unique file.
- Remote Virtual Disk, to provide access control lists and server configuration files. Each RVD file is unique.

More than 50 separate files are required to supply and control these services.

Because of its importance, Moira is frequently backed up. A replicated copy can operate while the master is being updated. After a server is updated, tests are run to verify the operational status before it is put back into service. In those cases where replicated server data exists, updates are provided sequentially so that service is not interrupted.

Moira clients do not access the internal database directly. This restriction shields clients from the internal details of the database so that it can be changed if necessary; it also helps to guarantee internal consistency. Instead, clients access the database through a set of Moira library functions. The library imposes the consistency requirements and also provides a set of consistency verification routines. Access to the Moira library is authenticated by Kerberos.

Each server obtains the data it needs in the format needed from the global Moira database. The data control manager selects the appropriate data subset from the global database and converts it to the specific format required by the server. Therefore, when a new service needs to be supported, the internal structure and data control manager can be modified in an isolated manner without unwanted side effects.

Transaction performance is not particularly important in Moira, because Hesiod acts as a high-speed front end for queries. Therefore Moira supports only relatively simple queries.

To obtain updates, a client sends requests via TCP/IP for data to Moira and receives replies. Requests can be of the form of queries or accesses. Queries are available as a limited set of predefined, named queries, allowing close control of database access. Queries exist in the categories of retrieve, update, delete, and append. Within these four classes are about 100 unique query types, such as

- get NFS quotas;
- get user information;
- add machine; and
- delete filesystem.

The database currently used in Moira is RTI Ingres. As Moira does not depend on any features of this database, it could be easily replaced by another relational database. The database contains several types of objects, with each object having an associated access control list [Rosenstein 88]. An audit trail is retained for all modifications.

All updates to servers are initiated by Moira. The system is designed so that partially completed updates do not cause loss of synchronization. Updates that fail are simply rescheduled.

If Moira is out of service, the system can continue to operate but cannot be changed. Because Moira is not needed for system operation, continuous availability is not too important. Maintaining database integrity in terms of retained data and internal consistency is important. Meeting this requirement calls for a database backup and recovery system to maximize recoverability.

Cron (a Unix facility that invokes programs at specific times) is used to run a data distribution program at scheduled intervals; each server has a different update schedule. When the data distribution manager runs, it scans the database to determine the servers that need updating. Only those servers that require updating are actually updated. A server-specific program (named in the database) is used to extract the necessary information and format it into the server-specific structure.

User Account Generation

Twice each year, the MIT's Registrar provides a tape of all registered students to Moira, Athena's service management system, which enters students not previously registered into a database of prospective users. The user services staff enters the names of interested faculty into this same database by hand. A new user can set up an Athena account without any staff intervention. When a prospective user decides to become a real user, the procedure is quite simple. The student can create an account by going to any workstation and logging in by clicking the "register" button on the log-in screen shown in Figure 6.7.

Figure 6.7   Athena log-in screen with registration button.

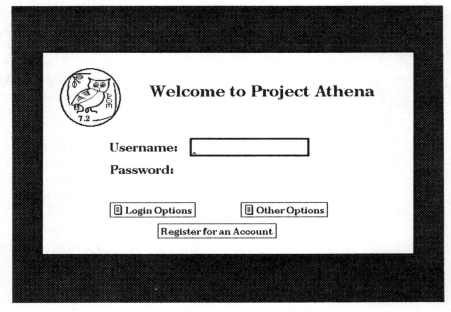

This action initiates a simple question-and-answer session that sets up the account with the necessary information. The student is prompted for a username, which is checked for uniqueness before it is accepted. Upon successful entry of a username, a home directory is allocated on the least heavily loaded file server, an initial disk quota is established, and a post office entry is established on the least heavily loaded post office server. An initial password is then solicited. Moira propagates these updates to the Hesiod name server, the mail hub, and the user's home file server. These updates can take up to 24 hours to become effective with the present update frequency.

The only communication between Kerberos and another service takes place at account creation time. The registration program checks with Moira to verify that the user's proposed log-in name is unique, and tentatively reserves it. Then the registration program tries to use the log-in name in a transaction with Kerberos, being prepared to back out of the Moira request if Kerberos indicates that the name is in use. Upon confirming that the log-in name is acceptable in both places, it passes the user's requested name and password to Kerberos, unseen by Moira. Meanwhile, Moira completes the rest of the account creation process.

Current Status

Moira currently manages about 15,000 user accounts, of which some 10,000 are active, and about 1300 workstations and some 100 network servers. It also manages the resource directories, such as the location of file servers and printers, and the data for system control, such as disk quotas. The current size of the Moira database is about 15 Mbytes.

Notification Server

The Zephyr notification server [Della Fera 88] provides a real time network-based notification service. In broad concept, a notification server bears some resemblance to electronic mail in that they both transmit messages from a sender to a recipient. In detail, however, they are very different. Whereas mail (specifically *sendmail* in the Unix system) is a batch operation with no notion of time, Zephyr transmits messages immediately. Whereas mail requires a static address for the recipient, Zephyr will determine whether the recipient is logged on anywhere in the system. Whereas the recipient must actively "read" mail, Zephyr delivers its message actively and without recipient intervention. When mail broadcasts a message to a large number of recipients, a separate copy is generated for each recipient. Zephyr generates only one copy of the message in the file system independent of the number of recipients. Whereas mail retains a message until read, Zephyr discards a message if it cannot be immediately delivered. Finally, in mail the sender determines who will receive a message. In Zephyr, the recipient determines who will receive messages based on the subscription service.

Because of these major differences, the appropriate kind of information sent using Zephyr is quite different from the appropriate kind of message sent by mail. Zephyr is designed to send time-sensitive messages, such as

- the printer in room E40–367 is now available for use;
- you have new mail;
- print queue status;
- message of the day delivery (MOTD), systemwide or user specific;
- on-line consulting;
- host status service;
- user location service *(rwho)*;
- talk or phone service;
- emergency notification to individuals or broadcast; and
- message service *(write)*.

Because of the class of messages intended for Zephyr, other changes have been made in its characteristics relative to mail. Because the messages are time sensitive, no queueing is provided. If the target recipient is not logged in, the message is discarded on the assumption that the time sensitivity of the message will quickly make it obsolete. Zephyr should be limited to messages of short, fixed length, preferably under 800 characters. Mail, however, is often used to send long messages of tens of thousands of characters.

Zephyr's architecture is similar to that of other Athena services. A Zephyr client library is provided; it supports the necessary services to client programs in terms of a reliable, authenticated (by Kerberos) notice transmission protocol. The library invokes a set of servers that control routing, queueing, and dispatching.

A notice from a client consists of routing information and a message. The Zephyr server creates a list of recipients based on routing attributes. The attributes can designate a single individual, or they can be based on a capability known as *subscription multicasting*. Each user can create a "subscription list" identifying the types of messages that are of interest. Attributes of messages to be sent are compared to attributes in the subscription list of each user. If there is a match, the message is sent to that user; if there is not a match the message is not sent to that user. This method can therefore be considered a "passive" mailing list in that only users who specifically request the message will receive it. In contrast an "active" mailing list is used by conventional list-based mailers, such as *sendmail,* that send messages to users whether they request them or not.

In all cases, the message is not interpreted by Zephyr. It may be in any format or character set and may even be encrypted. Interpretation of the message is the responsibility of the recipient.

Zephyr uses the Universal Datagram Protocol (UDP) of IP. Because of the limited capability but high performance of UDP, Zephyr clients must be able to suppress or accept duplicate packets, handle out-of-order packets, provide flow control, and provide reliable delivery.

Zephyr maintains a dynamic database to show the current location of all users logged in and also makes these data available to its clients. In order to protect privacy, a user may choose not to make log-in information publicly available. The user can also make log-in information available only to the system operations staff. If a workstation crashes, the log-in data may be temporarily invalid, remaining so until someone notices workstation unavailability or the user reboots the workstation.

Zephyr clients all run on the workstation and use the client library to send and receive messages. They communicate with a Zephyr server allocated at the time the workstation is booted.

Palladium Print System

The print spooler used in Berkeley Unix was developed for a centralized system and has many shortcomings in a distributed environment. The additional features desired in a distributed environment include

- the ability to place printers, users, and spool queues all on different machines;

- support of centralized management and logging for all workstations and printers;
- use of name service;
- authentication by an authentication server;
- support of printers that return information; and
- performance tradeoffs in favor of processors with large memories.

Although the Berkeley spooler [Campbell 83] had served Athena
well for several years, the system's growth to some 1000 workstations and 80 printers made development of a new print server desirable. In addition, Athena needed to implement print accounting in
order to allocate resources to students properly. The Palladium print
system [Handspicker 89] was developed to meet this need.

Palladium was developed by a multicompany group to meet
Athena's requirements and to operate in its environment. The goals
of the Palladium project were to support a distributed workstation
environment by using the client–server model, that is, the Kerberos
authentication service, the Hesiod name server, and the Moira service management system. Palladium was also designed to conform
to the European Computer Manufacturers Association (ECMA)
printing standard [ECMA 88] that was then evolving. Indeed, the
Athena requirements had a substantial influence on the ECMA
standard.

The remote procedure call (RPC) paradigm was used to provide
a simple interface to distributed services. The software chosen for
the RPC was the HRPC package from the University of Washington
[Sanislo 88]. This package is a common interface to a number of
RPC systems. It provides a generic interface for remote procedure
calls, and it keeps Palladium independent of the underlying communications protocols. Figure 6.8 shows the overall information
flow in Palladium (from [Handspicker 89]).

The information in the Palladium database consists of two general categories: static and dynamic. The static information describes
the capabilities and configurations of the printers, in a manner similar
to *tty* and *getty* for terminals in Unix. Each server and supervisor
reads the configuration file at startup and whenever commanded.
The static information in the database is normally generated by the
Moira service management system. The dynamic information in the
database consists of the print-job request information stored by the
server in the spool directory. The server is a set of library routines.

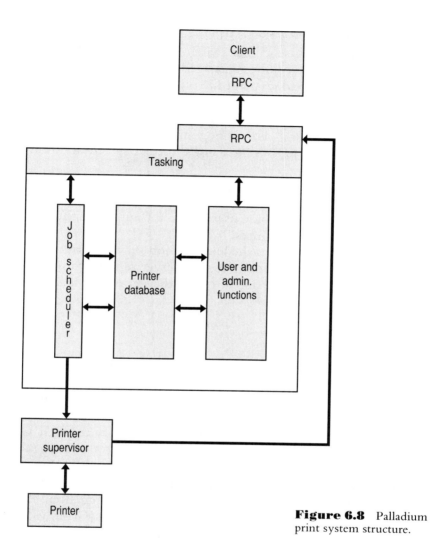

Figure 6.8 Palladium print system structure.

The sequence of events within Palladium is as follows. Upon receipt of a print command from the user, the print client contacts the name server to find an appropriate printer server (the print servers having previously "advertised" their presence, location, and functionality in the name server). The name server tells the client where to find the print servers (their IP addresses) that meet the user's request.

The client program creates a print task that is communicated to the Palladium server by an RPC. The task is entered into the server database. The job scheduler matches the job requirements with the capabilities of the printers managed by this server. Thus the server can support a broad range of file types and printer types.

The server database stores all queued print jobs. The scheduler passes responsibility for the job off to a specialized process called a "printer supervisor." The printer supervisor takes responsibility for printing a single job, using a single format specification on a single (type of) printer.

The print server tasking system allows multiple clients to make requests at the same time. As the name server may return more than one printer that meets the user needs, the application program must select among the responses.

The job scheduler schedules the job on the correct printer and tracks the progress of the job. The server reports status and significant events to the user and also logs the status information.

File Servers

As indicated earlier, keeping private files or extensive system files on the workstation is inappropriate. Alternative network file service can be either a global file system visible to all users at all times (such as the Andrew File System) or a large set of separately exported file systems advertised through an intermediate service, such as a name service. The Network File System conforms to the latter model.

To meet the various needs of the Athena system, three types of network file services are provided. These are the Network File System (NFS) [Sandberg 85, Sun 87] developed and licensed by Sun Microsystems, the Remote Virtual Disk (RVD) [Greenwald 86] developed by MIT, and the Andrew File System (AFS) [Satyanarayanan 85, Mauro 89] developed at Carnegie-Mellon University.

NFS

NFS is a distributed network file system for sharing files in a heterogeneous network of operating systems and workstations. Files that are physically remote can be "attached" to a local directory. Thereafter, all references to the directory and file appear to be local. Sharing is accomplished by logically attaching the remote file system to a local directory and then reading and writing files in place. Thus only one copy of the file exists for all users. All storage and files in the workstation network can be considered as part of a single pool of storage. As with the Athena design, NFS is implemented as a network service accessed through a specified protocol, not as part of a distributed operating system. This implementation as a network service avoids requiring the same operating system on all workstations.

In the Athena environment, NFS is accessed through the *attach* command. *Attach* performs a Hesiod lookup on the file system name. It then calls the NFS *mount* command, which forms the logical linkage of the remote file or directory to a mount point in the user directory. Before a file can be *mounted*, it must be exported to make it available for mounting. This step is required to control access to the file. Access control is granted for read/write to authorized machine names.

NFS uses a stateless protocol that does not retain information between accesses, which greatly simplifies recovery. Locking for exclusive write access is not part of NFS; instead, it is part of an external network lock manager.

NFS can communicate with incompatible systems through the External Data Representation (XDR) protocol. This protocol performs representation conversion for transmitted data. Access to remote files is accomplished through a Remote Procedure Call (RPC) to the remote NFS.

Although Athena uses NFS for storage of private files, it has a number of shortcomings. NFS categorizes all workstations as either "trusted" or "untrusted." Untrusted workstations cannot access any files. Trusted workstations are completely trusted, can masquerade as any valid user, and can therefore get access to almost any file, except those owned by *root*.

The version of NFS used by Athena had been ported to the VAX and modified at the University of Wisconsin, but further modifications were required. In the Athena modification, the NFS server obtains authenticated information from Kerberos at mount time. On each transaction, the user IP address and user identity from the service request are compared to information established at mount time. If it is the same, access is granted; if different, the access rights are set to be "no privileged access." At unmount time, the authentication information is deleted.

The addition of Kerberos authentication to NFS requires state information. Fortunately, this is state information that the client can easily recover should it be lost (for example in a server crash). Therefore recovery is not much more complicated than recovery without Kerberos. If an NFS server crashes, users have to issue an *nfsid* command or must log out and log in again.

This approach is not completely secure, because the control information is sent in clear text and could be forged. However, an attack can only be mounted while the user is logged on; no unauthorized access can take place when the user is logged off.

RVD

RVD was originally developed at the MIT Laboratory for Computer Science and subsequently enhanced at Athena. RVD provides the services of a remote disk server, which appear to be local to the workstation. All file system information is maintained by the workstation, and the RVD servers simply deliver requested disk blocks. An RVD pack may be used by many workstations in a read–only mode or by a single workstation in an exclusive read/ write mode.

Because of its lower overhead, RVD offers significantly higher performance than NFS. It provides access to the Athena system software library and to some of the applications software. As with NFS, RVD has been modified to provide authentication.

AFS

AFS is a distributed file system that uses a single root node for the entire directory hierarchy. The system is designed to be used nationwide or even worldwide over a wide area network. When a file that is not local is accessed, extensive caching is provided to improve performance. If write access is requested, locks are provided to synchronize updates. The logical file locations remain consistent regardless of the files' physical location or the platform on which they reside.

The AFS file hierarchy is decomposed into nodes, with each node being a local site. Each cell can be administered independently and can link to other (possibly remote) nodes automatically. Seven individual server processes comprise AFS.

- *File Server.* Delivers files to clients and stores files received from clients on demand.
- *Authentication Server.* Verifies user identity at log in and when requested in transactions.
- *Protection Server.* Provides access control to directories and their files.
- *Volume Server.* Aggregates files into logical units for easier management.
- *Volume Location Server.* Provides directory server for location of volumes.
- *Update Server.* Distributes new versions of server software to maintain configuration integrity.
- *Basic Overseer Server.* Assists in system administration of servers.

Because Authentication Server is compatible with Kerberos, and very similar to it, we do not discuss it further.

AFS extends Unix security in a number of ways. Rights of access are granted at the directory level, not the file level. Rights can be granted to individuals or groups, and different rights can be granted to every individual and to every group. The rights of access can be any or all of

- read;
- write;
- lookup (obtain status information about files in a directory);
- delete;
- insert (add new files to a directory);
- lock (obtain exclusive use of a file); and
- administer (change rights for the access control list).

The software for all servers is installed on every file server. However, only the File Server, Volume Server, Basic Overseer Server, and the client portion of the Update Server run on every file server. The other servers need only run on two or three file servers in any complex to provide services for all workstations. These other file servers maintain the replicated databases for the distributed system, namely, the Authentication Database, the Protection Database, and the Volume Location Database. Synchrony among the replicated databases is maintained by the *Ubik* utility in the database management library.

In order to reduce the amount of network communications, file caching is provided at the user's workstation by the *Andrew Cache Manager*. When a file is requested, the request first goes to the cache manager. If the file exists locally, it is delivered to the user program. If the file does not exist locally, the Cache Manager translates the request into remote procedure calls to the File Server. The File Server sends the requested file to the Cache Manager, which stores it in its own local cache before delivery to the user program. In order to synchronize the (now replicated) files, the File Server sends a *callback* to the Cache Manager along with the file if write access is requested. The using workstation is guaranteed exclusive access to the file unless the callback is broken.

Volumes can be moved from one File Server to another to balance loads. The location of a volume at any time is maintained by a directory accessed by the Volume Location Server.

A volume usually contains all of the files for a single user; the volume usually contains all of the files and subdirectories for a single directory. Volumes may be readwrite or readonly. There is only one copy of a readwrite volume, but there may be several (replicated) copies of a readonly volume, each located on a different File Server. The third type of volume is backup, for purposes of recovery.

Athena is currently evaluating AFS as a possible replacement for NFS. All Athena staff members have been moved to AFS. It appears to satisfy better than NFS the system's requirements for security, growth capability, and management.

The Andrew system at CMU was not only the first AFS cell, but it is also the largest in current use. It has 24 file servers, 1500 client systems, 8500 user accounts, and 27 Gbytes of data. Of the 1500 client systems, about 800 are workstations running the cache managers, and the remainder are personal computers. Andrew has developed a set of protocol software for allowing both industry standard and proprietary personal computers to access the AFS file tree, primarily for mail and bulletin boards. All incoming freshmen at CMU receive AFS accounts.

Dial-Up Service

Dial-up service has proven to be very popular with Athena users. Service is available from both analog phones (up to 2400 baud) and digital phones (DX25 service). The initial connection is made to a protocol translator. At that point, available commands include connect/disconnect, exit/quit, lock, rlogin, and telnet. Using these commands the user can log into an Athena time-sharing system. Presently eight Athena time-sharing systems are available on a hunt group. Each system is capable of supporting several users simultaneously. The system provides output suitable for character terminals.

SEVEN

The Athena Multimedia Workstation Project

Not long after initiation of Project Athena, it became evident that many subjects, primarily those outside of engineering, could not be adequately taught with only text, or even with text and graphics. Support of image, live video, and in most cases sound was required.

A *multimedia* workstation is one that provides substantially more sensory content in the human interface than do traditional workstations. This increased sensory content includes the use of still image, motion video, color, increased resolution, and audio. People are well endowed to obtain information efficiently from such a sensory environment, with about 40 percent of the brain cells devoted to vision alone. Traditional human interfaces to computer systems are "sensory deprived" in comparison to users' inherent capability, and therefore multimedia interfaces are able to deliver much more information much more efficiently than are traditional systems.

The sensory content of the human interface has been increasing since the development of interactive computing, beginning with low-speed hardcopy terminals and proceeding to ASCII video terminals, color, high-resolution displays, and sound. Multimedia workstations represent the next logical step in this evolution.

The Beginning

Early in Project Athena, several members of the MIT faculty, including Janet Murray (language), Steve Wertheim (medical), Patrick Purcell and Gloriana Davenport (Media Lab), Merrill Smith (architecture), Sheldon Penman (biology), Herbert Einstein (geology), and David Wilson (mechanical engineering) approached Athena and asked that multimedia support be provided.

In 1985, MIT faculty began using Digital's Interactive Video Information System (IVIS), supplied by Athena's applications development group. IVIS proved to be too limited to support the functions desired because of its analog video design. Athena brought Rus Gant in as a media consultant early in 1986 and added several other staff members late in 1986. A few months later, the Athena staff found a third-party board product that provided a digital approach to interactive video and that supported both Digital and IBM workstations. The advent of digital technology signaled the start of a serious multimedia program because of the substantially increased functionality.

By 1987, the people who had become involved with the video effort formed a group to look at the emerging issues, in consultation with interested faculty members. The particular form of the multimedia workstation developed at Athena is called the "Visual Workstation." The group implementing the project is called the Visual Computing Group (VCG) and is managed by Ben Davis. The VCG supports faculty members in the design of educational software involving audio and video materials as part of the content. The group offers expertise both in producing audiovisual materials and in developing the controlling software applications. Digital also supplies use of its professional corporate video studio for mastering video disks produced by VCG.

Based on the requirements identified during development of multimedia instructional modules, tools are developed to improve the efficiency and quality of the instructional materials. The MUSE authoring environment (described later) is one group of these tools.

To create an experimental delivery system to replace IVIS, the group modified a standard Athena workstation to support 256 color graphics as well as full-motion digitized video. The visual workstation uses either an IBM PC-RT or DEC MicroVax II workstation as a base, with a Parallax Graphics board added as the display subsystem.

Visual Computing Modules

Once a suitable hardware platform became available, work on multimedia course modules began. At present, some 20 applications using interactive video are in development, use, or both.

The largest visual computing project is a collection of three language teaching modules under Janet Murray's overall direction. The languages are French, Spanish, and Japanese. Major funding was provided by The Annenberg/CPB Project. The general approach taken is that of "artificial reality," in this case a novella where the user becomes an integral part of the action. Each of the language modules tests a different pedagogical approach. In the Spanish module, nodes represent scenes in the directed graph. User input navigates the user among scenes. In the French module, nodes represent still images, and navigation takes place among them.

In the language applications, one or more text streams can be synchronized to the video to provide subtitles for the video, as the student often is not able to understand the spoken material. A number of text streams can be used: One stream might be full text; a second, only key words; a third, in a different language; a fourth, annotations for editing. The user may pick which media (in this case text) stream to be displayed or to invoke all of them to be displayed. Different viewers can each have their own text streams.

The French language project, entitled "Direction Paris," is directed by Gilberte Furstenberg. The first segment, called "A la Rencontre de Philippe," is a fictional story about a young French writer who must solve his romantic problems or find a new apartment in Paris. Filmed on location, the story features numerous options for action and opportunities to use maps, answer phones, and use movie maps of authentic Paris apartments. Segments 2 and 3, "Dans le Quartier St. Gervais," provide an interactive video documentary of real French speakers in the actual neighborhood where the fictional story takes place.

The Spanish module, entitled "No Recuerdo" ("I do not remember"), is directed by Douglas Morgenstern. No Recuerdo is the fictional story of Gonzalo, a Colombian scientist who loses his memory while working on a secret biological material. The adventure was videotaped in Bogotá and features a mazelike series of plots and simulations for the student to help Gonzalo get his memory back before the amnesia plague hits.

The third module, used to teach Japanese, is an interactive broadcast program directed by Michio Tsutsui. "Goodbye This Year's Love" is a video drama taken directly from Tokyo broadcast television and re-edited into segments for comprehension exercises. It includes slide files of cultural events, maps, and art.

Another application is the Neuroanatomy Learning Environment project, directed by Steven Wertheim. This is a flexible learning environment for exploring the anatomy of the human brain designed for Medical and Neuroscience students. The four major components of the program are: an illustrated glossary, a 3-D model of the brain, a slide browser, and a brain dissection. This project uses 1400 text documents, images, and video segments of the brain. The various media documents are cross referenced to each other and to images and video. The application also closely couples image and text, allowing the student to ask questions about specific spatial areas of the images. Video segments and image libraries also provide expository information.

In Engineering, David Wilson and Seichi Tsutsumi directed development of a project entitled "Mechanical Design." This is an introductory course in mechanical engineering covering principles and concepts of mechanical bearings. The video disk contains animations, motion segments, and a still-frame library. The general program is planned to include an expert system front end for teaching bearing selection.

Three projects have been implemented by the School of Architecture: the "Boston Architecture Collection," the "Image Delivery System," and the "New Orleans: A City in Transition" study. Merrill Smith directed development of a multimedia presentation entitled "Boston Architecture Collection; Rotch Library Project." About 6000 images from the Boston Architecture Collection of 30,000 images from 1620 to the present were indexed and put on video disk. This image collection is now far more accessible than it was in hardcopy form. Images can be obtained in response to a database query, and all of the relevant images can be collected onto a "light table" or in a "picture book." This video disk and database provide excellent research tools for in-depth study of city planning, architecture, and transitional images from 1620 to the present.

Another project, the "Image Delivery System," is directed by Patrick Purcell of the MIT Media Lab. Using the material developed by Smith's group as a visual database, this system is being designed to deliver analog images to the workstation via MIT cable TV. A student can call for still video images from the Rotch Library by using the MIT cable TV system, which is connected to each multimedia workstation, and can associate the image with an on-line text database.

Gloriana Davenport of the MIT Media Lab directed the project "New Orleans: A City in Transition." Her group designed a video disk for teaching film and video editing concepts. Based on documentary footage of changes in the architecture of New Orleans during the World's Fair, this project has a visual database of more than five hours of still and moving imagery concerned with urban planning, design, and implementation of changes during a time of change. The module's display method is a high-level, video-disk-based editing system. The visual materials are used in a variety of projects related to urban planning and social policy, as well as for teaching the fundamentals of film editing techniques.

The Biology Department has implemented a multimedia teaching module entitled "Introduction to Cell Biology," directed by Sheldon Penman. This module is a set of basic biology learning aids written around existing video disks of biologic subject matter. Designed for first and second year biology students, the module takes advantage of still-frame and motion storage of visual molecular biology materials on commercially available video disks.

The Geology Department has implemented a multimedia teaching module entitled "Geology Engineering Educator," directed by Professor Herbert Einstein of the Civil Engineering Department. This project is an electronic book consisting of 250 short text documents and 500 photographic images that describe geologic features relevant to an introductory course for civil engineering students. All documents are indexed and cross referenced through hypertext-like linkages. These linkages allow students to traverse the pages by selecting words with the mouse and following the link to view a reference. The book is equipped with a table of contents and an index, both of which serve as conventional entry points and use the same point-and-click interface to traverse the network.

A companion "workbook" generates exercises that present images and ask students to identify geological features by name. It also asks them to locate features in the images by drawing closed polygon outlines directly on the image. These outlines are then compared with the ranges provided by the professor. The entire workbook is indexed to a reference manual, so that students can ask questions in the context of the workbook and immediately traverse to the appropriate manual page.

The "Navigation Learning Environment," developed initially by Digital, is an experiment in teaching ocean navigation by using interactive video disk technology. The context is a two-square-mile region along the Maine coast and utilizes a library of 10,000 images to represent the environment. The training is done in the context of an electronic document with seven variables representing boat heading, speed, compass reading, and the viewing angle. The user can direct the boat through an "artificial reality" using mouse manipulation of graphic controls on the display.

Another application is that of video editing. Markers can be time synchronized with the video to mark the beginning and end of segments. The various segments can be managed by MUSE. For this purpose, the metaphor of the "photo album" is used. The video editor can select pieces of video and then save them in miniature in the photo album for organization and annotation.

The album provides space for display of several images on a page. The pictures in the album are not limited to still images; they include video as well. The video can include all the sensory richness of the normal MUSE display, including text, graphics, and animated control devices such as scroll bars. The images can come from a number of electronic documents. The video editor can then combine the segments from the photo album into the new electronic document.

Hardware

One of Athena's rules is that all applications must run on the hardware of both sponsors. The project was fortunate in locating a board set that supported the desired functionality in image and video and that was available for both the VAXstation II (Q bus) and the IBM RT (PC/AT bus). The product, the Parallax Graphics board from Parallax Corporation, contains a high-speed frame grabber that digitizes a standard NTSC video signal at 30 frames per second. The workstation platform for Digital consisted of a VAXstation II. The Parallax boards replace the graphics processor and frame buffer boards in the VAXstation. The Parallax boards provide a 2048 by 2048 pixel frame buffer, which may be purchased in depths of 8, 16, and 24 bits. Athena used the 8-bit (256-color) version. Two color lookup tables are provided: one is a standard RGB table, and the other is a compression/decompression table for using 8-bit color with motion video. Switching between the lookup tables is controlled by a special bit plane and is switchable on a per-pixel basis. The monitor supported by the system provides a resolution of 1280 by 1024. The video image with a resolution of 640 by 480 occupies about one fourth of the screen. The off-screen part of the frame buffer can be used for storing images for quick recall. Figure 7.1 shows a diagram of the Athena visual workstation.

Using the digitized approach to video in the workstation offers significant advantages over the analog approach used in earlier systems because of the additional flexibility. Once the image has been digitized it can be stored and retrieved from any digital storage device. Single images can be taken from the video stream and displayed elsewhere on the screen or stored for later use. The Parallax boards also provided a high performance graphics processor, but relatively little use was made of this hardware.

Figure 7.1   Athena visual workstation diagram.

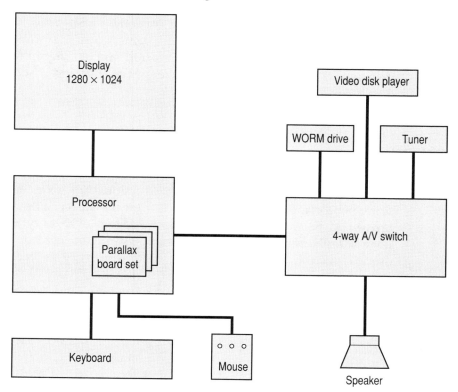

Athena developed software to present this digitized video in an X.11 window. The video window can be translated, scaled, and clipped as can any other X window. The system currently allows one window of full-motion digital video, but hundreds of windows can be created containing still images "grabbed" from the video source. The image facility can support sophisticated multi-image displays of a visual database.

Any NTSC video source can be used, but most applications utilize an optical video disk player with 12-inch media to obtain interactivity. Other sources used include cable TV, a video tape recorder, and a video camera. Extensive use is made of an analog write-once optical disk in conjunction with the visual workstation. The write-once disk uses 8-inch media and can hold 24,000 still frames or 13 minutes of motion video. It can also hold two channels of audio. This device is used to prototype applications that will ultimately be mastered on the 12-inch media and has about one fourth of the 12-inch media capacity. The fact that the write-once media can be written on-line is a significant advantage.

Source material comes from many places. Consumer-quality VHS camcorders are used to record meetings, interviews, and presentations at negligible cost. A 35-mm camera is used to capture images of documents, illustrations, overheads, and photographs, which then can be moved to the write-once optical disk and made immediately available on the workstation.

MUSE

One of the major problems that emerged in Athena was the lack of adequate tools for development of instructional software. Although some people anticipated this problem from the outset, its magnitude proved to be much larger than most realized. The only developmental tools available were those that system software developers used: Unix and C. Although these tools were very powerful (i.e., primitive), the development of instructional software using them was extremely time-consuming and required a high degree of skill.

The resulting cost was not acceptable to many faculty members. Various developmental systems were evaluated, but none was suitable. Although it became evident that there was nothing particularly unique about requirements for developmental environments for instructional software, still nothing was found. All of the develop-

mental problems experienced were magnified on the visual workstation with its interactive video and image capability.

The Authoring Environment

After an extensive survey of existing and planned authoring systems,
the VCG initiated design of an "authoring environment" called
ATHENA MUSE (hereafter, called MUSE) that would meet the
needs of the MIT instructional software developers. The dozen or so
video and image applications already in development had special
priority, but others expressed interest in more general applications.
Initiated in mid-1987 by Matt Hodges and Russell Sasnet, this project developed a prototype during the following year. The objective
of MUSE is to substantially reduce the time and skill level needed to
support the development of instructional software systems, especially those involving interactive video.

MUSE provides support for the creation of applications including text, image, graphics, video, and sound using an "electronic document" metaphor. It supports (at least) three different pedagogical
approaches [Hodges 89]:

- interactive presentations;
- simulation; and
- reference facilities.

MIT heavily based its pedagogical approach on exposition and
simulation. The exposition, either linear or branching, forms the basis for explaining the physical world to the student. Simulations allow the student to set up and control experiments quickly, with the
power of the computer handling input and output information
quickly. It also allows the students to test various trial situations
quickly, inexpensively, and safely. Reference facilities make large
amounts of information, especially graphic or image, available
quickly and inexpensively. Initial work is in process to provide
embedded tools that allow the student to combine and integrate these
resources into a single electronic document.

Functionality

The design of MUSE started with the human interface, and proceeded to lower levels of abstraction. In order to maximize existing
functionality of available software, MUSE is layered on the X

Window System and the X Toolkit. Figure 7.2 shows a schematic diagram of MUSE.

The screen layout and semantics of active objects of human interface are defined by a text file called an *Object Script,* created by the human interface designer. This file also links the active objects to the appropriate procedures and/or data structures. MUSE supports the object–oriented paradigm of combined procedures and data. A

Figure 7.2   MUSE schematic diagram.

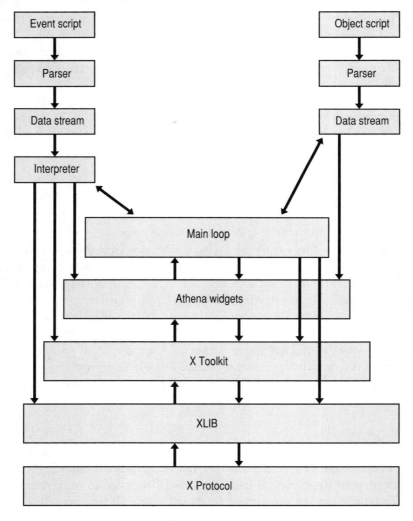

MUSE data model may include multiple media forms and link the various media forms into a compound electronic document. MUSE also supports a limited set of editors for creating objects which include the various forms of media. Hypertext and hypermedia structures are supported as subsets of the object-oriented capability.

One of the major problems in developing multimedia authoring environments is that of representing relationships among the media. After considerable study, the MUSE developers decided that four distinct methods of representing relationships were required:

- directed graphs;
- multidimensional spatial frameworks;
- declarative constraints; and
- procedural languages.

These four representational approaches are integrated so that an application developer can use any or all of them.

Directed graphs are used in two ways: to establish linkages among sets of multimedia documents (which may contain text, video, audio, and/or image) and to control the flow of control for user navigation. The Intermedia project at Brown University [Yankelovitch 88] established the value of nonlinear navigation through electronic documents, using the concept of hypertext and hypermedia. The hypermedia model of navigation is supported in MUSE as a subset of directed graph control.

The representation of multidimensional information is an important mechanism in MUSE. The dimensions are abstract and can represent any changing independent variable, including space and time. In the one-dimensional case, an abstract scale of dimension can be created (e.g., either time or space). Other variables may then be slaved to the independent dimension. For example, both video and text may be slaved to time in order to synchronize text to video. The number of dependent variables that can be linked to the independent variable is not limited, so a graphics object, such as a scroll bar, may be linked as well and synchronized to both the text and video.

In the two-dimensional case, images and video can be conveniently manipulated (for example, to perform pan and zoom). Because MUSE defines the image in a virtual space, it can automatically scale and translate the image appropriate to the user input. Text, graphics, and interface control mechanisms may be added as annotations as desired. Dimensionality beyond two can be supported: MUSE does not limit the number of dimensions that may be created.

Declarative constraints can impose relationships on variables. In MUSE, only two-way equality constraints can be imposed. The two-way constraint can be very useful, allowing, for example, the user to "grab" a scroll bar and drag it forward or backward to control the dimensions, such as video or text subtitles, linked to it.

MUSE is designed to minimize the use of procedural code, the use of which, however, is unavoidable at times. Therefore MUSE designers developed an interpreted language called *Event Script*. This language allows the developer to create and attach special purpose behaviors to display elements. The language is a simplified object-oriented system used to create event handlers for human interfaces, somewhat similar to Hypertalk.

Sample Capabilities

MUSE's functionality gives rise to several useful paradigms for organizing and presenting information. For example, synchronization of dimensions allows a scroll bar (graphical object) to be synchronized with live video. The scroll bar is useful in showing the fractional amount of a video segment that has been played. Because the video may be defined as slaved to the scroll bar, the user can "grab" the scroll bar with the mouse (assuming that it is suitably defined) and drag the scroll bar to a new location, and the video will also go to the new location (in time) automatically. If text were also slaved to the scroll bar, it would be dragged to the new location in time and would retain synchronization with the video. Similarly, a mouse-sensitive video control panel can be created with the desired user controls, say, play, stop, rewind, and double-speed buttons. With controls such as these, the user can solve an important problem in electronic documents, namely, moving through them easily.

A second and more serious problem is locating information in an electronic document. By its very nature, video information is difficult to search, because there is no concise way to represent objects in an image in symbolic form. Thus video cannot be searched for matches in the same way that databases or files can be searched. The preferred solution to this problem in MUSE is to use time as an independent dimension and slave other variables to it. Searches can now be carried out on other dimensions, such as text. Alternatively, the video can be annotated with text or numeric markers to assist in searching. In any event, moving the time line will cause all dependent media streams to move in synchronization with it and with each other.

Human Interface Benefits

Based on experience so far with the multimedia workstation, the following human interface benefits have emerged.

- *Combines visual, spoken, and written language.* These diverse forms of language have very different communication characteristics, and each has advantages in certain circumstances. They can also be effectively used in combination to improve speed or intelligibility.
- *Uses the expressive power of video.* Certain kinds of information, primarily spatial or temporal, can be presented by video more effectively than by any other means. Video is also very effective at including context information along with the main message. The video medium is also valuable in that it can be speeded up, slowed down, or used with freeze frames.
- *Speeds generation.* Video can be generated far faster than highly encoded communication such as text. This capability is very important where the time value of information is high.
- *Improves access.* Currently, access and playback of video are slower than with text. A stream of video, or even a single image, cannot be searched for a pattern as text can. MUSE provides a partial solution to this problem by synchronizing text and video so that indexing and text search techniques can be used with annotated video.
- *Provides a more powerful technique to insert geometric tags.* Use of tags, such as points and bounding polygons overlaid on the image, allows utilization of the search techniques from graphics to be used in an image and video environment. Again, technology will likely provide the solution in the form of powerful image processing capability.

Current Status and Future Plans

A cluster of 12 multimedia workstations has been installed and is available for public access. It is being used by several faculty application developers and researchers and for course delivery.

Project Athena has also been involved in a joint proposal to create a collection image system for the Native American Collections at the National Museum of Natural History at the Smithsonian Institution in Washington, D.C. This project (MITSI) will initially provide visual workstation support for curators and researchers using the Southwest Collections. Other prototypes involving curatorial and exhibition support are "Man Ray's Paris 1921–39," "Seeds of Change," "Flight of the Daedalus," "History of Technology," "Aspects of Visualization," and "Coastal Ecology."

The Visual Computing Group also works with MIT's Center for Space Research Man Vehicle Laboratory "telescience" experiments. By adapting the visual workstation to receive digital data, voice, and live satellite video links to the Kennedy Space Center, faculty and students will be able to monitor real time experiments anticipating the use of the multimedia workstation as a NASA system link to the Spacelab and Space Shuttle.

Other areas of interest include the use of image capture and storage devices, such as Write Once Read Many (WORM) optical media, CD-ROM databases, digital video camera input, networking of digital imagery, "jukebox" (video disk, WORM, and CD-ROM) delivery systems, digital imagery file systems, digital audio, and high-resolution graphics. Research is also under way to create a smaller, lower cost platform for the visual workstation.

Administration

EIGHT

Workstations in
Student Housing

_____

Part of the original plan to make Athena access easily available was to deploy workstations in most or all student housing facilities, such as dormitories, fraternities, sororities, and independent student residences. To date workstations have been placed in five such facilities. This description of that process and its results draws on a report commissioned by the MIT Project Athena study group. The study was managed by the Dean for Undergraduate Education and written by Gregory Jackson of MIT [Jackson 87, 88]. Material from the Athena specifications for living group installations [Erickson 87] also is used.

At first Athena provided only dial-up access to users that were off campus. Thus the benefits of workstations were not available to these users. Early in 1985, Athena developed guidelines and solicited proposals from the 39 student living groups at MIT for installation of Athena workstations, which would provide for greater student access to workstations. Athena offered to provide workstations, network connections, operating systems, and maintenance, if the living groups would provide space, power, and an organizational structure meeting Athena requirements.

This request for proposal generated considerable controversy. Some groups were concerned that those that got workstations would have an unfair advantage in attracting students. Others were concerned that workstations would upset the balance between dormitories and fraternities. Nevertheless, about half of the student living groups submitted proposals.

163

Groups had the option of installing workstations in a common area (called a "cluster") or putting them in the bedrooms (called the "intensive" installation). Generally, the physical arrangement of the building strongly encouraged one or the other of these options. (Other campuses make extensive use of living-group workstation access for education. Dartmouth's approach, for example, is to have a network access port "for every pillow." Dartmouth primarily uses personal computers purchased by students for educational computing.)

On-campus living groups were to receive direct access to the network with full performance, called an "on-campus" link. Those that were too far away for an on-campus line were to receive 14.4 Kb/sec access, called the "remote" link. In order to provide good response time, the remote sites were also to receive their own file servers and local network. In all cases, at least two printers were to be provided with the workstations. The servers provided to remote locations were to be adequate for them to operate in a stand-alone mode. The 14.4 kb/sec link was to provide a "trickle-path" between their net and the rest of the campus net. Workstation installation was to be funded by a special grant from the Provost's office.

The request for proposal guidelines also called for each living group to create an Athena committee of at least 3–4 people. One of the committee members was to be designated as the living group's contact person for Athena. Similarly, Athena was to designate a person as the contact with each living group. Another person from the living group, to be designated "cluster manager," would be a technical expert on running the system. The living-group committee was to be responsible for all contacts with Athena, as well as enforcing house rules regarding cleaning and security.

Upon system installation, the cluster manager was to be in regular contact with the Athena operations group (through its designated *droog*) and the Athena systems development organization. The cluster manager also was to be responsible for installing new elements released and notifying Athena of any system customization.

The following environmental specifications were established:

Space	28 square feet per workstation
Table	3 feet by 4 feet
Power	7 amps per workstation and 5 amps per printer
Phone	A phone must be in the cluster
Air-conditioning	1500 BTU per workstation or 3000 BTU per server

Carpet	Should be antistatic
Windows	Must be closed to minimize dust
Cleanliness	Room must be dusted and vacuumed once a week
Security	Room must be lockable
Liability	Individual and/or living group is liable for breakage, loss, and theft
Accidents	Covered by field service contract and Institute insurance
Access	Must be available to field service personnel on a reasonable basis.

The proposals were to be evaluated initially with respect to adequacy in meeting basic Athena requirements. Those meeting these basic requirements (the "short list") were then to be evaluated on the proposed set of applications and general creativity. Because the residences at MIT have strong individual cultures, various reactions to the type of workstation installation were expected. Thus an attempt was made to get some diversity in keeping with the concept of the installations as an experiment.

Proposals were due in December 1985. Ultimately, 19 living groups submitted proposals, and five of them were selected to receive equipment:

- Delta Upsilon, a fraternity (cluster, off-campus link);
- pika, an independent living group (cluster, on-campus link);
- Theta Delta Chi, a fraternity (intensive, on-campus link);
- Zeta Beta Tau, a fraternity (cluster, off-campus link); and
- 500 Memorial Drive, a dormitory (cluster, on-campus link).

Theta Delta Chi and 500 Memorial Drive are on the MIT campus in Cambridge. The pika residence is in Cambridgeport, about one mile west of the campus. Delta Upsilon is in Boston, immediately across the Charles River from the campus. Zeta Beta Tau, also across the Charles River but in Brookline, about 2.5 miles from campus, is MIT's most distant living group.

The Athena staff originally planned to prepare space and install the systems in the summer of 1986. However, many delays in space preparation, network installation, software, and hardware delivery occurred, which were relatively frustrating to all parties. The delays created some negative attitudes on the part of the living groups, because they had put considerable time and energy into developing the proposals and because a high level of expectation had been built up about getting the "advanced technology."

Workstations were installed in May 1987 (nine months late) in Theta Delta Chi, 500 Memorial Drive, and Zeta Beta Tau. Workstations were installed in pika and Delta Upsilon in December 1987, or about 15 months later than expected.

The living-group contact person was put on appropriate mailing lists. The contact is responsible for attending periodic meetings, creating mailing lists for the living group, and disseminating information from Athena to the living group. The contact is the "keeper of the keys," if there is a cluster installation, and is responsible for arranging for access to equipment by maintenance personnel. The contact is also responsible for maintaining supplies of expendibles such as documentation, paper, and toner.

Athena's Impact on Living-Group Life

At MIT each living group has a distinct identity, and lifestyles vary widely among them. Thus the response to Athena has varied considerably among the living groups that have received workstations.

Local modifications to make the system conform to the desires of the group were made sometimes. Although such modifications probably did improve usability of the system, they also caused many problems for installation of newer versions of system software.

The workstation clusters often became locations of social interaction. The new technology was a favorite topic of conversation, including how to use it and how to defeat its limitations. The clusters also attracted house "alumni" as well, who would return to see how the workstations were being used and would stay to talk in general.

Jackson summarized Athena's impact on living-group life in the following ways.

- *Residence as academic environment.* The workstations appeared to bridge the gap between academic life and residential life.
- *Athena as an integrator.* Athena seems to promote social integration of the members of the living group.
- *Group cost versus individual benefits.* The living group incurred the cost of installing the workstations, but the benefits went to specific individuals who made use of the system.
- *Cultural variations.* Tailored approaches unique to each group are required for success.

Let's take a brief look at the system's impact on the living groups that received the last three installations and then at the general experience with the system.

Theta Delta Chi

Theta Delta Chi fraternity has about 40 male members. The members are generally regarded as "well rounded," not, for example, as computer hackers. The rooms are largely doubles and triples. Workstations were installed in about 30 bedrooms, requiring that a cable be run to each of those rooms. In addition, three workstations were placed in the fourth floor library. Two printers were also installed. The system was connected to the campus spine and had full access to network services. Training was largely informal. Documentation played a minor role in training because it was often out of date. By the fall of 1987 the workstations had become a part of normal life, and they got considerable use.

The living-group workstations made course-related computing much more accessible than before, when members had to go to public clusters. Several individuals reached levels of workstation competence that they otherwise would not have attained. The younger members tended to take the workstations more for granted than did the older members. The planning and installation process generated considerable social interaction among house members, but overall impact on academic performance was modest.

500 Memorial Drive

This dormitory is the farthest from the academic buildings. It received a cluster of eight workstations for 390 student residents. Most rooms are doubles. Many delays occurred in installation, primarily for air-conditioning and networking. The cluster became operational in the fall of 1987. As demand for workstation access greatly exceeded supply, a signup system was installed. Documentation was largely inadequate, and most training was by word of mouth or provided by one of the house hackers.

The system was heavily used by a few individuals, and some never used it. Those who used the system appreciated its convenience. Academic impact was modest but positive. The inadequate number of workstations for the building population led to considerable frustration.

pika

Seven workstations, two file servers, and a laser printer arrived late in the fall of 1986. As with the others, long delays in installation generated considerable frustration. However, after installation, most residents came to use the workstations effectively. The workstation room became a kind of academic common space.

The pikans chose the basement cluster approach rather than the intensive approach to avoid the possibility that freshmen would pick pika for its computer access rather than for the people who lived there. A strong motivation for accepting the computers was the saving of the 20-minute walk to campus. This benefit was greatly appreciated.

General Experience

At the beginning of the experiment, considerable controversy developed over whether Athena would act as an integrator of residential life with academic life. Some students wanted increased integration, but others wanted to preserve a separation between residential life and academic life, perhaps as a shield against the pressure of coursework.

Jackson reports that the workstation clusters did in fact increase the integration of residential life and academic life and that it was generally viewed as positive. Members are now able to do work at the residence that would have required a trip to a campus workstation cluster. As a result, residents gained more workstation access and computing literacy. Few complained about academic encroachment on the residence refuge.

Workstation benefits were not evenly distributed among residents. The few who became heavily involved benefited significantly, especially those who acted as system managers or operators. Many benefited to some extent, and those who chose not to become involved received no benefits.

The acquisition and presence of workstations increased interaction among residents—initially in the planning and installation phase and later in using the workstations. The increased interaction was technical, academic, and social.

In those residences that installed clusters—and where there was a ratio of no more than five students per workstation—the impact seems to have been quite favorable. The workstation room emerged as a focus of informal academic interaction among students. At 500 Memorial Drive, the ratio of 45 students per workstation, among other factors, seems to allow little time for sharing experiences with other students. The signup system also restricted casual interaction among students. At Theta Delta Chi, the intensive installation model encouraged virtually all students to become involved with the workstations. The initial frustration at delays in getting the workstations faded when the systems were received.

The final score card reported by Jackson for the five installations is

- Theta Delta Chi—highly effective;
- pika—generally effective;
- Delta Upsilon—generally effective;
- Zeta Beta Tau—generally effective; and
- 500 Memorial Drive—generally ineffective.

The cluster model appears to be more successful than the intensive model primarily because of the increased interaction among residents in several ways. Most of the residents at all five sites reported some beneficial workstation experience. Jackson concluded that the key factors to success in utilizing workstations in a living-group environment are reasonable access to the workstations and some degree of commitment of members to use that access.

Future Plans

Although as late as July 1987 the plan was still to provide workstations to all student housing facilities, further installations were put on hold. Athena management decided to evaluate more fully the results of the first five installations before continuing. With the new campuswide twisted pair cable in place, planning for additional living-group installations resumed in the spring of 1989. However, none has been made, partly because of the considerable logistics problems and cost.

One of the major lessons learned from the living-group installations is that the effort required to plan, deploy, and maintain workstations in a student housing area is much greater than that required to provide the same services in classrooms. Moreover, off-campus locations require extra technical work and expenditures to configure a stand-alone system and the remote network connection.

NINE

Finance and
Organization

███████

In this chapter we describe the finance and organization of Athena. Financing was crucial to initiation of the project—and to its continuation. Later, organization was the key to its eventual success.

Finance

The initial estimate of the cost of development and installation of the Athena system was $70 million. Athena's supporters believed that this funding level would carry the project through five years of development to completion. The plan was then to integrate the system and support into MIT's normal administrative structure. Each of the two major sponsors, Digital and IBM, committed about $25 million in equipment, personnel, maintenance, and cash. In addition to the $50 million from the two primary sponsors, MIT agreed to raise $20 million from other sources. A list of these other sources is given in Appendix V.

At the end of five years, the project was far from complete. System development was only approaching completion, and instructional software development was still under way. However, the system appeared to be close to living up to expectations, and the sponsors had benefited significantly. Therefore both of the sponsors and MIT agreed to a three-year funding extension. Support annually by the sponsors would be approximately the same as for the first five years, bringing the total amount of support for the project from all sources including MIT to over $100 million for the eight years of development.

MIT realized prior to the start of the project that development of instructional software required a major effort. Very little instructional software existed at the start of the project, and little of what existed was based on workstations and Unix. The bulk of the instructional software had been written for personal computers or character-oriented time-sharing. Therefore MIT made $8.5 million available to the faculty to develop instructional software.

In some cases, the sponsors contributed additional money to the project. As the success of the project became known throughout the academic community, the project began to have many visitors. Throughout the extension period, 4 to 8 groups per week, averaging 3000–4000 visitors per year, visited the project. Because about one third of the visiting groups were Digital customers or employees, Digital contributed half the cost of a person to organize visits and make presentations. The other half of the funding for this position was provided by the MIT Industrial Liaison Program.

Resource Allocation

Because of the strategic importance of the Athena project in setting the model for campus computing for the next generation of systems, funding the project adequately was vital. This one-time funding of a leadership project could then be followed by deployment of the system to other institutions to assist them in using this technology. However, the scale of the Athena funding would not have to be repeated.

Digital provided a significant portion of the budget in the form of a grant that included hardware, software, equipment maintenance, and on-site services. These services were provided by software engineers who assisted in the development of the Athena system and application software.

The Digital hardware grant funds were allocated as follows:

File servers and peripherals	42 percent
Workstations	34 percent
Minicomputers	8 percent
Terminals	7 percent
Communications	4 percent

Printers   3 percent
Miscellaneous   2 percent

Although this allocation is reasonably accurate for the entire project, it is somewhat distorted by the acquisition of the initial time-sharing system. Later in the project, a rule of thumb was established that every dollar spent on workstations required about $0.80 to be spent in support equipment, including file servers, print servers, and communications.

Organization

The organization of Athena involved establishing and maintaining the following groups.

- Athena project staff: to carry out development and deployment.
- Athena Executive Committee: to set overall policy and provide oversight.
- Resource allocation committees: to fund pedagogical projects.
- Athena Study Committee: to evaluate project results.
- Athena Users and Developers Group: to improve communication between the project and the users and developers about new system capabilities.
- Athena sponsors: to ensure their full participation.

Although each group had its own mission, they interacted to a considerable extent.

Project Staff

When Athena began, two alternatives existed for its placement in the MIT organization. One alternative was to make it part of the Information Systems Department, and the other was to make it an independent project. The Information Systems Department already existed on campus and reported to Vice President James Bruce. This department was responsible for all administrative computing and central time-sharing services. It also was responsible for all campus communications systems, including the telephone system and local area networks. Moreover, at that time the department was absorbed in integrating several formerly independent computing systems.

However, the characteristics envisioned for Athena were unique and did not fit neatly into any existing MIT organizational framework. That is,

- nontraditional skills were required in Unix, C, workstations, graphics, and distributed computing;
- large equipment donations from the sponsors had to be kept separate from other computing operations;
- the project was temporary;
- the time scale of the project was relatively short compared to the size of the task to be done, requiring the ability to use expedited procedures; and
- the project was so large that it could benefit from being a separate organization.

These characteristics led to Athena's establishment as an independent project. Steve Lerman of the MIT Civil Engineering Department was appointed Project Director. His first task was to develop an organization. The Dean of Engineering had overall responsibility for the project and in turn was responsible to the Provost.

The initial project organization was fairly conventional, although the developmental aspects of the task, which were high priority at the time, were emphasized. The initial organization included a technical committee to design the system. This committee was adequate for the time-sharing system design but proved to be inadequate for the workstation system design. Therefore, 18 months into the project, a Technical Director was appointed to be responsible for the technical integrity of the system. The early organization also included a Manager of Systems Development.

When the project matured, emphasis shifted to operations. An Executive Director was appointed to handle day-to-day internal operations, while the Project Director handled strategic issues and external relations. Software development was merged with operations. Figure 9.1 shows the current organization, with its emphasis on operations and maintenance, which is quite different from the initial organization and its emphasis on design and development.

An early decision was made not to develop a separate Athena networking capability but, instead, to purchase those services from the existing campus Telecommunications Department. To ensure

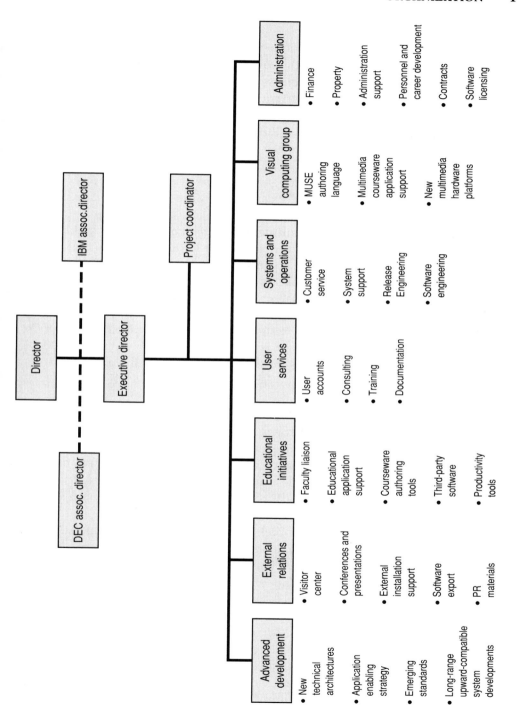

close cooperation between that department and Athena, networking personnel were colocated with Athena project personnel.

The MIT Athena staff increased in size over the life of the project, eventually reaching its current size: a total of about 85 full-time equivalent MIT people. In addition, each sponsor provided up to five software engineers on site. MIT retained veto power over sponsor personnel assigned to the project in order to maintain appropriate standards.

The Digital and IBM software engineers were assigned to MIT supervisors and were treated exactly the same as MIT personnel. Each sponsor also provided an on-site manager, who was responsible for meeting the staffing commitments for that company, for making sure that the appropriate contracts and other legal matters were taken care of, and for ensuring that technology transfer took place in both directions. The sponsor managers also assisted in selecting the appropriate products from the parent company and in making sure that orders were processed properly. In some cases the managers had strong technical skills and made significant technical contributions to the project.

All personnel from the sponsor companies are given appointments as Visiting Scientists or Visiting Engineers at MIT. In addition, the managers from the sponsoring companies are given appointments as Associate Directors. They participate in the day-to-day management of the project, along with the Project Director, Executive Director, and Manager of Operations. The MIT Vice President of Information Systems also participates in the day-to-day management of the project. He is able to bring campus MIS expertise to the project, and is able to coordinate Athena with other MIS activity on campus.

Initially there had been apprehension about comingling personnel from two competitors on a single team. In practice, there was never the slightest indication of competition or friction between personnel of the two sponsors. Indeed, it was difficult or impossible to tell which individual belonged to which company, as they all had the same objectives. These individuals approached their work objectively, and it was not unusual for a person to argue against the best competitive interests of his or her company and for the best interests of the project. (In this regard, the Athena experience is the same as that of the Microelectronics and Computer Technology Corporation (MCC) where members of competing companies often worked on the same technical teams.)

Athena Executive Committee

A high-level group was needed to establish project objectives from the MIT standpoint, generally oversee staff operations, set policy, represent the system users, and act as a board of directors. The Athena Executive Committee, chaired by the Dean of Engineering, was established to meet these needs. Although the membership changed from time to time, it generally included the

- Dean of Engineering;
- Director of Athena;
- Executive Director of Athena;
- Associate Director of Athena/IBM;
- Associate Director of Athena/Digital;
- Dean of Undergraduate Education;
- Dean of Humanities and Social Sciences;
- Vice President of Information Systems;
- Department Chairman of Electrical Engineering and Computer Science;
- Director of the Laboratory for Computer Science;
- chairpersons of the resource allocation committees (2); and
- several faculty members on a rotating basis.

The Executive Committee meets approximately quarterly. It usually receives a status and plans report from the Director of Athena and then considers other business brought it.

Resource Allocation Committees

In order to allocate the funds for instructional software, two resource allocation committees were established, one for Digital equipment for the School of Engineering and one for IBM equipment for the other schools. The two committees had similar functions but operated somewhat differently.

Initially, the participants felt that partitioning the campus between the two sponsors was important. Later, it became evident that separation was not needed, and equipment from the two sponsors was comingled to a large extent.

Procedures were established for faculty members to submit proposals to obtain funds and equipment for the development of instructional software. The proposals were to present the scope and benefits of the intended instructional development, the amount of funds needed, and the types and amount of hardware required. The funds supported faculty release time for the developmental effort, and students and professional staff to perform the programming.

The chairman of the Digital Resource Allocation Committee was selected from the faculty of the School of Engineering, as were the members. The Digital manager at Athena was a member of this committee. The chairman and members of the IBM Resource Allocation Committee were selected from other schools. The IBM manager at Athena was a member of this committee.

Project Athena Study Group

One of Athena's initial objectives was to provide information to support a decision on the MIT approach to educational computing after Athena. In order to provide a faculty evaluation of the project, the Project Athena Study Group was established during the summer of 1985. The group was chaired by Professor Jean DeMonchaux, Dean of Architecture and Planning. Membership was drawn from the faculty and Athena management. Funding was provided by the MIT Provost for a number of evaluation studies.

Athena Users and Developers Group

For the project, 1987 was a very hectic year. In order to obtain the functionality required, much of the new system's software had to be developed. At the same time, a large number of applications developers and system users were using it in a production environment and needed a stable interface. These two modes of use conflicted directly with each other, and the more the system developers improved the system, the more the interfaces changed, making existing software inoperable.

In order to resolve this conflict, at least to some extent, an informal group was created, called the "Athena Users and Developers Group." It held a series of meetings to inform users and developers of upcoming changes to the systems. With this information those affected could prepare for the changes. Moreover, they could comment on the relative value of changes compared to the cost in terms of additional application maintenance effort. The meetings were largely successful in resolving conflicts during the critical period until the system stabilized in 1988.

Faculty Registration and Deployment

All students are eligible for Athena accounts as a matter of policy. Any faculty member may register as an Athena user by calling the Athena Faculty Liaison office, followed by a registration session at a workstation. In addition, if a faculty member wants to set up a class locker for delivery of homework sets, programs, data, or whatever, a call to that same office can obtain a disk storage locker for that purpose. A project that involves development of new software usually receives a separate allocation of storage space for that development.

Many faculty members have also found it useful to request that their departments pay the cost of installation and network fees for an Athena-granted workstation for themselves or their teaching assistants. Such installations are subject to equipment and network availability. Proposing creation of a departmental facility may encounter fewer obstacles and lower total cost than proposing installation of several isolated workstations.

Restrictions on Use

By contract and by policy, Athena facilities are for educational use. As with most MIT policies, that policy is broadly interpreted. Students are encouraged to make use of the facilities in both curricular and extracurricular applications, within the general guidelines of a statement of "Principles of Responsible Use," which is posted at public workstation clusters and on-line. This document is reproduced in its entirety in Appendix IV. Faculty users are expected to follow the same general guidelines and to respect the boundary between teaching applications and research, administrative, and personal applications. Finally, faculty members are made aware that the security of the Athena network storage facilities is not adequate to maintain privacy of sensitive information, such as class grades and letters of recommendation.

Contracts

Two separate contractual arrangements were made in support of the project. One agreement was between Digital and MIT, and the other agreement was between IBM and MIT. This arrangement avoided the problem of having IBM and Digital contractually obligated to each other. The two agreements were based on similar principles but differed in detail, with each reflecting the interests of the contracting parties.

The agreement between Digital and MIT was split into two separate contracts. One contract covered the donation of equipment, software, maintenance, and on-site manpower. This was an outright donation, with nothing requested in return. The other contract covered the cash donation. In this case, Digital received certain nonexclusive rights to software developed at Athena. The IBM agreement was structured as a single contract, consisting of a donation.

MIT retains ownership of all intellectual property developed by Athena. However, because the primary objective of Athena is the improvement of higher education, all system software developed with Athena funding is made available to the public for a nominal media charge or at no cost, provided that the MIT copyright notice is retained. The X Window System Consortium has implemented this same policy.

The nature of the contractual arrangements between MIT and the two sponsors was crucial to the success of the project, in large measure because of the early decision that MIT would own all intellectual property developed by the project. Such ownership made it clear to the sponsors' employees on site that they were really working on an MIT project. This decision led in large measure to the elimination of corporate friction. This decision also allowed MIT to make the software generally available on extremely favorable licensing terms without consulting the sponsors' lawyers. As a result, developments such as the X Window System, X Toolkit, and Kerberos had a substantial advantage in the marketplace compared to competitive proprietary developments. This advantage ultimately benefited all participants in the form of industry acceptance and software portability.

System Cost

The original objective for the total steady-state cost of Athena, including operations, depreciation, workstation purchase (by the student), and maintenance was set at a maximum of 10 percent of tuition. Although selected somewhat arbitrarily, this cost was believed to be the maximum affordable by the students. Tuition at MIT is presently about $15,000 per year, or $60,000 over four years, and 10 percent of this total would be $6000.

An economic model of the project was developed in 1987, in which the best allocation of funds seemed to be about half this amount for the purchase of a personal workstation and about half for support of the infrastructure, including staff, depreciation of Institute-owned equipment, maintenance, and software. Thus workstation purchase would be 5 percent of tuition and all other costs would be 5 percent of tuition.

The initial startup of Athena is now over, and the annual cost is about $3.5 million, or about $400 per student. Of this amount, $2.5 million goes for operations and $1 million goes for development. Not included in this amount is overhead, equipment depreciation, and free maintenance provided by the sponsors. The total annual cost of the project on an ongoing basis is estimated at $6 million to $8 million, not including private workstation purchase but including public workstation and server depreciation. This amount is about 5 percent of tuition. Project costs based on current experiences are therefore meeting the original objective for infrastructure cost.

Purchase of a workstation meeting the MIT specifications for $3000 is not now possible, as indicated by the economic model. Recent product developments have used technological improvements to obtain higher performance rather than to lower cost. However, a workstation meeting the MIT requirements should not be much more expensive than a personal computer. Personal computers may be purchased for less than $2000, so it is possible that workstations meeting the MIT objective could be available for under $3000 in the near future (assuming an educational discount of 40 percent to 50 percent).

Economic Model

Steven Lerman developed the following economic model (updated with more recent information) to approximate the steady-state Athena costs to the user. All cost estimates are in constant 1990 dollars.

Capital Cost per Workstation

Basic workstation	$3000	Includes monochrome hardware and one network interface, system software, and documentation
Sales cost	300	10%

Annual Cost per User

Maintenance contract	$200	
Network connect	200	Operating cost only
Support	250	Includes training, consulting, software updates, and servers
Printing	25	Cost per page $0.05
Backup	tbd	Cost recovery

The assumed workstation cost of $3000 is the cost to the institution for 1000 units. The sales cost of 10 percent represents the markup of the campus computer store. As with textbooks, most of the purchases will be made in September, and the organization must be prepared to cope with this highly peaked activity.

Cost to Institution

The cost of providing the educational computing service at an institution will vary widely, depending on the type of service provided, the distribution of costs, and the local cost rates. The following is an approximation of the costs projected at MIT for the service just described on a per user per year basis in 1990 dollars. The costs assume that there are about 10,000 users and are not necessarily linear for much smaller or much larger user populations. These costs are approximate and will vary significantly by institution.

Networking labor	$ 60	
Operations labor	80	Includes hotline support
System software	70	
User services	60	Includes training, documentation, consulting
Administration	50	
	$320	Per user per year, or $3.2 million per year for 10,000 users

The Athena experience is that an Ethernet network drop averages about $1000. The cost of installing an Institute-owned workstation has averaged $2000–$2500, including renovation of space, furniture, light, power, security equipment, and labor. This cost is dropping substantially as the size of the network has increased and as workstation power consumption has decreased.

These costs do not include the capital or maintenance costs of the servers or network. As a first approximation, these capital costs will be somewhat larger than the workstation hardware cost.

TEN

Assessment

⎯⎯⎯⎯

Assessment of a project such as Athena is difficult, because there is no generally accepted standard against which to judge it. The following qualitative assessment is based on discussions with people involved with Athena, such as system developers, application developers, and users.

Assessment of Athena began shortly after the project was initiated and has been carried out, officially and unofficially, by many organizations. The Project Athena Study Group (PASG) was established during the summer of 1985. It was a faculty committee appointed by the Provost and chaired by Jean DeMonchaux, Dean of the School of Architecture and Planning. The primary question to be answered by the study group was: What should be the MIT approach to educational computing after the Athena experiment and its external funding ended? The PASG reports included the living-group assessments by Jackson [Jackson 87, 88] and the teaching/learning impact assessment by Turkle [Turkle 88].

Athena also carried out its own assessment, although for different purposes. Rather than trying to establish a strategy for the post–Athena period, project management wanted to assess and improve its ongoing operations. Toward this end, Athena carried out nine semiannual studies, using anonymous surveys by Karen Cohen.

The Cohen studies [Cohen 87] showed that 95 percent of incoming MIT students have had prior computer experience, which in most cases is extensive. About half of MIT students have personal computers. Half of the personal computers run DOS and the rest are

Apple Macintoshes. About one third of the personal computers have modems. Most of the DOS computers were purchased before the students came to MIT, whereas most of the Apple systems were purchased from the MIT Microcomputer Center after the students arrived on campus.

The usage patterns of Athena closely approximates student populations with regard to gender, class year, school, and residence. The most common uses of the workstations, in percentage of time spent each week, are:

Word processing	27 percent
Programming	19 percent
Problem sets	18 percent
Mail	12 percent
Data storage	7 percent

The most positive aspects of Athena reported by students were the ability to visualize abstract concepts, such as equations, and to be able to use the computational power of the computer for simulation and other calculations. Students also reported positive educational impact from the ability to explore "what if" situations with computer simulations.

The most negative factors reported by students [Cohen 88] were:

- printers not working;
- waiting for access to a workstation (required 24 percent of the time) (Note: Waiting time was reduced to a negligible amount a year later when an adequate number of workstations were deployed.);
- problems with the system (crashes, hard to use); and
- inadequate storage space (then limited to 600 K byte per student, but now 1.2 Mbyte).

Surprises

Many of Athena's results could be predicted once it became clear that the project was going to successfully reach its system objectives. However, there were some outcomes that no one expected. These included the impact of cluster size on student use and the impact of the *Zephyr* real time message system.

The largest Athena cluster is in the Stratton Student Center, which presently has 120 workstations and six printers. This cluster is the most heavily used (on a percentage basis) of all clusters. The reason is that a large cluster fits student needs better than a small cluster. People are always around to help in case someone runs into problems, printer service can be relied on, and workstations are always available. Floor space is adequate for sleeping, and food service is readily available. The cluster is busy much of the day, even at 3:00 A.M. The popularity of this cluster was unexpected.

The other surprise is the impact of the *Zephyr* real time message system on students and staff. The system creates an "artificial reality" for those who use it intensively, making it seem that they are in the same "room" with the other person, even though they are physically separated.

Zephyr at its simplest may be thought of as a type of electronic mail, sending messages from one user to another. However, the ability to send messages in real time and to subscribe to "classes" and "instances" of messages (analogous, basically, to a set of hierarchical mailing lists), has proven to be far more valuable and interesting. For example, consider the "consult" instance. Anyone subscribing to this instance receives all messages sent to it. Its purpose is to provide a channel for Athena's student consultants to communicate with each other as a group when trying to answer a user's question or to inform each other that something of interest happens (e.g., a file server is down). The instance becomes a party line, or a form of electronic conferencing. In addition to the consultants, though, a great many users listen to it to pick up interesting tidbits or just to keep abreast of system events.

The interesting thing that has occurred is that some instances spontaneously come into being, last for a while (sometimes a long time), and then disappear. A number of (admittedly masochistic, or bored) users listen to *all* nonpersonal messages on all instances. If someone creates a new instance, these users will notice and may start a conversation over that instance. If there are enough users, the instance may stay around, forming a small community. The "communities" come complete with their own codes of ethics, and the group will often "gang up" on users who prove too obnoxious or tiresome, chastising them in public (over the instance) for transgressions. The most avid *Zephyr* "talkers" are often those who are traditionally considered the least "sociable" of MIT types: the hackers. The hackers have, in fact, been very social in their own forums (typically electronic, such as the Usenet, or any number of computer bulletin boards), and *Zephyr* has provided a real time, flexible forum for discussions.

The sense of community extends not only to particular instances, but also in some ways to all of Athena. Someone tells a joke, and people all over campus laugh; a system goes down, and suddenly a dozen people send messages informing the operations staff that something is wrong. (A resultant problem, of course, is that sudden deluges of messages can make an instance impossible to keep up with!) With news of the earthquake in California in October 1989, a "quake" instance appeared, and any and all updates and news bits were posted as they were heard.

Many people have questioned the benefit of networking in instructional computing. They maintain that instructional software can be easily distributed on floppy disks and that the other benefits of communications systems are not worth the cost. Those who feel that communications have value in instructional computing point to *Zephyr* as a system that is heavily used and that has greatly increased peer help and the interaction within informal groups.

Assessment by Accreditation Committee

During the spring of 1990, MIT was visited by an accreditation committee to review curriculum quality. The committee devoted a substantial portion of its report to a review of the Athena project. Among its findings were the following.

> Athena's goals apparently were achieved or approached in a number of courses by devoted instructors who rethought their subjects and then translated their new conceptions into courseware that enabled them to project their ideas in more powerful and efficient ways. We saw, and were impressed by, the creativity of newly designed instructional software employed in courses on physiology and biophysics, the writing program, and a course on dynamic systems in mechanical engineering. We were equally impressed that undergraduate students in the Department of Electrical Engineering and Computer Science had been deeply involved in the development of this software. Although not part of its original goals, Athena had provided a group of gifted undergraduates with an invaluable opportunity to work on challenging and creative problems.

> Athena, when viewed as a campus-wide experiment, can claim success of various kinds. It gained or regained for MIT its reputation as a leader in computer design and applications to education, giving to its participants, both faculty and students, a sense of pride in being associated with a major innovative effort in the field. It also heightened the aspirations of those who worked with it, in some cases forcing them to rethink their subjects and pedagogy. It permitted the exchange of ideas about the use of electronic media in the curriculum, and strengthened those shared software design skills.

But we also recognized, as many within the MIT community already have, that the ambitious goals of Athena had been approximated for only a small segment of the undergraduate community. Perhaps 30 or 40 courses have been designed or redesigned to use the special resources of the Athena system; somewhat more have used its interactive capacities without much change in the basic design of the course. The broad availability of the workstations was welcomed by students, who used them for the most part as they would have used any networked consoles for word processing, electronic mail, and games. Important technical improvements were made to the system over time, some of which will have continuing application beyond the Athena system, but this continual tinkering often made the system more difficult to use.

Moreover, large segments of the campus, including the science departments and management programs, tended not to adapt their courses to Athena. Others, in a variety of subjects, developed sophisticated forms of educational computing outside Athena, sometimes because Athena was not adaptable to the special needs of the course (as, for example, a course on music and music theory) or for other reasons.

The accreditation report then discusses the CAC90 report and its recommendations.

CAC90 Assessment

In the summer of 1989, the MIT Provost convened the "Committee on Academic Computing in the 90s and Beyond," abbreviated as CAC90. The charter of this committee, chaired by the Dean of Undergraduate Education, was to "take a comprehensive look at the educational computing needs and possibilities for MIT's undergraduate and graduate students and faculty, establish objectives for MIT's educational computing, assess the technology which will be available in the 1990s, consider the costs and management of educational computing at MIT, and recommend options to the Provost." The ultimate objective of the committee is to develop the strategic direction for academic computing at MIT for the decade of the 1990s and then to recommend a set of options at differing levels of resources and capabilities that MIT can pursue. In conducting the study, the committee considered the likely evolution of computers and information technologies, academic computing at other leading colleges and universities, academic computing at MIT, and the balance between common and individualized academic computing environments.

The committee formulated a set of issues and objectives to be considered in instructional computing after 1991, in which cost played a major role. The committee surveyed instructional computing at other institutions, including Brown, Carnegie-Mellon, Stanford, Dartmouth, Drexel, and the University of Michigan. It also assessed the results of Athena at MIT. Finally, the committee formulated instructional computing options for MIT to pursue in the 1990s and beyond, with the likely costs and benefits of each. The Provost, in consultation with the faculty, selected from among these strategies in charting MIT's course for the decade.

We describe the CAC90 recommendations for the future of computing at MIT in Chapter 11. However, we present here that part of CAC90's findings related to an assessment of Athena's results.

CAC90 Findings

The 1979 estimate of the cost of computing resources likely to be in place in 1989 was $18.8 million (in 1989 dollars). The actual value of computing resources in place in 1989 was estimated by CAC90 [CAC90 90] at $101.3 million, or five times the estimate made ten years earlier.

The CAC90 report provides a census of computing resources available at MIT in early 1990. It shows a total of about 13,000 computers of all types, including about 10,100 personal computers, 2800 workstations (including 1100 Athena), 93 minicomputers, 6 main frames, and one supercomputer. In 1989 the Microcomputer Center sold 2400 microcomputer systems, of which about 90 percent were proprietary personal computers.

The CAC90 report defined academic computing to consist of

- research, to develop and explore new ideas without regard to specific applications;
- development, to translate ideas into useful devices or software packages;
- service delivery, to operate systems and facilities;
- user support, to provide technical assistance to users and developers; and
- assessment and planning, to provide high-level studies and long-range planning for the above.

The report's summary of Athena results development to date stated that the system

- has more than 1000 workstations and supporting infrastructure in operation;

- has been reliable and stable for two academic years;
- is based on de facto industry standards (Unix, X, Motif, Kerberos);
- can accommodate multiple vendor hardware;
- is Cray 2 accessible and compatible;
- has a core of supported applications; and
- is heavily used by students (over 90 percent).

The committee also found that an effective infrastructure was in place for training, documentation, consultation, and interaction with the faculty. Tools were also available for self-registration and on-line consulting.

The committee further found that more than 100 faculty members were involved in educational computing and that substantial sharing of software was occurring on campus. About two thirds of the departments had departmental clusters and good progress was being made in installing workstations in the offices of faculty members who wanted them.

Technical Assessment

Development of the system software must be considered a major success from a technical standpoint. Athena successfully created a high-quality layer of software on top of Unix that corrects its major shortcomings in a distributed workstation environment.

Athena's functionality remains that of Unix with the addition of a portable standard interface to the display (X Window System), augmented by third-party software and instructional software developed locally. A major shortcoming in functionality is the lack of tools to develop interactive applications. Work is under way to improve this situation, but today it remains a serious impediment to the development of instructional software. Another shortcoming Athena shares with all Unix-based systems is that the system's human interface is hard to learn and difficult to use. The planned solution to this problem is to use the graphic human interface software developed by the Open Software Foundation, to which both major sponsors belong.

The Athena system is presently operational and provides good service to its users. Over its life, concerns have always been expressed about various aspects of the project. In 1987, the concerns were about functionality; in 1988, about reliability; in 1989, about stability of the application programming interface; in 1990, about support of personal computers.

Several areas have been identified as requiring improvement. Some of the needed improvements come from experience with the system. Others come from the significant advances that have been made in technology.

Cost of Operation

Currently, Athena's operations cost is low in comparison to other similar systems but is high enough that it remains a burden. However, this cost is expected to decline as maintenance tools and skills improve, as the installed hardware base is updated, and as more users are added to the system.

Opportunities for great reductions in personnel and skill requirements in any one area are not apparent, but many opportunities for smaller reductions are available. Advances will be made in reducing Athena's operations labor requirement in certain areas as part of ongoing maintenance. One area in which cost reduction is possible is in automating backup. The present method of backup is to write the files to a second disk over the net, following by copying that disk to a tape, which is labor intensive. An automated backup operation to an optical jukebox would require less staff at lower cost, or a larger quantity of storage could be managed by the same staff.

Tight Network Coupling

Athena is completely dependent on connection to the network for operation. If the network stops, the workstation stops. Unfortunately, the network is not completely reliable, and when it stops several hundred irate users are on the telephone almost simultaneously. While tight coupling may be appropriate for public workstations, it is of marginal benefit for an individual's workstations, such as that on a faculty member's desk. Presently, public and private workstations are managed in exactly the same way to conserve labor.

Workstations can now be obtained economically with enough local mass storage to store much of the system and most private files. Therefore the network connection might be used only as required for access to mail and infrequently accessed files. Similarly, kernel updates are now virtually simultaneous on all workstations. If a private workstation could store its own operating system, updating could be done at the user's convenience rather than as mandated by the operations group.

Support of Personal Computers

Coherence has greatly simplified the task of application development, including instructional software. Unfortunately, it makes the support of personal computers difficult—and just when personal computers of several different architectures are becoming very popular because of their low price. The system must support personal computers in some manner. The present plan is for Athena servers to interoperate with personal computers in file storage and transfer, printing, mail, and communications, but not to try to achieve full coherence (i.e., support workstation instructional software on PCs).

Human Interface and the Cost of Applications Software Development

The cost of developing application software, especially instructional software, is so great in terms of labor, skills, and money that it is seriously hindering full achievement of the project's pedagogical objectives. Despite the large amount of effort used in developing the human interfaces of applications, the results fall short of those desired. Consistency among applications is inadequate, and the quality of results varies considerably.

Problems also exist in the human interface to the system. The user interface to Unix at Athena is the C shell *csh*. As is well known, this interface is difficult to learn, is error prone, and imposes a large memory burden on the user. It is, of course, very powerful in the hands of the expert user, but most of the users of Athena are not expert. Athena users, however, even in departments far removed from computer science, become moderately expert users of programs such as *csh* and *emacs*. Whether this is good or bad is the subject of debate.

The Athena distributed services are largely transparent to the user, and when they are fully operational and used properly, the need for a human interface is not great. However, when the services "break" or are used improperly, the user has great difficulty coping with the problem because of the hidden mechanisms of the system.

Although these problems are not directly related to distributed aspects of Athena, they remain a serious impediment to further expansion of use. The current plan for solution is to import the *Motif* user environment component from the Open Software Foundation to provide a de facto standard and more powerful tool set for the development of human interfaces. Beyond that, the MUSE authoring environment is under development to reduce the cost and skills required for development of applications having good user interfaces.

Printing

A decision was made early in the project to provide high-quality laser printing at no cost to the user, which encouraged, to some extent, excessive printing. The project has now installed a cost-recovery system for printing to make sure that it is used responsibly. Each user receives a quota of 1200 pages of free printing per year, but printing beyond this point requires payment of a fee. The quota system is supported by the Palladium distributed print system [Hart 89], developed for Athena by an informal group of leading computer manufacturers.

Large versus Small Clusters

The Athena experience is that supporting workstations in a few large clusters is much easier than supporting many small clusters. Large clusters are easier to maintain and simplify provision of printing and consulting services. Unfortunately, space for clusters has always been scarce and is now a seriously limiting factor in deployment of additional clusters of any size. Installing a modern network in buildings that are nearly 100 years old is also very difficult.

Backup

Backup of user files remains difficult simply because the files are so large. The solution has been to dump to tape, but time to dump and logistics of handling 15 G bytes of tape are quite difficult. These problems are getting worse as the capacity of disks continues to increase rapidly. Moreover, they are compounded because Athena file servers are physically distributed.

Implementation

The computer industry has a 40-year history leading to a set of well-known procedures for implementing a large MIS project successfully. Athena's supporters initially viewed it as a simple turnkey installation of off-the-shelf hardware and software by a single vendor. This scope gradually grew (because of external influences) into a far larger and more complex project, requiring extensive development of innovative software. At some point the project should have been treated as a large MIS implementation, and the traditional tools and management skills of the MIS discipline should have been used. The magnitude of the task was not recognized until three years into the project, at which point the problems were very difficult to solve.

A tangible shortcoming is in the number of public workstations deployed. Initial plans were to deploy about 3000 public workstations, but the goal was continually reduced over the life of the project to 2000 in 1985, 1500 in 1986, and 1000 in 1987. The actual number deployed at the end of the first five years was 750, of which 500 were for students and 250 were for developers. It is important to ask whether 3000 workstations was ever the correct number. A major problem was insufficient space (always in short supply at any institution). Thus ever installing many more than 1500 public workstations now seems impractical. Indeed, whether depreciation on 3000 public workstations could have been afforded is now questionable. The new strategy is to limit the number of public workstations to about 1500. The present deployment of 1300 workstations seems to be adequate, except during the peak load on the last few days of spring semester. Quite possibly, 1500 workstations always was the right number.

Use of Athena by Others

One measure of the success of the project is the extent to which it is used by others. To date, Athena has been installed at several other locations, in some cases for testing and evaluation and in other cases for operational use. Athena's use by other organizations is described in Appendix I.

Relationship with the Faculty

The MIT faculty was initially oversold on the implementation schedule and capability of the system. The inevitable disillusionment set in initially when schedules slipped by years and intensified when the system failed to meet tool, stability, and reliability expectations. Further, the faculty saw the project as being too autonomous, pursuing "technical goodies" for their own sake rather than doing things of value to the faculty.

The faculty was (and to a lesser extent still is) far from agreement in its view of the proper role of computing in higher education. At one extreme, some are skeptical of any substantial role of computing in education, preferring analytic solutions to numeric approaches. Many wanted only to use PCs or Macs to do simple things simply. Perhaps many believed the early claims about the power and functionality of the system and were expecting an ideal solution. A few understood the magnitude of the difficulties faced and were willing continually to strive to develop effective software on the system for their classes despite repeated and long-term problems. In the end, this last group was successful and made an essential contribution to the Institute, but the cost was high. Now that the system is stable and reliable, wooing the disillusioned faculty back is proving difficult. Given Athena's scope and the innovations required, some of these problems were inevitable, even with highly experienced and skilled personnel.

Benefit to Sponsors

Both IBM and Digital believe that they obtained significant benefits from participating in Athena. It was the flagship external research project for Digital, much as Andrew was the flagship project for IBM. Digital's top management has historically had close ties to MIT, and most of Digital's central engineering and central research are located within 40 miles from MIT. The benefits to Digital included

- development of product prototype;
- development of product requirements;
- testbed for product evaluation;
- testbed for concept evaluation;

- showcase account; and
- developer of people.

IBM obtained similar benefits. In some instances, the technologies were prototyped at Athena and then developed into products elsewhere. In other cases, the concepts were stimulated by activities at Athena and prototypes were developed elsewhere. Athena developed people—both new hires and those on rotation—and built consensus—both intracompany and intercompany. The X Window System, X Toolkit, 3-D extension to X (PEX), video extension to X (VEX), and Palladium distributed printing software are all examples of intercompany cooperation that Athena fostered.

Pedagogical Assessment

Ideally, we would assess the pedagogical success of Athena by carrying out a controlled experiment. A course would be taught to two matched groups of students with all variables controlled, except that one group would be taught with Athena and the other without Athena. The results would then be compared. This type of evaluation is not likely to be done for funding and ethical reasons.

The best assessment is that likely to come from the experience of the faculty in aggregate. Many faculty members have taught the same course with and without Athena. Although this kind of assessment is much less satisfactory than a controlled experiment, it does provide some data. Some faculty members believe that they can teach more effectively with Athena than without it. At least one faculty member states that he can cover about 30 percent more material with Athena than without it.

When evaluated against its major goals, Project Athena must be judged successful. In considerable contrast to the situation in 1983, the use of high-quality educational computing today at MIT is widespread. Students are now graduating who have never known life at MIT without Athena and (based on student interviews) cannot imagine life at MIT without it. About 96 percent of the undergraduate students and 70 percent of the graduate students use Athena. The system is stable, documented, reliable, and affordable. Athena software provides a coherent and logically integrated computing environment campuswide, despite a high degree of physical distribution and heterogeneity of equipment.

However, Athena has been much more successful technically than pedagogically. Although anecdotal evidence that Athena has improved the quality of education at MIT is substantial, the improvement is far from uniform and has yet to be documented. Until pedagogical improvements become more generally available and documented, final judgment on the pedagogical success must be withheld.

ELEVEN

Quo Vadis Athena

In this chapter we describe the future of Athena in three respects:

- continuing and new initiatives based on current plans;
- desired future workstation characteristics;
- recommendations of the Committee on Academic Computing in the 1990s (CAC90) for MIT.

In order to place the future educational computing objectives of MIT in perspective, we also compare them to CMU future computing objectives.

Continuing and New Initiatives

Initiatives facing Athena are the following.

- *Continue deployment of public workstations.* The 1300 workstations that are in place are not an adequate number, as students often must wait for access. Moreover, the better the system gets in terms of stability and function, the more demand there is for access. The current strategy is to extend twisted pair Ethernet throughout buildings and to continue the installation of public workstations. More emphasis is being given to working with departments to establish department clusters.
- *Improve the human interface.* The C shell is not an appropriate interface for the students to use with the operating system. It is

simply too hard to learn and too complex to remember. More importantly, development of instructional software is very costly in terms of personnel and skill level because of the lack of appropriate tools. This problem is so serious that faculty developers cannot make the investment needed to use the system widely for education. The current strategy is to use the Open Software Foundation *Motif* human interface development environment as the standard instructional environment. The use of *Motif* will provide a more powerful and de facto industry standard development environment. This use is additionally attractive because both Athena sponsors belong to the Open Software Foundation. Those involved hope that the use of a standard development environment will promote the ability to import and export instructional software at MIT.

- *Continue instructional software development.* Additional funding needs to be found to continue this essential activity.
- *Move to private ownership model.* To date, all Athena workstations are owned by MIT and are made available to students and faculty at no cost. When prices for a workstation meeting Athena standards drop to an appropriate level (currently seen as $3000), MIT will sell workstations to students and faculty members through the Microcomputer Center. Eventually the number of workstations supported (primarily privately owned) will approach 10,000. The network, servers, and infrastructure must be provided in accordance with the number of workstations in a transparent manner.
- *Shift to vendor-supported software.* The strategy of Athena is to move away from the Berkeley Unix to a vendor-supported Unix. The reason for this strategy is to gain better access to applications. As both major sponsors belong to the Open Software Foundation, the use of the OSF/1 operating system looks attractive. (Athena also belongs to the Open Software Foundation and has a research grant relationship with it.)
- *Support automatic software update and integrity check.* Installation of a major new version of the system software is a major undertaking, because it requires a visit to every workstation. Tools are now being developed to allow installation of a new version of the system software over the network and verification of its integrity after installation.
- *Reconfigure networks dynamically.* One of the most common current problems for Athena workstation installation is that of an

incorrect Internet address. Experiments are under way to assign this address at boot time. In addition, when Athena begins to allow privately owned workstations, it must be possible for a user to unplug from one network connection and reconnect at a new location without notifying the network administration. Work on dynamic reconfiguration is also in process.

■ *Support personal computers.* The widespread availability of personal computers with screen resolution of 300,000 pixels makes their support attractive. A project to provide Athena services to personal computers, both open system and proprietary, is under way.

■ *Support public databases.* Publicly available databases are believed to have great value on campus, providing access to libraries, course catalogs, research descriptions, and schedule information. A first step has been taken in this direction through the development of *TechInfo,* a new on-line information system available via the campus network. Information presently available on *TechInfo* includes

> academic schedules;
>
> weekly campus events;
>
> lab supplies catalog;
>
> information systems articles; and
>
> weekly job postings from Personnel.

■ *Establish a courseware development resource center.* A high-priority task is to provide faculty developers with well-publicized and easily obtainable information about ongoing activities in courseware development and to encourage the sharing of code, expertise, and resources. To facilitate this task, plans are now being made to create a centralized group to develop the following.

> Developers' kit, to be mailed out on request, containing reading material describing alternative approaches to courseware development.
>
> Clearinghouse for up-to-date information on projects, including principal investigator, contact person, and project descriptions.
>
> Programs that may be shared, including source and executable files and documentation.
>
> Information on relevant third-party software.

A developers' database, containing information such as sample makefiles, reusable code, and on-line documentation.

On-line users' group and mailing lists.

Pool of student programmers for hire.

Sample courseware modules.

Advanced topics.

- *Deploy to other institutions.* Part of the vision for Athena was to make it available at no cost to other research labs and universities once it was fully operational. Late in 1988, part of the system was installed at Digital's Cambridge Research Lab. During early 1989, the entire distributed system was installed at Bond University, a new, private university in Australia. Since then, the system has been installed at additional locations, as described in Appendix I, and more are planned.

Desired Workstation Characteristics

Based on the experience gained in developing the Athena system, minimum characteristics are envisioned for the next generation of workstations at MIT. Two different workstation configurations are required: monochrome and color. Thus monochrome configurations do not have to be upgradable to color ones. Little or no documentation in paper form is assumed; that is, all documentation other than for installation is to be in electronic form.

Monochrome Workstation Specifications

The minimum desired specifications for workstations at MIT in the 1990s are as follows.

Processor performance	3 MIPS
Screen resolution	800 K pixels
Screen size	15 inch
Chromatic resolution	4 bit pixels
Main storage	6 Mbytes, expandable to 16
Communications	1 RS-232 port
Input	Keyboard and mouse
Floppy disk	1.4 MB industry standard format
Hard disk	70 MB (preferably 3.5 inch)
External interface	SCSI (two ports minimum)

The unit does not need a bus with plug-in slots for adapter cards. However, having a bus connector port available with an optional bus expansion unit and related power supply and board slots would be desirable. (The preferred type of external interface is still under review.)

The hard disk is used for the root file system, swap space, and temporary and private storage. The operating system, utilities, and productivity software modules are stored on the file servers or an optional CD-ROM.

The available plug ins for the SCSI interface should be

- Ethernet;
- token ring;
- CD-ROM player; and
- 70 or 140 MB disk.

All documentation should be obtained electronically over the network or from the CD-ROM player. An optional modem or printer can be attached to the RS-232 port or SCSI port.

The system should be usable in two ways: on net (usually on campus) and off net (usually off campus). In the on-net case, the SCSI interface is used to support the LAN interface, either Ethernet or token ring. In the off-net case the SCSI would normally plug into the CD-ROM player to provide large amounts of read-only storage. Some form of caching method will usually be needed to keep as much data as possible on the hard disk.

The CD-ROM allows workstations to be used at home and is essential to obtaining a significant number of off-net users. A preferred method of delivering third-party software to the user is to have all available software on the disk, whether it has been purchased or not. The user would receive a decryption key when the software is purchased.

Power consumption, heat dissipation, noise levels, RF emissions, and temperature levels must be consistent with deployment in closed offices, dormitories, and homes. Some means of providing physical security is required. The workstation should be easily attachable to a table or wall bracket.

Color Workstation Specifications

The requirements for color workstations are the same as those for the monochrome model, but with 800 K pixels of 8 bits each on a 15-inch monitor. At MIT, only about 10 percent of the public workstations will be color. At other colleges and universities, the proportion may be much different.

Software

Independent of the hardware utilized, the following software must be provided, either by the manufacturer or by third-party software suppliers.

- System software
- Operating system, Posix compatible

    C, FORTRAN, Common Lisp compilers

    X windows version 11

    EMACS

    Andrew File System

    NFS
- Productivity software

    Numerical library

    Spreadsheet

    WYSIWYG editor for text, image, and graphics with Post-script output

    Mathematics symbolic manipulation package

    Database system

    Electronic mail

The server software described in Chapter 6 will be supplied by the Institute.

Future of Instructional Computing at CMU

We describe the future of instructional computing at MIT in the next section. Before that, let's examine the future of computing at CMU for purposes of comparison.

In November 1988, with Andrew fully functional and an integral part of the campus infrastructure, CMU President Cyert established a new "Computer and Network Planning Committee" to review past accomplishments and current status, and to recommend future approaches. That review [Eddy 89] showed that most of the objectives established in the 1982 Newell report had been accomplished. Computing had become both widespread and deeply ingrained in the educational process. The great diversity of computation forecasted had indeed occurred, but this diversity had created a fundamental dilemma for both students and faculty. Different user groups had widely differing expectations of computing, and these expectations often did not match the widely varying resources available.

The report therefore recommended that steps be taken to reduce this diversity. To do so required establishing a minimal computation resource that would be available to all students, regardless of department affiliation. Students would be encouraged, but not required, to own private microcomputer systems. The administration was encouraged to provide all faculty members with desktop workstations suited to the needs of their disciplines. Also recommended was creation of a set of standards that would be mandatory for all computer systems acquired or recommended by CMU, in order to maximize integration with research activities. An important management recommendation was that the university should continue to encourage decentralized management of the campus system. In spite of the recommendation of decentralized management, the report favors an integrated computing environment for administration, research, and education. Whereas the 1982 report proposed universal access to computing provided by "3M" class workstations, the 1989 report identified the current and future challenges to be "distributed resources, diverse applications, and decentralized management," or the "3D" model.

Instructional Computing at MIT after 1991

We described the charter, objectives, and assessment of CAC90 in Chapter 10. Here we summarize the rest of the CAC90 report [CAC90 90], first describing the findings and then presenting the recommendations.

The Committee found that attitudes toward academic computing vary greatly at MIT. These differences exist among and within the major constituent groups of faculty, students, and sponsors. Attitudes within the faculty varied from some who wanted much more academic computing to others who wanted much less. The actual or intended use of academic computing also varies widely among faculty members. Some use it for analytic tools, some for simulation, some for computer-based instruction, some for database access, some for personal productivity tools, and some for presentation of information.

Organizationally, some faculty members prefer leaving academic computing to individuals or departments; others prefer various degrees of centralization. Technically, some faculty members prefer the sophisticated networked capability of Unix workstations and supercomputers; others prefer the simpler environment of isolated PCs.

Attitudes toward academic computing vary significantly by school. The School of Engineering supports academic computing more generally than their colleagues in the other schools. It believes that an advanced academic computing environment supports MIT's preeminence in higher education and is a necessary prerequisite for engineering education. The school strongly supports the present Athena design and coherence.

The School of Architecture and Planning has aggressively utilized Athena as part of a larger heterogeneous computing community. It would like to see greater decentralization of academic computing to assist it in initiating future computing initiatives. The school is also very supportive of heterogeneous environments and more curriculum development projects.

The School of Humanities and Social Science has had little involvement with Athena, although some of its projects (e.g., language instruction and Educational On-line System) have been among the most innovative. Many of its faculty members believe that Athena is a major failure and that the money spent has been wasted. The School of Management (Sloan) has had minimal involvement with Athena but would like to become active.

The School of Science has had some involvement with Athena, and its faculty members use computers extensively in research. Most of the faculty believe that computers contribute little to undergraduate education beyond routine calculation. They also believe that educational computing should be used to improve research skills of students in the junior and senior classes and beyond. Many believe that students should be required to provide their own computing resources and skills.

The committee learned that undergraduates want simpler access to Athena network services, and that they value free, powerful computing. Graduate students have only recently been given access to Athena and continue to use other sources of computing, especially research and laboratory computers. In addition, the committee found the following.

1. Athena has met many of the expectations of its founders and supporters. The project has developed a successful, large-scale, distributed workstation network that leads the field and is increasingly copied. It has developed award-winning instructional software.
2. The academic computing environment at MIT is heterogeneous. Almost all faculty members have office computers, mostly DOS-based PCs. About half the students own computers, evenly divided between DOS and MAC/OS systems.
3. Students use Athena for many purposes, some requiring networked workstations and others not. Students use Athena about one third of the time for word processing, one third for subject courseware or technical tools and programs, and the remaining third for communication. Two thirds of students' personal computer use is for word processing.
4. MIT experience with academic computing is consistent with experience elsewhere. The patterns of use experienced at MIT are similar to those found at Dartmouth, Brown, and CMU.

MIT Spending Compared to Other Organizations

Much of the report is devoted to cost analysis. As part of its findings, the report compares expenditures on academic computing at MIT with those of peer organizations. Current spending on academic computing at MIT from all sources was about 0.6 percent of total budget. This level compares to a typical expenditure level by information-intensive organizations of 2 percent to 4 percent for activities comparable to academic computing. The current budget for the MIT library system is about double that of academic computing. The average spending level by peer institutions is about $352 per student per year. Specific examples are Stanford at $406 and CMU at $384, compared to MIT at $231. MIT has been able to spend minimally on academic computing because of Athena sponsor generosity.

Recommendations

The report proposed two simultaneous strategies, which overlap and complement each other but which address different objectives. The first is to make a set of basic educational services and tools available throughout the MIT community. The second is to support the development of a set of educational development projects. Closely related to the second strategy is a plan to provide strong user support services.

Basic Educational Services and Tools   Basic educational services and tools include the Athena services described earlier but extended to personal computers running DOS and MAC/OS. This extension requires less coherence than for the workstations. Coherence with workstations provides a set of applications and services that run on every system, with the ability to interchange programs and data. This level of coherence is to be retained for the workstations after the personal computers are added to the system. The personal computers would utilize the Athena services of

- printing;
- file access;
- communications;
- mail;
- on-line consulting;
- on-line teaching assistants;
- bulletin boards;
- access to databases;
- real time notification; and
- registration.

They would also be able to interchange text data. They would run the X Window System and TCP/IP, including *rlogin, telnet,* and related services. They would not be able to run the workstation applications locally. Instead, they are able to run the large number of "shrink wrapped" software packages available for personal computers. The personal computers could run instructional software that has been ported to them and that has been modified to work with the lower resolution screen. One way to get access to workstation applications and instructional software would be to run them on a workstation client and use the personal computer as an X terminal server.

   Athena services for personal computers would be supported within the context of the personal computer user interface to the extent possible. For example, in a DOS system the network files would be supported as additional "disk drives," and Athena printers would be supported as virtual local printers in DOS. The services would be provided using the Athena authentication service and name service.

Educational Development Projects   Educational development projects would develop tools and software modules for teaching specific courses.

Investment Options

CAC90 proposed three different options for academic computing, depending on availability of funds. These are, in order of decreasing cost: the "target option," which was strongly recommended by the report; the "first-step option," which should be considered only as a transition to the target option; and the "retreat option," which provides only minimal academic computing.

The committee recommended several principles that would apply to all three options. Academic computing should be offered on the three or four most common platforms in use at MIT. Commercial software and software developed elsewhere should be used wherever possible to minimize the need for development. User support staff should be deployed along with the hardware to help faculty members and students. The organizational structure for academic computing should parallel other academic activities, primarily along departmental and school lines, except where centralization can produce clear benefits.

The target option embraces all the committee's recommendations. In brief, it would continue Athena as it now exists and add support for DOS and MAC/OS, support for instructional software development, and funds for more user support. This option would provide

- 904 workstations in all locations, or equal to the current number of public Athena workstations deployed;
- 300 personal computers in public clusters;
- a full set of basic educational services and tools;
- support for 40 ongoing educational development projects;
- extension of the network to 4600 ports in clusters and student housing; and
- a user support staff of 44 people.

The cost of this option is about double the current cost of Athena, including central expense and excluding related departmental costs. This option responds fully to the diverse needs for academic computing at MIT and should maintain the Institute's preeminence in academic computing.

The desired workstation for this environment is a 10 MIPS, 1 million pixel system with a 70 million byte disk and local area net connection.

The two other platforms to be supported are DOS and MAC/OS computers. If funds are insufficient to support the entire option, the educational development projects should receive lower priority.

If funds are not immediately available to implement the target option when Athena external funding terminates, the committee recommended the first-step option as a transition to the target option. The first step option provides

- a subset of the basic educational services and tools;
- about 12 ongoing educational development projects;
- 210 personal computers;
- 266 workstations;
- 3000 ports; and
- 36 user support people.

The cost of this option is about the same as current Athena cost. However, it reallocates funds from workstations and educational development projects to basic educational services and tools and personal computers.

Below the first-step option, serious retrenchment would occur. The retreat option would support

- 100 personal computers;
- 70 workstations;
- a few tools and services;
- 10 ongoing educational experiments; and
- 21 user support staff.

This option would cost about 40 percent of current Athena cost.

The three options are compared with current Athena in the following table.

Component	Athena	Target	First Step	Retreat
Public workstations	904*	904*	266	70
Personal computers	50	300	210	100
BEST projects	†	15	11	5
EDP projects	‡	40	12	10
Student net ports	715	4634	2876	170
User staff	24	44	36	21

*Does not include 400 private workstations.
†Athena ported its services to DOS and MAC/OS systems in the final months of the project.
‡Athena funded the development of 125 EDP projects early in the project but none during the last two years.

Organization

CAC90 recommended that Athena be broken up and its functions allocated to existing and new organizational units. It recommended that management of the workstations and personal computers be taken over by the existing Information Systems group. Faculty members would initiate and implement educational development projects, assisted by graduate students and support staff. An existing administrative unit (not named) would implement the basic educational services and tools. Research would be carried out by existing research groups using external funding.

The committee recommended that the following new organizations be created.

- An academic computing directorate, reporting to the Provost to coordinate academic computing across departments and schools to minimize redundancy and inconsistency. It would coordinate fund-raising and advise the Provost on academic computing policy.
- A set of panels to bring together MIT individuals who share common interests in academic computing. Panels might exist for fund-raising, network-related distributed services, intercollegiate cooperation, and to critique policies.
- A council on academic computing to provide feedback from users.
- An external review group appointed by the Provost to visit MIT periodically and appraise academic computing. It would function more as an accreditation team than a visiting committee.

Detailed Recommendations

Within the major themes described, the committee formulated several strategic principles [CAC90 90a], which it grouped under the categories of educational focus, intellectual community, and implementation and organization. These recommendations stated that

- educational computation should advance *innovative* educational practice, especially where current practices are unsatisfactory;
- access to computing should be ubiquitous;
- commercial software is preferred to in-house development;
- work on advanced systems should be done outside the academic computing organization by research groups and with external funding;

- the Institute should provide a basic level of computing resources and that departments needing additional resources should be responsible for providing them;
- the network should be enhanced to provide access from student housing, local homes, and faculty residences, but at perhaps a slower speed;
- MIT should encourage students to own personal computers or workstations; and
- resources should be made available for research in computer-intensive learning environments.

The Decision

The Institute selected the first-step option as a guaranteed minimum level of academic computing to be supported by internal funds. Every effort is being made to go beyond this level toward the target option by raising funds externally.

Somewhat independent of the future of academic computing at MIT, many colleges and universities are adopting the Athena architecture of combining workstations and personal computers for educational computing. They are doing so for the same reasons as MIT, whether starting from personal computers and moving toward workstations, or the reverse. The only real question to be decided is the degree of coherence desired.

In the long term, the MIT model of educational computing is expected to become the model for implementation around the world. Thus the CAC90 report is of considerable import in shaping not only the future of educational computing at MIT, but also educational computing in general around the world.

Comparing the Futures of Athena and Andrew

The strategies adopted by MIT are both similar and different in several important respects to the strategies adopted by CMU. The similarities include the goals of providing ubiquitous access to high-quality computing for students and faculty. Both provide a basic level of computing resource for the entire campus, with departments encouraged to supply additional and more specialized resources as appropriate. Both systems include a mixture of workstations and personal computers, linked by a local area network and supported by a variety of network services.

The differences between the two strategies include the following.

Strategic area	CMU	MIT
System management	Decentralized	Centralized
Integration of administration, research, and education	Yes	No
Diversity of computing resources	High	Medium

Concluding Remarks

Most of the issues in educational computing outlined at the beginning of Athena remain unresolved. Athena has been forced to take a position on most of them, but there is little, if any, better consensus as to the "correct" position now than there was then. However, progress has been made in understanding the context and tradeoffs available so that the issues now are much more sharply focused. Perhaps because of this sharper focus, attitudes seem to be more polarized now than at the beginning of the project.

The proper role of computing in education remains a topic of debate. The question of whether there is a "sacred inner core" of science that should not be relegated to computers remains unresolved. Alternative pedagogical models of teaching with computers are not well understood, and the relationship of course content and computer support remains an open question. In spite of the great faculty interest and effort in developing educational software for their courses, the relationship of such activities to tenure continues unresolved.

In the area of workstations in student housing, the Athena experiment has provided some answers. Workstations can be effective in student housing under the proper circumstances and do not appear to be an unwelcome intrusion into student housing as a bastion against academic life.

Despite the unanswered questions, education at MIT has been changed forever. Workstation computing is ubiquitous on campus. Most students use and like Athena, and many say that they cannot imagine education at MIT without it. Students are now graduating who have never known MIT without Athena.

Some lessons from Athena are clear. Long-term partnerships between academia and industry can work, even in high-pressure developmental situations. Conflict between competitive industrial partners need not be a problem, as proven by experience at both Athena and MCC. In addition to the two main sponsors, Athena has significant relationships with Hewlett-Packard/Apollo, Apple, GTE, Parallax, and several other firms. Given the magnitude of current research projects, partnerships may be the only viable approach to making significant progress. The policy established at Athena that MIT owns all intellectual property from the project also seems to work, as indicated by the success of the X Window System, X Toolkit, Kerberos, and the overall Athena system itself. The policy of making software available at no cost and with minimal licensing requirements also seems to work, both for the academic institution and the industrial partners.

Some of the assumptions made by Athena probably were wrong or at least premature. Workstations meeting the MIT price objective are not yet available. The personal computer has become very popular, as has DOS. Application programs and software development tools have emerged first on personal computers and are only now slowly finding their way into workstation systems. DOS has emerged as the de facto standard for much instructional software. Nevertheless, there are those who continue to believe that workstations and Unix are the right platforms for MIT, regardless of other considerations. They also believe that the next few years will prove them right as Unix replaces DOS.

Human interface issues have proven to be much more important and difficult than initially realized. Athena remains a hostile and formidable system for some students and faculty. Although progress is being made, it is too slow. The objective of network transparency is laudable and valuable so long as the system works. However, when the system breaks, transparency breaks. Provision must be made for users to cope with system problems when transparency vanishes. Nevertheless, progress has been made. It is important to realize that as system capability rises, expectations also rise. Generally expectations rise faster than system capability.

Ubiquity of computing access has proven to be very important. The fact that the faculty knows that all students have access to workstations has made a substantial difference in faculty use of the system. Indeed, ubiquity has proven to be more important than performance. Centralized management also works very well, giving high-quality service at relatively low cost. Some departments at MIT that have their own computer systems are evaluating their support cost and aggravations against those of Athena. In several cases Athena is adequate for the purpose—and at much lower cost.

New technology can be very seductive. Often it falls short of easily solving the problems for which it is intended. As Jerry Saltzer says, "There is no such thing as free software." Extending old technology into new areas is very risky as evidenced by the effort of Athena to use time-sharing Unix in workstation networks. The Athena experience is that new technology can indeed solve important problems—but at great cost.

MIT students, while being very critical of the system, were always able to cope with complexity and change. Students generally felt that learning the system was part of the educational experience. However, the faculty had very different expectations of and attitudes toward the system. They had great difficulty in coping with the inherent conflict in Athena's twin goals of rapid development and production service delivery. Some of the faculty became alienated from Athena early in the project and are only now taking a serious second look.

A common criticism of Athena is that it represents overkill for the most common applications, such as spreadsheets and word processing. An alternative view is that Athena is ahead of its time and that eventually others will catch up. So far, faculty and students alike believe that networking has significant benefits. Workstation prices and proprietary personal computer prices are converging, and the MIT objective of a $3000 workstation may be in sight. Time will tell whether Athena made the right decision.

The technical advances made by Athena appear impressive. The X Window System, X Toolkit, and Kerberos authentication server appear to be important technical accomplishments and are becoming de facto industry standards. However, these advances must be kept in perspective. Now that a suitable system platform is in place, MIT is positioned to make far greater advances in the next few years in pedagogical and technical applications than all the benefits achieved to date. Applications, in the final analysis, deliver visible benefits to users.

Perhaps the best summary and most concise statement of Athena's results is that made by Dean Gerald Wilson, the strongest supporter and most severe critic of Athena. In his letter to the faculty of the School of Engineering dated April 5, 1990 he said, "Although we (MIT) did not accomplish all of our visions and dreams for this effort, Project Athena is hailed as the most successful program of its kind across the country and internationally."

As stated at the beginning, the Athena approach to educational computing is clearly not for everyone. All campuses are highly individual, and a system that works well at MIT may fail elsewhere. At a minimum, the system must be highly specialized in terms of the particular needs of the installing campus. The installation and use of Athena at the other campuses described in Appendix I will help provide answers to the question of the general applicability of the Athena approach.

Ten years hence it will be interesting to look back at the Athena of 1990 to determine the true value of these accomplishments, which were obtained at such high cost. Of course, they will look incredibly primitive. The computing resources available today could be only dimly foreseen, if at all, in 1979 for a time 10 years hence; because the pace of development is so much greater today, we are even less able to forecast the computing resources and information services that will be available in the year 2000. Regardless of what becomes available, it will be built on earlier efforts, and Athena likely will be seen as a necessary step in the achievement of the wonderful things that are to come.

Our best hope is that, as Dan Geer says, "Athena will be the shoulders on which developers of the future will stand to build their new systems." Nevertheless, Athena's most important accomplishment may be that it provided a successful model of how industry and academia can work together effectively to achieve something that neither can do alone—and in the process change the world of computing forever.

APPENDIX
I

Deployment
of Athena

Athena has been installed in several locations other than at MIT, in some cases for test and evaluation and in other cases for operational use. Test and evaluation installations include those at the University of Texas at Austin, New York University (NYU), and the University of California at Santa Cruz. Of principal interest is testing and evaluation of the *Kerberos* authentication system.

Kerberos by itself is used at several locations and is supported as product by both IBM and Digital. It is an integral part of the DEcorum distributed computing environment, developed by Open Software Foundation, and the Open Network Computing system, developed by Sun Microsystems. It is being used at CMU as part of the Andrew system.

The first installation of Athena for full operational use outside of MIT was at Bond University in Australia (near Brisbane on the east coast) in February 1989, where the system is called "Kowande" after an aboriginal hero. This system is relatively small, with about 35 workstations and two server systems. Subsequently, much larger installations have been made at the University of Massachusetts at Amherst, Stanford, North Carolina State University, Iowa State University at Ames, Nanyang Technical Institute in Singapore, and the Royal Technical Institute of Sweden (KTH).

In order to make installation at these locations easier, Digital ported the Athena system to a Digital product environment. This port included moving the Athena software from the Berkeley UNIX base used at MIT to an Ultrix base, and removing or generalizing the MIT-specific elements of the software. The new software system resulting from this porting process is called "DECathena." Existing Athena or DECathena installations are shown in the following table, along with information on the name, scope, funding source, and installation.

Comparison of Athena Installations

User	System Name	Scope	Funding	Application	Resource Allocation
MIT	Athena	Campus	DEC/IBM	Education research	Athena
Bond	Kowande	Inf. dept.	Self	Education research	Inf. dept.
UMASS	Pilgrim	COINS	DEC/Mass	Research	COINS
Stanford	SPLICE	Campus	Self	Education	Campus
NTI	NTI	Campus	Self	Research	Campus
NCSU	EOS	Eng. dept.	Student fees	Education	Eng. dept.
ISU	Vincent	Campus	U.S.	Education research	Dept. heads
KTH	Bifrost	EE dept.	Self	Research	EE dept.

Note: all but MIT and Stanford have DECathena.

University of Massachusetts/Amherst

During February 1990 the system was ported to the University of Massachusetts/Amherst. The system built around Athena there is called "Project Pilgrim," as in the definition, "one who travels looking for truth." Project Pilgrim is a cooperative research relationship among Digital, the University, and the Commonwealth of Massachusetts. It is expected to significantly build on innovations such as X Window System and the Athena distributed system environment. It is a three-year, $6 million project designed to dramatically improve the quality and accessibility of computers used for education and research.

Pilgrim is based in the Computer and Information Science (COINS) department's research computer facility and the College of Engineering's Computer Services facility. It involves the design and implementation of a software system that links the two facilities. Together, they have a collection of approximately 500 workstations and 40 multi-user systems. The linkage provides a cohesive computing environment that can be used easily by all 3000 members of COINS and the College of Engineering, from undergraduates to advanced researchers. Faculty also use the project as a test system for research and courseware development. Current work that might benefit users includes development of "intelligent" computerized tutors; sophisticated three-dimensional graphics tools; and software for a wide variety of advanced scientific and administrative applications.

Project Pilgrim will develop a unified network of workstations that could strongly influence how computers are used in the 1990s. Ultimately more than 3000 engineers, scientists, and students on the Amherst campus will have access to this open network from various manufacturers' workstations. The University of Massachusetts at Amherst is the largest public research university in New England.

Stanford

The Stanford Academic Computing organization installed many of the Athena modules in late 1989 and achieved operational status in February 1990. Their system is called SPLICE (Stanford Program for Location Independent Computing Environment). The system is used primarily for education. Presently they have nearly 200 workstations running the SPLICE environment or parts of it, with plans to extend this to several thousand workstations over the next few years.

Rather than getting their software from Digital, they obtained their code directly from MIT. They modified the MIT code substantially to fit within the Stanford environment. They participated in the development of the *Kerberos* authentication service, and provided code for some sections of it. They have ported the SPLICE software to additional platforms for both clients and servers, and have plans to install a number of additional Athena modules.

The use of the Athena software at Stanford differs in an important way from the use of the same software at MIT. At MIT, hardware that executes server software is always different from hardware that runs client software. In the Stanford environment, clients and servers often run on the same hardware. This leads to greater flexibility and efficiency in operation, but can also lead to more difficult security problems.

North Carolina State University

In June 1990 Athena was installed in the Engineering Department at North Carolina State University (NCSU). Figure I.1 shows a system diagram of the configuration. The name of Athena at NCSU is "EOS," after the Greek goddess of the dawn. The project was implemented by the School of Engineering, and initially only engineering students (including Electrical and Computer Engineering) use the system. Later, the plan is to extend the system to the entire campus. There are about 7000 engineering students in a total student body of 25,000. The first phase is an installation of 200 workstations in four clusters of 50 each. Three of the clusters are in the same building. Each cluster is on one Ethernet subnet, and each has system file servers. Initially the workstations are of a single architecture, but later other architectures will be added.

The first students to use the system were entering freshmen in the fall semester of 1990. No students at a higher level will be allowed to use the system. As successive freshmen classes enter the university they are to be added to the system. All students that use the system are required to take a two-credit course in using the system during their first semester. This course is limited to system and applications use and does not include programming. An optional second-semester course in programming is offered. All engineering students pay a system use fee of $100 per semester. Tuition at NCSU is presently $500 per semester, so this represents a 20 percent increase in cost. Printing in excess of some threshold is an extra cost.

Workstations will be added to the system to maintain a ratio of 10 students per workstation until 750 workstations are available. As at MIT, the type of work that can be done on the system or the hours of use are unrestricted. Each student is given 3 MB of disk storage, and all clusters are staffed. A few high-speed laser printers are used instead of many small ones, because the cost per page of expendibles is far lower.

One dormitory was designated "computer dorm." The students who live there pay extra and are given special access to computer facilities in the dorm. They also work on special computer projects and provide informal consulting services to other students. They

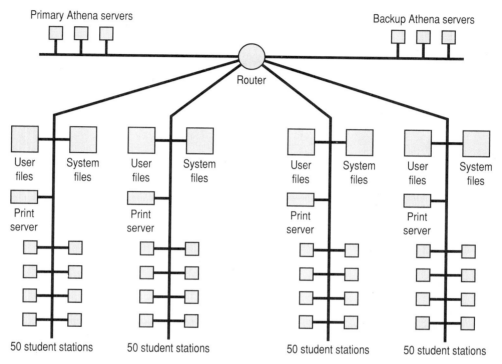

Figure I.1   System configuration of North Carolina State University installation.

seem to function somewhat like SIPB at MIT, and they probably will play some role in system improvements.

Iowa State University

Athena was installed at the Iowa State University (ISU) at Ames in June 1990. The name of Athena at ISU is "Vincent," honoring John Vincent Atanasoff, who invented the electronic digital computer at ISU. Use of Athena at ISU is different from that at MIT: It is used for both research and education, rather than for education only. Moreover, with Vincent all computing resources are allocated to department heads, and they in turn allocate the resources to research and education in accordance with department priorities. Figure I.2 shows the block diagram of the system.

The system includes 350 workstations, all using the reduced

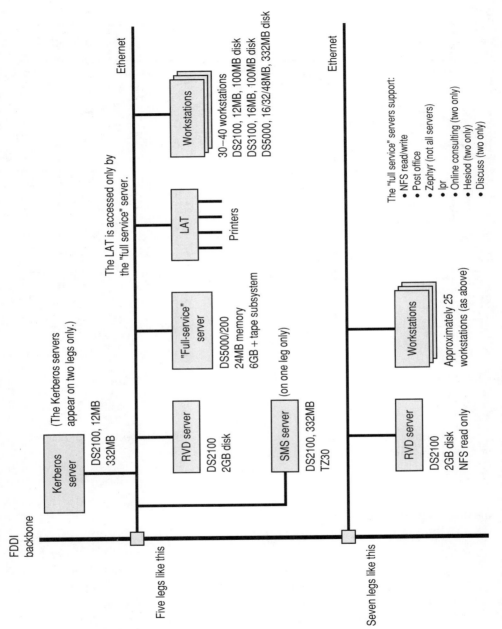

Figure 1.2 Vincent system at Iowa State University at Ames.

instruction set architecture. Rather than dedicating one server to each service (such as a name server), as Athena does as a matter of policy to simplify administration, Vincent combines many services on a single server. This approach reduces cost and is quite feasible because of the much higher performance of newer systems. Another difference is that the performance of Athena workstations was relatively uniform, even though they came from different manufacturers. The Vincent workstations vary widely in many parameters, including processor performance, memory and mass storage size, and color capacity, ranging from 1 bit per pixel to 96 bits per pixel. This range of performance is consistent with research-use requirements.

The Vincent system is composed of two groups of subnets, with subnets within each group being quite similar. The first group has five subnets and supports all server types in the system. Within this group, one subnet supports a *Moira* server, two subnets support *Kerberos* servers, and all subnets support LAT, RVD, and "full-service" servers. Each subnet also supports 30–40 workstations. The full-service servers support

- NFS;
- post office;
- Zephyr notification;
- lpr distributed printing;
- on-line consulting;
- Hesiod naming; and
- Discuss network conferencing.

The other group contains seven identical subnets. Each supports an RVD server and about 25 workstations. All 12 subnets are connected by a fiber digital data link (FDDI) backbone operating at 100 million bits per second.

Nanyang Technical Institute

Athena was installed at Nanyang Technical Institute in July 1990. This installation was unique in that it was the first time that Athena was installed on a workstation network in heavy production use. The Athena system installation did not disturb ongoing production work. Another unique aspect of the installation was that it included the first support of diskless workstations by Athena.

NFS file server software was installed on two VAX 3500s. These two VAX 3500s supported some 50 VAXstation 3100 diskless workstations. In addition, one server supported the mail hub, post office, and name service. The other server supported notification, authentication, and time services.

APPENDIX II

Guidelines for Athena Installation

These guidelines for installation of an Athena-like system in an academic environment are drawn from the experience at MIT and were developed for Bond University. Bond is a new, private university built in 1988 in Australia and modeled after MIT in many respects.

Requirements

Athena software should only be installed after 15–25 workstations are in place and running vendor-supplied Unix. Using the Athena system to bring up a totally new hardware system is not appropriate.

All campuses are different, and the Athena software must be customized for each specific environment. This requirement is especially true of the *Moira* system management module, which is highly adapted to the MIT environment in its present form. Other modules are more portable. Absolutely no support is provided for the Athena software by MIT.

What You Get and How to Get It

Athena software can be obtained from MIT layered on Berkeley Unix or from Digital layered on Ultrix (DEC-Athena). In either case it comes as a 6250 BPI magnetic tape or it can be copied over the net. To obtain the tape from MIT, contact the Athena Information Officer and request the "PANSS" tape. To copy the software over the net, do an anonymous *ftp* to node *athena-dist.mit.edu*. MIT makes the Athena system software (but not the instructional software) freely available to all. The only restriction is that the MIT copyright notice must be retained in the source code.

To obtain the source from Digital, receiving organizations must show evidence of a valid Ultrix source license for at least the system that will be used for system builds. Valid Berkeley 32V and AT&T Unix source licenses are also required. A valid Ingres binary license is required (from RTI) if the *Moira* service management system is to be used. The TRANSCRIPT software must be acquired from Adobe or elsewhere for use with postscript printers.

The Athena modules provided include

- *Kerberos* authentication service;
- *Hesiod* name service;
- network mail system (including POP and XMH);
- *Zephyr* notification service;
- *Moira* service management system;
- X Window System and clients, Version 11;
- NFS modified to work with *Kerberos*;
- RVD Remote Virtual Disk file service for read-only files;
- on-line consulting package;
- *Discuss* public bulletin board system; and
- Boot service.

Sources for these modules are provided on the tape. The system must be compiled for the local environment. Tables reflecting the local hardware configuration and network assignments must also be developed.

For non–United States locations, the Kerberos authentication service cannot be provided by MIT because of export restriction laws. Instead, a replacement for *Kerberos,* called "Bones," is provided, which will allow the system to operate but without the ability to perform encryption, decryption, or authentication. If there is a need to print Athena documentation from electronic sources, a SCRIBE binary license will also be needed. Some public domain software, such as Gnuemacs, will also be provided.

Organization

The Executive Committee

Long experience with MIS systems has shown that for a system installation to be a success, policy and objectives must be set by the users of the system. In this particular case, the users of the system are the faculty. It is recommended that a committee of leading faculty members representing major departments or schools be established. The policy decisions, and ultimately the support, of this committee were of crucial importance to the ultimate acceptance and success of the Athena system.

The Development and Support Organization

In order for the system to be initially installed and then maintained at a receiving campus, there must be a resident development and support group. The leader of the group should have a title something like "Director, Workstation System Management." This position requires someone with tertiary teaching experience so that he or she can relate well to the faculty. This person must also have traditional MIS experience in the development (not just operation) of a large workstation–based computer system, preferably using Unix and TCP/IP.

The following groups will report to this individual:

- Development;
- Networking;
- Operations; and
- User Services

The Development group is responsible for system software, must consist of "Unix wizards," and must be experts on the internals of the type of Unix that you are using. Unix is a very flexible and complex system and requires a great deal of low-level detail work to keep it operational. A principal activity of the Unix wizards will be to customize system management software and to build the entire system from sources to fit the local environment. A Release Engineering group within the Development group is responsible for providing the Operations group with a complete, documented, and tested system in binary form plus installation kits and instructions.

The Network group designs, installs (or oversees the installation by a contractor), and maintains the network, including the assignment of network addresses, the ongoing monitoring of network performance, and the planning for capacity upgrades. This group is also responsible for installing and maintaining the modem pool for dial-up service. It is assumed that the network supports other systems on campus beyond the ones discussed here.

The Operations group is responsible for taking orders for equipment, getting quotes, placing orders, and keeping track of equipment. When equipment is received, the Operations group inventories and warehouses it. The group then installs it, attaches it to the network, loads it with system software (preferably over the net), and tests it. The necessary configuration tables in the system management software are modified to reflect the new hardware. This group is responsible for working with Physical Plant personnel to obtain modifications to power, walls, cabling, air-conditioning, etc.

While unattended operation is appropriate for the server hardware, there needs to be an operations office (not in the machine room) with several workstations on the network. Some of these workstations (perhaps two) will be dedicated to monitoring network and server activity, rather than being used by operators as interactive terminals. There should be a remote temperature sensor for each machine room, with indicators in the operations office. This group needs access to warehouse space for the equipment received but not yet installed.

It would be advisable for the Operations group to maintain an inventory of equipment and spare parts to minimize down time when failures occur. The group is responsible for ordering service when a failure occurs. It is advisable that Operations provide space for vendor maintenance people to maintain a small office and storage space for tools, documentation, and parts.

The User Services group delivers training, consulting, documentation, "hot line" support, and notifies the maintenance group when action is required. Athena user documentation is available from MIT upon written request. This group also establishes the requirements for purchased third-party software (editors, text formatters, spreadsheets, graphics packages) and evaluates available products, procures and supports them. This group also helps new users establish accounts.

For large systems (i.e., more than 500 workstations), the positions of Assistant Director and Technical Director might also be desired. The Assistant Director is responsible for the day-to-day operation of the staff, freeing the Project Director for more strategic and externally oriented activities. The Technical Director is responsible for the overall integrity and consistency of system architecture.

If a significant number of purchased software packages is to be used, a position needs to be defined to manage this activity. Based on Athena experience, this activity could take the full time of an individual.

A set of position descriptions drawn from the MIT experience is included at the end of this section.

Standards

The recommended standards for this system are:

- Berkeley compatible Unix with the BIND name server
- TCP/IP
- X Window System V11
- Postscript
- GKS (2-D)
- C and FORTRAN
- Common Lisp
- SQL
- PHIGS (3-D)
- AFS
- Ethernet

Configurations

System configuration is ultimately set by the number and type of users. If there are no privately owned PCs or workstations, a ratio of about ten students to each public workstation is a good working minimum, although five students per workstation would be better. If there are student-owned PCs or workstations, a ratio of 10–20 students per public workstation might be used.

These workstations should be placed in public clusters, along with printers. The number of workstations per public cluster might range from 20 to 200. The MIT experience is that large clusters are much more popular with students than small clusters and that large clusters are much cheaper to operate than small clusters. Most of the MIT clusters are unattended.

If low-speed printers (i.e., eight pages per minute) are used, about one printer per eight workstations, but at least two per public cluster, should be available. At least in theory these low-speed printers can be unattended. However, operational problems arise in this approach, with students trying to load paper, unjam mechanisms, and "repair" faults. In any event, at least a nominal charge for printing, equal to or greater than copying cost, should be made. Experience at MIT indicates that each student prints about 500 pages per year at a materials cost of about $40.

In addition to the low-speed printers, some high-speed printers capable of about 40 pages per minute for large documents should be provided. High-speed printers can have much lower expendibles cost (by a factor of two) than slower printers. In all cases, these devices should be in places convenient for students—for example near classrooms, in student unions, or in libraries.

In order for the system to not have single points of failure, at least two of each of

- authentication servers,
- name servers (preferably 3 minimum),
- system disk servers, and
- notification servers

should be provided. These servers may be dual ported (each disk subsystem interfaces to two processors) for additional reliability. Dual porting looks very attractive but has not been tested at Athena.

The following assumptions seem reasonable in view of the Athena experience at MIT for use in sizing the system. Only one type of workstation—a VAXstation or DEC station with 12 MB main memory and 100 MB hard disk—would be utilized. Servers like Microvax 3900s, low-speed printers like LNO3s, and high-speed printers like LPS-40s would be provided. (The experience at MIT is that high-speed printers such as the LPS 40 are not appropriate for direct student access but instead should be a "behind the counter" operation. They are suitable for direct staff access.)

The following storage requirements are based on Athena experience.

- 1–3 MB private storage per undergraduate student
- 4–8 MB private storage per graduate student
- 8–10 MB private storage per staff member

- 500 MB system software binaries (includes 50 MB for third-party software)
- 500 MB instructional software

The following instrumentation data were obtained on Athena with regard to disk usage. At the time these data were gathered, the default disk quota was 1.4 Mbytes, although this quota could be increased upon suitable justification.

- 25 percent of the users use 40 KBytes or less.
- 50 percent of the users use 300 KBytes or less.
- 90 percent of the users use 1100 KBytes or less (95 percent of quota).
- 95 percent of the users use 1440 KBytes or less (default limit).
- 5 percent of the users use 40 percent of the space (usually staff members with large quotas).
- 10 percent of the users use 50 percent of the space.
- 50 percent of the users use 93 percent of the space.

A policy of overcommitment of file space is followed. At the time these data were gathered, the total disk space available was 6.4 Gbytes. However, 10 Gbytes was committed to users via quota. This approach of overcommitment works relatively well.

The size of the NFS servers is determined by the amount of space given to the users for private files in aggregate. Instructional software may also be stored in the NFS servers. The RVD servers hold the system binaries and some instructional software. The RVD server is provided in addition to NFS because it has much higher performance with read-only files.

No MIT instructional software is supplied with the system. Instructional software must be obtained individually from its faculty developers.

The LAN communications system should correspond approximately to the MIT campus communications system. A backbone link should connect the major buildings and Ethernet subnets provide intrabuilding communications.

"Firewalls" in the network are important to prevent problems on one subnet from propagating and bringing the entire net down. In particular, the backbone should be protected from each subnet.

Based on the MIT experience, a good approach would be to bring all subnets back to a single point. All communications equipment then could be installed and maintained in a single room, along with the servers. This approach would greatly ease installation, modification, and maintenance.

Subnets with more than a few workstations should have their own RVD servers. The Athena experience is that these servers are not compute bound. One RVD server is required for each 100 workstations, and maintaining one RVD server as a hot spare on each subnet may be advisable. The number of NFS servers required is determined by the amount of storage that can be put on each server.

Backup on Athena is accomplished by copying to disk across the net at night when the load is light and the files are relatively stable. The next day the backup disk is copied to tape during normal working hours when operators are available. The number of tape drives required for backup is flexible. This is principally a function of support staff and geographical distribution of servers. Given wide distribution and a reasonable staff, having a tape drive on each NFS server provides the greatest throughput and greatest sense of security. RVD servers back each other up, because all the data is the same on each.

A main frame system of at least 3 MIPS, 16 Mbytes of main memory, and 1.6 Gbytes of disk storage should be provided for system builds. This system should also have access to a 6250 BPI tape drive.

The following table suggests sizes for the configuration based on the preceding assumptions and recommendations. Sizes are given for both 3000 and 9000 students.

Students	3000	9000
Workstations	300	900
Subnets	5–10	20–30
RVD servers/subnet	1	1
NFS servers	15	45
Authentication servers	1 master, 1 slave	1 master, 2 slaves
Mail servers	1 hub, 2 POs	1 hub, 4 POs
Name servers	3	5
Notification servers	1	4
Service management servers	1	3
Low-speed printers	25–30	70–90
High-speed printers	2	5

If there are too many subnets, there will be too many RVD serv-ers. If there are not enough subnets, there will be too much traffic on the subnet and the servers.

Training Users

MIT offers the following training courses in Athena, which are both necessary and reasonably sufficient. Any campus supporting an Ath-ena-like system should consider offering similar courses. The courses are one hour in duration unless otherwise noted.

1. Introduction to Athena
   This course is an introduction to Project Athena and Athena workstations. It shows how to get started on the system. The topics presented include

   getting an account (authorization to use Athena);

   where to find Athena workstations;

   logging in;

   using files and directories;

   using X windows; and

   finding help and documentation.

   Prerequisites: None
2. Basic word processing on Athena
   An introduction to text processing on Athena:

   how to create and change files using the *Emacs* text editor;

   sending electronic mail around the campus, the country, or the world;

   using *Zephyr*—note passing to other Athena users; and

   using Athena's laser printers.

   Prerequisite: Introduction to Athena
3. Advanced word processing
   All you need to produce a simple class paper:

   the remaining *Emacs* fundamentals; and

   basic text formatting with Scribe.

   Prerequisite: Basic word processing

4. Scribe reports (report)
   The Scribe techniques needed to produce a fully formatted report, including

   chapter numbering;

   footnotes;

   tables;

   cross-references;

   table of contents; and

   bibliography.

   Prerequisite: Advanced word processing
5. Scribe thesis
   How to produce a document that meets all the formatting requirements for an MIT thesis.

   Prerequisite: Scribe reports
6. Scribe math
   How to include mathematical symbols and expressions in Scribe documents:

   numbered equations;

   special symbols;

   complicated fractions;

   Greek letters; and

   superscripts and subscripts.

   Prerequisite: Advanced word processing
7. RS/1
   An electronic lab notebook that provides facilities for

   tables;

   x–y plots;

   3-D graphs;

   data analysis; and

   curve fitting.

   Prerequisite: Basic word processing
8. Programming in C
   A six module, video-based course with six 40-minute video presentations and corresponding programming exercise sets. Assumes knowledge of at least one other programming language.

Physical Security

The file servers and authentication servers must be kept in locked rooms with controlled access to prevent tampering. The number of people with access to the authentication servers should be kept to a minimum.

Public clusters should be secured by entrance through a door that has some sort of lock, perhaps a ten-key pad. Experience with unattended operation at MIT has been satisfactory. Telephones should be available in the cluster rooms to allow calls for hotline assistance. The logic modules, if desktop units, need to be physically attached to the desk or table by a cable or cage. Loss of unsecured keyboards and monitors at MIT has not been a problem.

Athena Software

The following is the set of software licenses that Athena has found useful. This list may not be complete, but at least gives the major items.

Software Available on Athena

Support Category

Cat. 1 = Athena supported

Cat. 2 = Third Party supported (non-SIPB)

Cat. 3 = Not officially supported but SIPB will answer questions

Cat. 4 = Beta (evaluation, limited distribution/license)

Cat. 5 = Special development (interim workstations, visual)

Cat. 6 = Unsupported

(Athena supported means the project will make bug fixes and issue new releases. Third party means vendor will do this.)

Documentation

A = Athena (Essential document, in racks, or through on-line-help)

V(1) = Vendor or 3rd party documentation available in the racks

V(2) = Vendor or 3rd party documentation available on-line

V(3) = Vendor or 3rd party documentation available for purchase (send mail to mwmoor for more information)

H = On-line help within program only

M = man page only

— = no documentation

continues

Training—'Yes' means that this topic is covered in one of our minicourses.

Name	Support Category	Description	Documen-tation	Training
Languages/Compilers				
C (pcc)	1	C compiler	A	Video
gcc, gdb	2	gnu C compiler	V(1)	
Saber 2.0	1	C interpreter/debugger	A, V(1)	
hc (RT's)	1	C compiler	A	
dbx	1	debugger	A	
F77	1	FORTRAN compiler	A, V(1)	
LISP	4	Allegro Common LISP	—	
KCL	1	Kyoto Common LISP	V(1,2)	
Pascal	6	Pascal compiler	—	
PostScript	2	Page description language	V(1)	
Prolog	6	Prolog compiler	—	
Scheme	2	Scheme	A	
clu	2		—	
shell scripting	1		A, V(1)	
System Utilities				
Kerberos	1	Authentication/authoriz. sys.	A	
mh	1	Mail handler	A, V(1)	Yes
xmh	1	X version of mh	M	
mh-mail (motif)	4	Motif version of mh	—	
Zephyr	1	Notification service	A	Yes
SMS (Moira)	1	Service Management system	A	
Discuss	3	Conferencing system	A	
xdiscuss	3	X version of Discuss	—	
Turnin/pickup	1	Courseware utilities	M	
Transcript	1	PostScript utilities		
psrev			A	Yes
enscript			M	
ps4014			M	Yes
X Window system	½	Window system and related util., libs. and toolkits	V(1)	Limited enrollment
messages (andrew)	5	Mail handler	V(2)	

Name	Support Category	Description	Documen-tation	Training
Productivity Tools				
Andrew ez	4	WYSIWYG editor	A, V(2)	Yes
Andrew table	4	WYSIWYG table/ spreadsheet	V(2)	
Andrew zip	4	WYSIWYG drawing	V(2)	
Andrew eq	4	Equation processor	V(2)	
Andrew raster	4	Image processor	V(2)	
20/20	6	Spreadsheet	V(2)	
ditroff	6	Device independent troff	M, V(1)	
GNU Emacs	1	Text editor	A, V(1)	Yes
INGRES	4	Relational database management system	V(3)	
MACSYMA	1	Symbolic manipulation pgm	V(1)	
MatLab	4	Interactive matrix pgm	V(3)	
MATRIXx	6	Matrix manipulation pgm	V(3)	
SIMNON	6	Non-linear systems analysis	V(3)	
Minitab	4	Statistical package	V(3)	
NAG	2	Numerical routines library	V(1,2,3)	
Scribe	2	Text formatter	A	Yes
LaTex	3	Text formatter	A, V(1)	
viewdoc	4	PostScript text previewer	—	Yes
xps	3	PostScript previewer	—	
xdvi	3	TEX previewer	—	
RS/1	1	Electronic lab notebook	A, V(1)	Yes
olc	1	Online consulting program	A	
olh	1	Online help system	A	
olta	4	Online course TA	—	
whatsup (postit, bulkpost)	1	Activities online listings	M	
Graphics				
ProChart	1	Presentation Graphics pgm	V(3)	

continues

Name	Support Category	Description	Documen- tation	Training
GKS	6	Graphics Kernel System 2D	V(3)	
IGKS	4	Graphics Kernel System	—	
Movie.BYU	4	Graphics 3D modeling pkg	—	
Penplot	6	Vector graphics library	V(3)	
PostScript	2	Page description language	V(1)	
Hoops	4	3D graphics	—	
xmath	4	Function plotting package	H	
xfig	3	General graphics pkg	—	
idraw	3	General graphics pkg	—	
ped	6	Picture Editor	—	
Development Tools				
BLOX	5	User interface generation Tools	V(3)	
Andrew Toolkit	4	Interface generator	—	
Muse	5	Courseware Authoring	—	
Motif uil/toolkit	4	Interface generator	V(3)	
Others				
Kermit	6	File transfer	A	
gctl, galatea	5	Video Soft Switch server	A	
rrn	3	network news	A	

Other Considerations

UPS power should be considered for the servers critical to operation, especially the authentication server and name server.

The annual operating budget should contain a line item for depreciation approximately equal to 25 percent of the replacement cost of the hardware, including workstations, servers, and printers.

Faculty use of the workstations will be different from that of students. Faculty patterns of use should be considered in the design.

Interface to the library and administrative system should be considered.

Personnel, location, and method of delivering training, documentation, trouble-shooting, and consulting need to be considered. DECwindows, *Motif,* or some similar graphical interface to Unix should be used to ease training problems.

Position Descriptions

The following are position descriptions, including the skills necessary to support Athena on campus. These descriptions are drawn from the MIT descriptions of such jobs and reflect MIT's organizational structure.

System Architect

Responsibilities. Responsible for overall system architecture, design, and improvements to an advanced Unix-based distributed workstation operating environment using the MIT Athena distributed services software.

Qualifications. Candidate must have 7–10 years experience in system design and architecture, with emphasis on Unix-based distributed workstation systems. Must understand the architecture of Unix thoroughly and must be able to develop highly detailed solutions to difficult problems in operating system operation. Must be well versed in the TCP/IP communications protocols and its relationship to Unix. Must have in-depth knowledge of the client–server model of distributed computing and its implementation in a Unix environment. Must have some demonstrated understanding of the performance issues in distributed workstation computing systems. Must have detailed knowledge of NFS and related distributed file systems.

Unix Specialist

Responsibilities. Continue development and maintain advanced Unix-based distributed workstation operating environment using the MIT Athena distributed services software.

Qualifications. Must have five years experience and detailed knowledge of the internals of Berkeley Unix. Must have a thorough knowledge of device drivers. Must be able to find difficult bugs in

Unix operation based on dump analysis or symptom analysis and must be able to fix the bugs rapidly without introduction of additional problems. Must be able to design and implement or find bugs in distributed aspects of Unix operation. Must be proficient in C language programming. Education requirement is Bachelor's degree or equivalent combination of experience. Must have demonstrated ability to work with others in integrated team. Experience with X11 Window System is also desired.

Instructional Software Consultant

Responsibilities. Provide consulting to students and faculty using standard end user software and on-line consulting tools: provide feedback to User Services about operations in the field and technical training to users. Positions deal with delivery of educational services and development of training programs. Will supervise the administration of day-to-day operation of on-line consulting tools and evaluate prerelease software.

Qualifications. Bachelor's degree or equivalent combination of education and experience necessary, as well as two or more years of experience in computer programming or system administration and demonstrated ability to work well with computer users and technical staff members. Computing experience in a university setting: experience with Unix and with a variety of end-user software, as well as ability to train other technical staff preferred. Proven supervisory skills, strong technical skills, extensive experience using Unix utilities, and computing experience in a networked environment desirable.

Deployment and Installation Manager

Responsibilities. Develop policies and procedures for the deployment, installation, and maintenance of workstations in a large distributed network. Develop budget and accounting procedures for equipment purchase and maintenance of stocking levels for inventory. Perform database development to maintain accurate records of equipment configurations and locations. Extract report generation material from database for management review. Provide management to Supervisor of Hotline for all vendor and internal trouble calls. Maintain two shifts of technicians for repair of hardware and software. Coordinate installation of workstations with all other involved departments.

Qualifications. Candidate should have five years experience in project and operations management in telecommunications and/or with computer vendors. Experience with workstations and networking and excellent communications skills are required.

User Support/Administrator

Qualifications. Must have five years experience in user support and administration in a Unix-based distributed workstation system. Must have a good appreciation of user needs and the ability to work well with people in different situations.

Unix Communications Specialist

Responsibilities. Develop and maintain TCP/IP communications environment supporting advanced workstation distributed network systems.

Qualifications. Must have five years experience in design and implementation of TCP/IP communications systems on Ethernet in a Berkeley Unix environment. Must have experience developing Ethernet gateways or bridges, and should understand tradeoffs involved in developing similar technology. Must be able to program in C and Unix.

Instructional Software Development Programmer

Responsibilities. Assist faculty working on educational software and implementation—in particular will provide proposal formulation assistance and identification of funding sources for projects, consult on user interface and application design, and write software in support of courseware development in a Unix environment using graphic display processors.

Candidate will implement applications programs, standards, and libraries and maintain contact between the faculty and staff. Will research appropriate software and hardware avenues to meet faculty needs and will provide assistance in resolving technical problems. Will install and modify applications packages obtained from vendors.

Qualifications. Bachelor's degree or equivalent combination of education and experience necessary. Also required are good communication skills and one year or more full-time experience with at least two of the following: Unix, C, computer graphics in a scientific environment, and X11 window and toolkit system.

Applications Developer

Responsibilities. Will assist faculty members working on educational software and implementation—in particular, will write device drivers and other system software in support of visual courseware development in an Unix X11 environment using graphics display processors such as the Parallax board; implement applications programs, standards, and libraries; and maintain contact between faculty and staff. Will research appropriate software and hardware avenues to meet the needs of the faculty and will provide assistance in identifying and resolving technical problems users may have. Will provide conceptual, technical, and standard information to users and communicate user needs requirements to developers. Will install, document, maintain, and modify applications packages obtained from vendors or other computing facilities.

Qualifications. Bachelor's degree or equivalent combination of education and experience necessary. Requires good oral and written communication skills and good interpersonal skills, and one year or more full-time experience with at least two of the following: Unix, C, interactive computer graphics in a scientific environment, interactive videodisc, device drivers, and X11 toolkit. Familiarity with optical file systems desirable.

Systems Developer

Responsibilities. A Systems Programmer is required for work with the Systems Development Group. The candidate will be specifically responsible for development of extensions and modifications to a distributed operating environment layered on Unix. These activities require a thorough knowledge of C, Unix device drivers, and kernel internals.

Qualifications. Bachelor's degree or equivalent combination of education and experience necessary. Experience with construction and tuning of DMA driven board level processors a plus. Experience with project leadership and a proven ability to deliver a necessity. Ability to work with others at all skill levels, both as coworkers and as clients, a requirement. X11 server experience a definite advantage.

Technical Writer

Responsibilities. To write and update documentation; work with faculty and staff to determine needs; work as member of documentation delivery team; test prerelease software; investigate on-line documentation delivery strategies.

Qualifications. Bachelor's degree or equivalent experience and one year technical writing experience necessary. Strong technical background, including knowledge of at least one programming language, text editors and formatters, Unix system, and application areas. Experience in university setting strongly desired. Writing samples required.

System Consultant

Responsibilities. To provide consulting to students and faculty using standard end-user software on the Project Athena computer system; learn and use standard end-user software and on-line consulting tools; provide feedback to Athena staff and users about operations in the field; provide technical leadership and training for the consulting team; prepare and distribute technical information to other members of the consulting team and interested members of the Athena staff; hire, train, and supervise student consultants; supervise the administration and day-to-day operation of on-line consulting tools; design and implement utility programs, and modify existing programs; evaluate prerelease software and monitor changes to the release system from the point of view of end-users; and work with the documentation and training staffs to help provide documentation and training for end users.

Qualifications. Bachelor's degree or equivalent combination of education and experience necessary, as well as two or more years of experience in computer programming or system administration, a strong facility for acquiring and assimilating information about application packages and the configuration of a distributed computer system, and a demonstrated ability to work well with computer users and technical staff members required. Experience with Unix, computing experience in a university setting, experience with a variety of end-user software, and evident ability to train other technical staff preferred. Proven supervisory skills, strong technical writing skills, extensive experience using Unix utilities, and computing experience in a networked environment desirable.

End-User Consulting Manager

Responsibilities. Plan, hire, manage, and supervise a staff to provide consulting to users of Project Athena's resources. Channel user feedback to User Services (particularly Faculty/Course Liaison and Documentation) and Systems Development. Provide status information and workarounds to users when operational problems occur. Procure the necessary on-line programs and tools to deliver these services and provide consulting programs for end users of Athena's standard applications and systems software.

Qualifications. Bachelor's degree in Computer Science. First-hand experience with Unix and Unix utilities and a variety of end-user software; familiarity with one or more programming languages; computing experience in a networked or distributed environment. Experience establishing consulting services; proven supervisory skills; ability to work well with users, students and other staff, and to resolve conflicts between them. Excellent communication skills, both oral and written, required.

Computing experience in a university setting, experience with large-scale computer systems, systems administration experience, and systems programming experience on Unix highly desirable. Familiarity with the design of user interfaces, experience providing direct day-to-day user or customer support, fluency in C and experience with hardware (including network) maintenance desirable.

Hotline Supervisor

Responsibilities. Coordinate all vendor and internal repairs of hardware/software. Supervise two shifts of technicians for repair of hardware/software. Supervise the day-to-day operation of an on-line hotline database. Provide feedback to Athena users of nonfunctioning equipment. Generate quarterly reports of hotline activities.

Qualifications. Must have at least three years experience within operations/telecommunications environment. Ability to work well with computer users and technical staff members. Experience with computers and workstations. Position requires good communication skills and good interpersonal skills. Experience in Unix helpful.

APPENDIX III

Other Issues in Instructional Computing

■■■■■

This section provides additional background information in instructional computing for higher education in the areas of

- alternative design approaches;
- alternative ownership models; and
- role of private industry.

Alternative System Design Approaches

Of the many design approaches that may be taken in the use of workstations at higher education institutions (see [McCredie 83] for further information), those of particular interest here include

- workstations versus personal computers;
- networked versus not networked;
- institution ownership versus private ownership;
- disk versus diskless; and
- standards versus laissez faire.

These design issues interact strongly with each other: That is, a decision relative to one strongly influences the resolution of other issues. For example, if a university has only institution ownership of workstations and all workstations are on campus (i.e., tightly coupled), a diskless approach may be attractive. Conversely, if the university has (mostly) privately owned workstations and if many are off campus, the diskless approach may be very unattractive.

Resolution of these issues are not mutually exclusive, and in most cases universities will implement multiple approaches. For example, a university may have both institution and private ownership of workstations. It could also have both networked and nonnetworked workstations. Thus the questions are not which approach is to be taken, but rather how much of each approach is to be used and how they are to be integrated.

The advantages and disadvantages of each approach may be relatively complex, but some tradeoffs can be easily described. If the workstations are networked, the system can support mail, shared files, public databases, and easy exchange of all forms of information. The disadvantage is a substantial cost increment. Of course, networking can be accomplished by Local Area Networks (higher cost and performance) or modems (lower cost and lower performance). There are also many intermediate approaches.

Diskless workstations have the advantage of lower cost compared to workstations with disks. Other advantages of a diskless configuration flow from the resulting statelessness of the workstation: All software distribution is to the servers that provide storage; library service for the workstation and backup can be handled centrally.

However, diskless workstations put a substantial extra burden on network channel loading and on server storage. Experience indicates that no more than about 40 diskless workstations can be supported by one file server in read–write operation with locking (the normal case). More subnets may be required to handle the increased network traffic.

The mix of choices must be made in a local context. However, some general interactions of solutions can be discussed.

The question of whether a hard disk should be a required feature of a workstation is a hotly debated one. In situations where all workstations are

- institution owned,
- centrally administered, and
- required to be attached to a high-performance network,

workstations may be deployed with no hard disk. Whether there is an economic advantage in the smaller physical configuration at the workstation and a net economy of scale from sharing large disks at the server is a cost-engineering question that has not been definitively answered. Moreover, the answer changes frequently with changes in technology.

In any case, there are also environments in which the three conditions just listed do not hold and therefore in which a diskless configuration is simply not usable. In particular, when students own their own workstations they expect them to be useful when standing alone. One reason is so that they can take them home over the summer or contemplate living in an apartment away from the campus network. Even for the on-campus student, there is a strong psychological barrier to laying out a substantial sum of money for an object that is usable only when plugged into a system with limited geographical range and whose services are completely under someone else's control.

Alternative Ownership Models

Models of ownership range from workstations owned by the institution and provided as part of the educational environment to the students, to workstations purchased by the students on a voluntary basis, to workstations purchased by students on a required basis.

Private ownership may be mandatory or voluntary. The institution may require that purchased workstations conform to established standards, or it may allow users to purchase any type of workstation (laissez faire). Centralized servers (file servers, print servers, etc.) normally are owned by the institution.

If students purchase workstations, the most senior students will have the oldest equipment. If the institution provides workstations to students through a lease plan, arrangements can be made to provide the most senior students with the newest equipment.

Important characteristics of institution ownership are that the cost burden is directly born by the institution and all students have access to the facilities. The cost is passed on to the student through tuition or to the public through taxes. Whether this is an advantage depends on local circumstances. Institution ownership can be established as policy, regardless of whether funding is public or private. With institution ownership, delivery of education arguably will be more equitable, because all students can have equal access to computing facilities regardless of personal budget. However, if all students are required to purchase workstations upon entry to the university (perhaps as part of tuition), comparable equal access could be achieved.

A likely long-term ownership model for MIT is that of private ownership of most workstations, and Institute ownership of servers. There would also be Institute ownership of a significant number (e.g., 1500) of publicly available workstations on campus. If the private ownership approach were supported in the future, the privately owned workstations would be purchased by students and staff members from a variety of sources, including but not limited to the campus microcomputer store. The number of privately owned workstations could grow to about 10,000 over time.

Delivery of Required Services

Services required to support delivery of educational computing include

- sales of hardware and software;
- maintenance;
- user training;
- consulting (both on-line and personal);
- documentation;
- network installation;
- network support; and
- workstation installation.

Various colleges and universities have widely differing needs for support of computing services. At one end of the spectrum, the university may be highly self-sufficient in one or more (perhaps all) services. At the other extreme, the university may contract for essentially all services. The two sources of the required services are the institution and private industry.

Role of Private Industry

In this context, *private industry* refers to computer and workstation manufacturers, and third-party suppliers of products and services, such as software, maintenance, network services, and consulting.

Private industry must be able to support educational institutions across the spectrum of computing needs described. In those instances where the institution is able to provide a service, it normally can do so at a much lower cost than can private industry. For example, a college or university can support the sales function with a markup on the order of 10 percent, whereas private industry needs a much higher markup. Likewise, the labor rates for a college or university to perform maintenance are far lower than they are for private industry.

In the following scenario, two extreme situations are described: one in which the institution offers essentially no services and one in which the institution is essentially self-sufficient. In any real situation some combination of these extremes would exist. Industry must have the flexibility to meet such diverse, situation-specific requirements.

In the case of minimum institutional services, private industry is required to provide nearly all services. The workstation manufacturers or other marketing organizations open stores on campus to sell hardware, software, documentation, and maintenance services for their workstations. Workstation installation must be easy enough that the purchaser can do it, preferably with no more than one page of instructions and in no more than 15 minutes. Ideally, the software can be loaded over the network if the institution has purchased a site license (and has appropriate servers and networks); otherwise the software must be loaded locally.

In the case of a self-sufficient institution, a very different situation exists. Here, the institution is treated as a value-added retailer. The institution operates the computer store very much as the manufacturer does in the preceding case. The store sells a range of products approved for use on campus. Private industry sells products and services, such as hardware, software, repair parts, product brochures, and other information, to the computer store wholesale. Substantial training services—for example, product training, maintenance training, and consulting training—are required by the institution.

The self-sufficient model is very close to the one selected at MIT for the post-Athena period.

APPENDIX IV

Athena Policies

The two documents presented here should be of interest to developers or administrators of systems such as Athena. They are:

- Principles of Responsible Use of Project Athena; and
- Athena Rules of Use.

The Athena staff developed these policies on the basis of experience gained early in the project. They apply to all users.

Principles of Responsible Use of Project Athena

STEVE LERMAN
Project Athena Director

Project Athena is an eight-year experiment in the use of a large, networked computer system as part of the educational process at MIT. Athena's distributed computer system will open up entirely new ways for members of the MIT community to share information. One consequence of linking the entire community together, however, is the potential for improper use of the system, a violation of MIT's high standards of honesty and personal conduct.

Intended Use

The hardware granted to Project Athena, and the software licensed for that hardware, are intended only for educational use by MIT community members. Use of Athena resources by anyone outside MIT requires approval of the Provost, and the sale of such use is prohibited. The use of Athena resources for financial gain is similarly prohibited. Use of Project Athena's facilities for sponsored research activities that normally would make use of other MIT facilities is not permitted, except by permission of the Director.

Privacy and Security

The UNIX (UNIX is a trademark of Bell Laboratories) operating system used by Project Athena facilitates sharing information and software among its users. Security mechanisms for protecting information from unintended access—from within the system or from the outside—are minimal. These mechanisms, by themselves, are inadequate for a community the size of MIT's, for whom protection of individual privacy is as important as sharing. Users must supplement the system's security mechanisms by using the system in a manner that preserves the privacy of others.

For example, users should not attempt to gain access to the files or directories of another user without explicit authorization from that user (unless that user has intentionally made them available for public access). Nor should users attempt to intercept any systems communications, such as electronic mail or terminal dialog. Programs should not store information about other users without the users' prior knowledge. Personal information about another individual, which a user would not otherwise disseminate to the MIT community, should not be stored or communicated on the system without the other individual's permission. Such information includes grades, evaluation of students, and their work.

System Integrity

Actions taken by users intentionally to interfere with or to alter the integrity of the system cannot be permitted. These include unauthorized use of accounts, impersonation of other individuals in systems communications, attempts to crack passwords or encryption, and destruction or alteration of data or programs belonging to other users. Equally unacceptable are intentional efforts to restrict or deny access by others to any of the resources of the system.

Intellectual Property Rights

Some software and databases that reside on the system are owned by users or third parties, and are protected by copyright and other laws, together with licenses and other contractual agreements. Users must abide by these restrictions. Such restrictions may include prohibitions against copying programs or data for use on non–Athena systems or for distribution outside MIT, against the resale of data or programs or their use for noneducational purposes or for financial gain, and against public disclosure of information about programs (e.g., source code) without the owner's authorization. It is the responsibility of the owner of protected software or data to make any such restrictions known to the user.

Athena Rules of Use

At times, Athena's computer resources are stretched to their limits. We need your help to keep things from getting out of hand. It is likely that some Athena facilities will develop additional local rules of use to meet the needs of their facilities. We do not intend to police Athena facilities to enforce these rules. Instead, we expect voluntary compliance and group pressure to be the most effective enforcement mechanisms.

1. **Do not eat or drink in Athena clusters.**

   Food and drinks can damage equipment.

2. **Do not lend your Athena password.**

   Do not lend your Athena password to anyone, including friends, or even to members of the Athena staff. Giving someone else your password is like lending someone the key to your house or giving someone your charge card.

   Your Athena username identifies you to the Athena user community. Anyone who has your Athena password can use your account and anything they do that affects the system will be traced back to your username. If your username is used in an abusive manner, you will be held responsible. We have had incidents of misuse of the mail systems involving people using other people's usernames to send abusive messages.

Every student (undergrad and grad) and every faculty member who wants an account can have one; there's no need for borrowing.

3. **Do not print Athena *olh* modules.**

Athena-written documentation is meant to be read on-line. Printed copies are available for purchase at the Graphic Arts Quick Copy center in 11-004.

4. **Do not use Athena printers as copy machines.**

The Athena printers should be used to print only one copy of a document. To make additional copies, please use copy machines. You can use the copy machines at Graphic Arts for 3 cents a page, or send your output to the Xerox 9700 printer, which costs about the same. You pay the fee when you pick up your output.

5. **Do not be a printer hog.**

Please do not print a large or complicated document which takes longer than 10 minutes to print on the printers in the public clusters. Doing so ties up the printer for a long time, and other users won't be able to get printouts. If you have such a document, either break it into sections which you print out when the printer doesn't seem to be busy, or send it to the "linus" (LPS-40) printer behind the I.S. Dispatch Desk in Building 11.

If you have a scribed document and don't need a printout of all of it, you can use the psrev command to print just a portion. See directions on psrev in the OLH module on printing from an Athena workstation.

6. **Do not leave your workstation unattended for more than 20 minutes.**

If you are using a workstation in one of the public clusters and intend to keep using it but must leave it briefly unattended, you should limit your absence to less than 20 minutes. Please leave a note on the workstation indicating the time you left the machine and your intention to return.

If you are gone longer than twenty minutes, another user who needs a workstation may log you out or reboot the machine if you leave a public workstation in a "locked" state.

7. **Observe priorities for the use of workstations.**

If a cluster is crowded, the highest priority goes to course-related work—running or developing course software. Middle priority goes to text processing, sending mail, exploring the system or just hacking. Lowest priority goes to game-playing.

Some clusters have workstations which are reserved for specific course use or which have special features—for example, color or special peripherals such as a videodisk player. If you are using such a workstation for a purpose other than its special purpose and someone who needs its unique feature asks you to surrender it, please do so gracefully.

8. **Do not play games if the cluster is busy.**

Games are the lowest priority software on the system. Do not play games if there are only a few workstations free or people are waiting for workstations.

If a user needs a workstation for higher priority work while you are playing games, the user can ask you to give up your workstation.

9. **Do not make a lot of noise in the public clusters.**

Public clusters are similar to the MIT Libraries in that students who use these facilities have to be able to concentrate to do their homework. Please do not play music, shout, or engage in loud conversation in the clusters.

10. **Do not copy copyrighted software.**

Many Athena programs are protected by some kind of copyright restriction.

11. **Do not turn the power off on Athena equipment.**

Do not turn the power off on Athena equipment, such as workstations, monitors, or printers. Turning the power off can permanently damage the hardware. The exception to this is if it smells or looks like it is burning. In that case, please turn it off and call the Athena hardware hotline at x3-1410.

12. **Do not reconfigure the cluster.**

Moving equipment will often break it, and may cause it to be reported as stolen. If you believe the configuration of a cluster needs to be changed, please call the Athena hardware hotline at x3–1410. In particular, please don't unplug or move keyboards, as this can result in permanent damage to the hardware.

13. **Do not forward electronic chain letters.**

The proliferation of electronic chain letters is an abuse of the mail system and the network. You may lose your Athena privileges if you support this abuse by creating or forwarding such letters.

Thank you for your cooperation.

APPENDIX
V

Athena Donors

————

The two primary sponsors of Athena are Digital Equipment Corporation and IBM. In addition, many other donors contributed to the project, providing in aggregate about $16 million. The following is a list of these donors who did not ask to remain anonymous.

Addison–Wesley Publishing Company
Amoco Foundation
The Annenberg/CPB Project
AT&T Bell Laboratories
Boston Edison Foundation
CBS Publishing Group
Alexander and Brit d'Arbeloff '49 '61
Abraham I. Drantz '48
Max E. and Robert J. Gellert '48 '53
Leopold R. Gellert Family Trust
General Electric Foundation
General Motors Foundation, Inc.
Kenneth J. and Pauline S. Germeshausen '31
Houghton Mifflin Company
Hughes Aircraft Company
Edward C. Johnson III
Lockheed Leadership Fund
McDonnell Douglas Foundation
Robert M. Metcalfe '68
Harold J. Muckley '39

Welrose Newhall '22
A. Neil Pappalardo '64
Stratford Foundation
Westinghouse Educational Foundation
3COM Corp.

Others who contributed technology or resources include:

Adobe Systems, Inc.
Apollo Computer, Incorporated
Apple Computer Inc. (USA)
Bolt Beranek & Newman Inc.
Carnegie–Mellon University
Codex
Franz Manufacturing Co., Inc.
GTE Corporation
Hewlett-Packard Company
Integrated Systems Division of Litton Industries, Inc.
MIT Industrial Liaison Program
Open Software Foundation
QMS, Inc.
Salomon Brothers Incorporated
Tektronix Incorporated
Transarc Corporation
University of Wisconsin
Visix Software, Inc.

APPENDIX VI

First Athena
Press Release

■■■■■

The following is the first Athena press release, provided by the News Office of MIT, given to the press on May 27, 1983. The press contact at MIT was listed as Eric Johnson, Assistant Dean, School of Engineering.

MIT Launches Major Experimental Program To Integrate Computers Into Education; Digital Equipment Corp., IBM Providing Support

Can computers really help undergraduates learn faster and more effectively? Educators at the Massachusetts Institute of Technology think so, and to find out how, MIT has launched a major experimental program to integrate the next generation of computers and interactive graphics into undergraduate education throughout all five of its schools.

Digital Equipment Corp. and IBM Corp.—the world's two largest computer manufacturers—are working independently with MIT in what they see as an exciting opportunity to develop ways of tapping the extraordinary flexibility and power of the computer to help students gain a deeper understanding of a wide range of academic disciplines.

The companies are providing a total of nearly $50 million in equipment, software, service, maintenance, support, research grants, and on-campus personnel over the next five years. DEC's contribution is the largest single gift it has made in its corporate history. In addition, MIT has begun a campaign to raise as much as $20 million in grants from other organizations and individuals in order to provide funds to sustain the project.

The unique program, announced today by MIT President Paul E. Gray, is called Project Athena after the Greek goddess of wisdom. Project Athena is based on the premise that computers with advanced computational and graphics capabilities represent a revolutionary new medium for learning.

"This may be the largest step forward in MIT's long history of contributions to education" President Gray said. "The Institute has traditionally played a pioneering role in many areas from curriculum development to novel approaches to teaching."

A key MIT goal unique to Project Athena will be to develop "coherence" among the suppliers' computers such that all machines will function with the same operating system interface and use the same languages. Coherence will enable students and faculty eventually to move easily from one manufacturer's equipment to another.

"Athena will integrate computers into the educational environment in all fields of study through the university in ways which encourage new conceptual and intuitive understanding in our students" President Gray explained. "Central to the project will be the creation of an extensive, coherent network of computers that will enable individuals to share each others' information and programs, and to work together on problems and ideas in creative new ways."

Professor Michael L. Dertouzos, Director of the MIT Laboratory for Computer Science, added that "Project Athena, with its key notion of coherence, is as big a technical challenge as it is a promise that our MIT community will use its newest technology in the service of its oldest goal—improving the education of our students."

President Gray described faculty planners who have been working on Athena for more than a year as "extraordinarily enthusiastic and excited" about the possibilities of producing sweeping changes in the teaching of everything from history and literature to engineering and architecture, from foreign languages, political science, and economics to physics, chemistry, and mathematics.

"Our faith in the success of this experiment is based on the great strength of the MIT faculty and student body," according to Joel Moses, Head of the Electrical Engineering and Computer Science Department. "We are fortunate to have obtained the computer resources and services needed for the project. Now we must begin the task of translating the vision into reality."

In the School of Engineering, for example, professors are planning to use this new computational and graphics power to develop new ways to help students grasp abstract concepts. In particular, the system could improve the effectiveness of teaching electromagnetic field theory. It could instill an intuitive or physical feel for structural behavior. Computer graphics could be useful to help teach fluid mechanics and the intricacies of crystal structure, fields which involve two- and three-dimensional spatial relationships.

"The intensive use of computers is by no means limited to computer specialists or to engineering majors," said President Gray. "Foreign language teachers are already exploring use of personal computers to make learning a second language faster and easier. And political scientists, economists, and managers are studying new ways to use computers to help them visualize dynamic models."

Project Athena will involve thousands of terminals, including interactive graphics terminals, personal computer stations—many with color graphics—organized into regional networks around campus. Supporting these networks will be scores of mainframe computers, storage devices, and printers, all serving the classroom and homework needs of students throughout the Institute.

Digital and IBM will each independently provide local area network technology to organize their computers into clusters to be connected with an overall "spine" network. MIT experts will work with each manufacturer to develop the new interface technology needed to achieve the coherent distributed computing.

"An important point to remember is that this is an experiment" said Dr. Gerald L. Wilson, Dean of the MIT School of Engineering. "We believe we can help students learn by using personal computers and computer graphics in new ways, but nobody is sure exactly how. Our experience suggests, however, that computers can aid the teaching of difficult concepts, give new life to laboratory experiments, help in developing the skills, knowledge, and insights needed for design problems, and especially, help nurture that elusive talent we call intuition."

"But just having computers and graphics isn't the key" he added. "If it were, we could put all the material we have on videotape and give every student a television set. The key is for the student to interact directly with the graphics, to change a component to see what happens, and to play 'what if.' That direct and personal interaction makes this project so exciting."

Dean Wilson suggested several novel possibilities that may arise from this undertaking, such as textbooks with floppy disks inside the cover, and computers serving as expert aids for tutoring. Such tutoring could guide the student's progress according to his or her interests and abilities, as well as encourage experimentation.

Some 2000 of MIT's sophomores, juniors, seniors who major in engineering and all of the Engineering faculty will use DEC hardware and software. IBM systems will be used in programs for all first-year students and by faculty and majors in MIT's Schools of Science, Architecture and Planning, Management, and Humanities and Social Sciences.

Each company will have at least five representatives stationed at MIT. These representatives will work closely with faculty and students to blend computers and graphics into the educational process. One person from each company will serve on the project's steering committee, functioning as an associate director.

Athena will be carried out in two phases—the first two years starting next Fall constituting Phase I, and the remaining three years Phase II.

During Phase I, DEC will provide MIT with a mix of more than 300 alphanumeric display terminals, personal computers, and advanced graphic workstations, as well as some 63 VAX 11/750 and 11/730 minicomputers. IBM, during this phase, will provide 500 high function personal computers.

During Phase II, DEC will provide Athena with about 1600 advanced personal computers and IBM will supply about 500 advanced single user systems. Precisely what this equipment will be is not yet known since the specific functional characteristics required will be strongly influenced by Phase I experience.

Bibliography

Anderson, D. P., et al. "The Dash Project: Issues in the Design of a Very Large Distributed System." *Technical Report 87/338*. Berkeley: University of California Computer Science Division, Department of Electrical Engineering and Computer Science, January 1987.

Athena staff "Introduction to Project Athena." MIT report, October 1983.

Avril, C. (ed.). "Windows on Athena." MIT report, August 1989.

Balkovich, E., Parmelee, R. P., and Saltzer, J. "Project Athena's Model of Computation," *Project Athena Technical Plan,* section C. September 1985. Cambridge, Mass.: MIT.

Balkovich, E., Lerman, S. R., and Parmelee, R. P. "Computing in Higher Education: The Athena Experience." *Communications of the ACM* November 1985a: pp. 1214–1224.

Birman, K. "Replication and Fault Tolerance in the ISIS System." *Proceedings of the Tenth ACM Symposium on Operating Systems,* December 1985.

Birrell, Levin, Needham, and Schroeder. "Grapevine: An Exercise in Distributed Computing." *CACM* April 1982: pp. 260–274.

Black, A. "Supporting Distributed Applications: Experience with Eden." *Proceedings of the Tenth ACM Symposium on Operating Systems Principles* December 1985.

Bloom, J. and Dunlap, K. "A Distributed Name Server for the DARPA Internet." *Usenix Conference Proceedings,* Summer 1986, pp. 172–181.

CAC90 (MacVicar, M.) *Computing for Education at MIT: Final Report.* Cambridge, Mass.: MIT, June 22, 1990.

CAC90a (MacVicar, M.) *Computation and Education Community: A Background Paper.* Cambridge, Mass.: MIT, March 22, 1990.

Campbell, R. "4.3 BSD Line Printer Spooler Manual." Department Electrical Engineering and Computer Science, Berkeley: University of California, July 1983.

Cheriton, D. "The V Distributed System." *CACM* March 1988: pp. 314–332.

Cohen, K. C. "Project Athena: Assessing The Education Results." *1987 ASEE Annual Conference Proceedings,* August 1987.

Cohen, K. C. "Project Athena—Year 5 Student Survey Findings, 1988." MIT Report, June 1988.

Coppeto, T., et al. "OLC: An On-line Consulting System for Unix." *USENIX Conference Proceedings,* Summer 1989.

Davis, D. "Project Athena's Release Engineering Tricks." *Proceedings of Usenix Workshop on Software Management,* April 1989.

Davis, T. L. and Mark, R. G. "Teaching Physiology: The Cardiovascular Simulator Project." *Project Athena: The First Five Years,* Vol. IV. 1988, pp. 69–75. Maynard, Mass.: Digital Equipment Corp.

DellaFera, et al. "The Zephyr Notification System." *Usenix Conference Proceedings,* Winter 1988.

Dertouzos, M., and Burner, W. *Report of the Ad Hoc Committee of Future Computational Needs and Resources.* Cambridge, Mass.: MIT, September 1978.

Dyer, S. P. "Hesiod." *Usenix Conference Proceedings,* Winter 1988.

ECMA. "Standard ECMA—Document Print Service Description and Print Access Protocol Specification." European Computer Manufacturers Association, Group TC35-TG5, September 1988.

Eddy, W., and Wactlar, H. "The Future of Computing at Carnegie Mellon: 3M Workstations in a 3D World. Pittsburgh: Carnegie-Mellon University, The Computer and Network Planning Committee, November 1989.

Erickson, A. "Specification for Living Group Workstation Clusters." MIT Project Athena internal report, June 1987.

Greenwald, M., and Sciver, J. *Remote Virtual Disk Protocol Specification.* Cambridge, Mass.: MIT, 1986.

Handspicker, B., Hart, R., and Roman, M. "The Athena Palladium Print System." MIT report, February 1989.

Hart, R. "Palladium Printing System Design Document." MIT report, September 1989.

Hodges, M., Sasnet, R., and Ackerman, M. "A Construction Set for Multimedia Applications." *IEEE Software,* January 1989: pp. 37–42.

Jackson, G. "Living with Athena: Effects of Powerful Computing within MIT Living Groups." MIT internal report, 1987.

Jackson, G. "Settling Down with Athena." MIT internal report, August 1988.

Jul, E., et al. "Fine-grained Mobility in the Emerald System." *ACM Transactions on Computer Systems* February 1988: pp. 109–133.

Kent, S. T. and Voydock, V. L. "Security Mechanisms in High-Level Network Protocols." *ACM Computing Surveys,* June 1983.

Lerman, S. "Project Athena Overview." MIT report, September 1987.

Levine, P. J., et al. "Service Management System, Section E.1." *Project Athena Technical Plan.* Cambridge, Mass.: MIT Project Athena, 1987.

Mauro, T. "An Overview of the Andrew File System." Pittsburgh: Transarc Corporation, 1989.

McCredie, J. W. *Campus Computing Strategies.* Bedford, Mass.: Digital Press, 1983.

Mendelsohn, N. "A Guide to Using GDB," Version 0.1. MIT Project Athena internal report, 1987.

Milgram, J. H. "Using the Athena Laboratory Computer." MIT Project Athena report, January 1987.

Miller, S. P., et al. "Kerberos Authentication and Authorization System." *Project Athena Technical Plan.* Cambridge, Mass.: MIT Project Athena, December 1987.

Mockapetris, P. "RFC 1034—Domain Names—Concepts and Facilities." USC/Information Sciences, Institute, November 1987.

Mockapetris, P. "RFC 1035—Domain Implementation and Specification." USC/Information Sciences Institute, November 1987.

Morris, J. "Make or Take Decisions in Andrew." *Usenix Conference Proceedings*, Winter 1988.

Mullender, S. J., and Tanenbaum, A. S. "The Design of a Capability-based Distributed Operating System." *The Computer Journal* 29(4) 1986: pp. 289–299.

Mullender, S. J. "Amoeba as a Workstation Operating System." *Proceedings of IEEE Workshop on Workstation Operating Systems*, Cambridge, Mass., November 1987.

Murman, E., LaVin, A., and Ellis, S. "Enhancing Fluid Mechanics Education with Workstation Based Software. *Proceedings AIAA 26th Aerospace Sciences Meeting*, Reno, Nev., January 11–14, 1988.

Nachbar, D. "When Network File Systems Aren't Enough: Automatic File Distribution Revisited." *Usenix Conference Proceedings*, Summer 1986.

National Bureau of Standards. "Data Encryption Standard." *Federal Information Processing Standards Publication 46*. Washington, D.C.: U.S. Government Printing Office, 1977.

Needham, R., and Schroeder, M. "Using Encryption for Authentication in Large Networks of Computers." *CACM* December 1978: pp. 993–999.

Neuman, B. "Issues of Scale in Large Distributed Operating System." *Report FR-35*. Seattle: University of Washington Department of Computer Science, 1988.

Newell, A. *The Future of Computing at Carnegie Mellon University*. Pittsburgh: Carnegie-Mellon University, 1982.

Notkin, D., et al. "Interconnecting Heterogeneous Computer Systems." *CACM* March 1989: pp. 258–273.

Ousterhout, J., et al. "The Sprite Network Operating System." *Computer* February 1988: pp. 23–36.

Paradis, J. "Teaching Writing in an On-line Classroom." *Harvard Education Review* May 1988: pp. 154–170.

Raeburn, K., et al. "DISCUSS: An Electronic Conferencing System for a Distributed Computing Environment." *Usenix Conference Proceedings*, Winter 1989.

Rashid, R. "From RIG to Accent to MACH: The Evolution of a Network Operating System." *CMU Computer Science Department Research Report*. Pittsburgh: Carnegie-Mellon University, 1987.

Rand Corporation. "The Rand Message Handling System: User's Manual." Irvine: University of California at Irvine Department of Information and Computer Science, November 1985.

Relational Technology, Inc. *Ingres Reference Manual Release 5.0 Unix*, 1986.

Rose, M. T. "Post Office Protocol" (revised). Newark, Del.: University of Delaware, 1985.

Rosenstein, M., Geer, D., and Levine, P. "The Athena Service Management System." *Usenix Conference Proceedings*, Winter 1988.

Russo, G. and Smith, J. "A New Method of Computer-Aided Thermodynamics." *Computers in Mechanical Engineering* January 1987.

Sandberg, R., et al. "Design and Implementation of the Sun Network Filesystem." *Usenix Conference Proceedings*, Summer 1985.

Sanislo, J. "An RPC/LWP System for Interconnecting Heterogeneous Systems." *Usenix Conference Proceedings*, Winter 1988.

Scheifler, R., and Gettys, J. "The X Window System." *ACM Transactions on Graphics* April 1986: pp. 79–109.

Schiller, J. *Campus Networking Strategies*, Arms, C. (ed.). Bedford, Mass.: Digital Press, 1988, pp. 112–126.

Schroeder, M., Birrell, A., and Needham, R. "Experience with Grapevine: The Growth of a Distributed System." *ACM Transactions on Computer Systems* February 1984: pp. 3–23.

Sherwood, B. "An Integrated Authoring Environment." Carnegie-Mellon University report, June 1985.

Slater, J. H. "User's Guide for Program Growltiger." *Athena CATS Research Report No. CATS87-1.* Cambridge, Mass.: MIT, 1987.

Steiner, J. G., Neuman, B. C., and Schiller, J. I. "Kerberos: An Authentication Service for Open Network Systems." *Usenix Conference Proceedings,* Winter 1988.

Sun Microsystems. "Yellow Pages Protocol Specification, Networking on the Sun Workstation." Sun, 1986.

Sun Microsystems. "NFS Protocol Specification and Services Manual Revision A." Sun, 1987.

Swick, R. "The X Toolkit: More Bricks for Building Widgets." *Usenix Conference Proceedings,* Winter 1988.

Tanenbaum, A. S., and Van Renesse, R. "Distributed Operating System." *Computing Surveys* December 1985: pp. 419–470.

Taylor, E. F. "Spacetime Software: Computer Graphics Utilities in Special Relativity." *American Journal of Physics* June 1989: pp. 508–514.

Treese, G. W. "Berkeley Unix on 1000 Workstations: Athena Changes to 4.3BSD." *Usenix Conference Proceedings,* Winter 1988.

Turkle, S., et al. "Project Athena at MIT." MIT report, May 1988.

Walker, B., et al. "The LOCUS Distributed Operating System." *Proceedings of the Ninth ACM Symposium on Operating System Principles,* October 1983, pp. 49–70.

Yankelovitch, "Intermedia: The Concept and the Construction of a Seamless Information Environment." *Computer* January 1988: pp. 81–96.

INDEX

Abstract concepts, visualizing with
    computers, 44
Academic computing, 37–39. *See also*
    Instructional computing.
    attitudes toward, 203–205
    costs of, 205
    role of, 211
Access privileges, management of, 106
Accreditation committee, assessment by,
    186–187
Active mailing lists, 137
Address, defined, 80
Ad Hoc Committee on Future
    Computational Needs and Resources,
    1979 report by, 4–6
Administrative computing, 37–38
Adventure workstations, 15
Aero-Astro, courses using Athena, 64–65
Affordability
    Athena distributed systems model, 90,
    95
    as system requirement, 79
AFS, *see* Andrew File System (AFS)
Agamemnon, 25
AIL (Artificial Intelligence Laboratory),
    118
Amoeba, 82–83, 85
Andrew, 7, 10–12, 82, 83
    assessment of, 202–203
    vs. Athena, 85
    Athena Writing Project and, 48

compatibility, 89
future of, 210–211
objectives of, 12
Andrew Cache Manager, 144
Andrew File System (AFS), 83, 85, 100–
    101, 140, 142–144
Animation, benefits of, 52
Annenberg/CPB Project, 149
Annotator, Athena Writing Project and, 48
Aphrodite, 25
Apollo, 25
Apple Macintosh, 183–184
    faculty preference for, 71
    student purchase of, 39
Application coherence, 89, 94. *See also*
    Coherence.
Applications developer, position
    description, 240
Applications development group, 46
Applications programming interface,
    coherence and, 94
Applications software, 40, 191–192. *See
    also* Instructional software; Software.
Architecture, multimedia projects, 150
Architecture, School of, MIT, 150–151,
    204
Argus, 110, 114
ARPAnet, 10
Artemis, 25
Artificial Intelligence Laboratory (AIL),
    118

Trademarks and Sources

The following are trademarks of Digital Equipment Corporation: DECstation, DECwindows, the Digital logo, ULTRIX, VAX, and VAXstation. The following are trademarks of The Massachusetts Institute of Technology: ⚉ , Athena, Hesiod Name Service, Kerberos Authentication Service, Moira Service Management System, Palladium Print Service, Project Athena, X Window System, and Zephyr Notification Service. RT/PC and PS/2 are trademarks of IBM. NFS and Network File System are trademarks of Sun Microsystems Inc. MS/DOS is a trademark of Microsoft Corp. UNIX is a trademark of AT&T. PostScript is a trademark of Adobe Systems Inc. Macintosh is a trademark of Apple Computer, Inc. NeXT is a trademark of NeXT, Inc. Motif and OSF/1 are trademarks of the Open Software Foundation. AFS and Andrew File System are trademarks of Transarc, Inc.

Chapter 5 is an expansion and update of an article, "Project Athena as a Distributed Computer System," published in *IEEE Computer,* September 1990. It is published here with the permission of IEEE. Chapter 9 is an expansion and update of an article, "Organization and Management of Project Athena," published in the *Journal of the Society of Research Administrators* (Spring 1991), and is printed here with their permission. Figures 1, 2, 6.2, 6.3, 6.6, 6.7, and 9.1 are used with the permission of The Massachusetts Institute of Technology. Figure 6.5 is used with the permission of Bolt, Beranek and Newman, Inc. Figure I.1 is used with the permission of North Carolina State University. Figure I.2 is used with the permission of Iowa State University. The Athena logo is used with the permission of The Massachusetts Institute of Technology.